50

GREAT WORLD CUP MATCHES

...and why you should watch them

50

GREAT WORLD CUP MATCHES

...and why you should watch them

DOMINIC HOUGHAM

pitch

First published by Pitch Publishing, 2024

Pitch Publishing
9 Donnington Park,
85 Birdham Road,
Chichester,
West Sussex,
PO20 7AJ
www.pitchpublishing.co.uk
info@pitchpublishing.co.uk

A CIP catalogue record is available for this book from the British Library.

ISBN 978 1 80150 724 0

Typesetting and origination by Pitch Publishing

Printed and bound in India by Thomson Press

Contents

Acknowledgements

A HUGE thanks must go out to my family. To my wife Annelise – throughout 27 years of marriage, you have been there for me always, supporting my passions, and every day with you has been special – you are the best. And to our boys, Jake and Sam, thanks for putting up with my many hours of football viewing and for giving me the idea to write this book in the first place. I also need to thank my parents. My lovely mother, who sadly passed away during the pandemic – thank you for ingraining a love of Brazilian football in me at an early age; my father for taking me to my first matches, letting me stay up late to watch *Match of the Day* and endless hours of taking me to the park in all weather, having to be goalkeeper. I still look forward to our footballing chats. I'd also like to thank Omar Saleem at *These Football Times* for publishing my first attempts at football writing during the pandemic and supporting my development along the way – your website and magazines are truly awesome! Thank you to Jane Camillin at Pitch Publishing for taking a punt on a first-time author and guiding me through this new world. And finally, thanks to my many international work colleagues, who, when I used to organise a group competition during each World Cup, said, 'You really should write a book about it.' Well, I finally took your advice and did it.

Introduction

I'VE ALWAYS loved the World Cup. My first consciousness of it as a child was the 1974 tournament, held in what was then West Germany. I remember getting the Panini sticker book and slowly filling it through pocket money and a lot of parental begging. And as each sticker went in, the fascination just grew. At that innocent time of no internet and limited coverage on TV, there was no way of knowing who all these international players were. Pages would start to build of the Brazilians in their vibrant yellow shirts, but then also of countries like East Germany, looking austere, and Haiti, who I could not even find on a map back then. Next came the wallchart, taped up on the bedroom wall, ready to fill in as each game ended. There would be footballs sold with the country names on them and kids during park games adopting names such as Cruyff and Müller.

The 1978 World Cup was enjoyed during a school summer holiday, when I was free to watch every game if I so wished. I was mesmerised by the ticker tape as Kempes strode majestically around the pitch. And I can link World Cups with key events of my life – the 1982 edition fell during my O-level school exams, the 1986 edition fell during my second-year university exams (I sometimes feel that the 2022 Winter World Cup was genius – FIFA needs to give serious consideration to exam schedules!). Subsequent World Cups became harder to watch so thoroughly as a work career was started, I moved to California and a family evolved. I recall trying to watch the 1998 World Cup in the US where at that time the only places where you could see games were dodgy bars after begging them to turn it on. How things have changed now!

With the modern game now flooded with money, allowing a few teams to dominate through financial strength, international football still has a refreshing aspect of non-financial bias. If you are England, you cannot just go out and buy players to strengthen your team. You are limited by your population and who is available. It allows golden generations to come and go and for countries such as the Netherlands and Croatia to be competitive. Yes, the bigger countries still have an advantage, and richer countries will have better infrastructure etc, but it is still a more level playing field than the Premier League, for example.

Watching the recent 2022 World Cup with my sons and other American friends, it struck me that there was a need for a book targeted at them and it is this that I hope to achieve. I have friends who, like me, are deeply into football – we can bore anyone around us with endless conversations about the Netherlands' Total Football system and how it evolved from the 1950 Hungarians – and there are many fine books available on such topics. There are 250-page books dedicated to single World Cups and even just to single World Cup teams, such as Brazil 1982 and Denmark 1986 – and they are fantastic reads. However, I felt that the casual fan needs a general entry point, and it is that which I hope this book achieves.

My thought therefore was to write a book that could work in two ways – for the newer fan, it could give them a starting point without overwhelming them, while for the deeper fan it could provide a nice collection of all the key matches. I decided to go for the 'recommended games' approach because these should fire passion for football, rather than slogging through highlights of 0-0 draws or low-action matches. Those low-action encounters may be important and enjoyable to some, but could also stop others dead in their tracks, and I wish to promote the love of football.

We are lucky to live in an era when so much video content is available to us on platforms such as YouTube. Some heroic people have put on highlights of almost any game you can think of while whole matches are also available in many cases. They are available in a mix of languages – and it is often more fun to watch a Brazil game with the passionate local commentary than just sticking to English. But the flip side is that there is so much out there now available, so if you are starting to explore old World Cups, where to start?

Given that my hope is for the reader to enjoy these matches through viewing, I have chosen to start with the 1974 World Cup. I found that when I listed great games, using that as a starting point gave me a perfect 50, plus for me it is the first World Cup that I remember watching. Of course, there were many great games in prior World Cups, although video coverage is often scarcer and more limited, with 1970 especially being a classic. But they were before my time.

I have written about the games in chronological order, but the reader can choose whether to go that route or to just dip into whichever tournament takes their fancy. The advantage of chronological viewing is that it allows you to see how the game changes and develops over time, from strict 4-4-2 formations to Total Football, implementation of the back-pass rule, pressing etc. But if you just want to dive into Spain 1982 first, for some reason, I encourage that too.

I have taken a three-step approach to discussing each game. Firstly, and to me this is hopefully the most interesting step, I have set out why you should consider watching it. And this is where I have tried to provide the reader with context. Picking a match that is not in here as an example, so I don't spoil it ahead of time, let's say Denmark 1 Scotland 0 in 1986, I could just describe the action, but that is available on video anyway. What I have tried to do is to set context ahead of watching the game – so for example with this one I would talk about how Denmark were the up-and-coming team, 'Danish Dynamite' etc. Then, when you watch the game, you will have an appreciation for what is occurring and some knowledge about why the fixture was eagerly awaited.

Secondly is the match itself. You will find that I have placed the score at the end of each game rather than in the introduction. I have done this purely because, when I watch a match, I always prefer not to know the score ahead of time. I feel it adds to the excitement and so if you are reading about a game of which you have no prior knowledge, it may be preferable to read the description without knowing beforehand how it ends. A minor point but one that I hope helps.

Thirdly comes the aftermath – what were the subsequent events that were shaped by this game? It could be as simple as the victors going on to win the tournament or more detailed such as a golden generation fading or a team rethinking how it plays. But big games can have big consequences and so it is important to consider those.

I have then thrown in some additional thoughts such as the teams and interesting trivia facts.

But my key hope in writing this is that it sparks further interest within you, the reader. Ideally it would pique your interest in certain teams or tournaments, and you then go to the next level of research. It should give you an overview of the key teams and games for each tournament, but it is just that – a tasting menu. Maybe one reader will become fascinated by the 1986 Denmark team and want to learn more. They can then turn to more dedicated books such as the excellent *Danish Dynamite* by Lars Eriksen, Mike Gibbons, and Rob Smyth. Hopefully this will be a roadmap to learning more about this great game.

Lastly, you will have noticed that I have made no attempt to 'rank' the matches, with good reason. It is a thankless and impossible task. Who am I to say that Argentina v England from 1986 is better than Uruguay v Ghana in 2010? And everyone will have their own opinion anyway – it is subjective. And what does it really matter in the end? We are not judging here but just highlighting great games. I have however marked those that I consider World Cup Classics to help point to those matches commonly considered greats – but that is as far as I have taken it.

So please enjoy this trip down memory lane and I hope that you enjoy learning about, and subsequently watching, the games as much as I enjoyed researching them. If there are games here that you have never watched, I envy you – there are some great matches within, where I wish I could wipe my memory clean and watch them again, unaware of the drama about to unfold. And I would encourage you to watch them in your preferred format – for some, a ten-minute highlight reel might be perfect while for others they might want to watch the whole game. Whatever works for you; it is your journey.

May this be a first step that leads to many hours spent going down online rabbit holes and the building of an impressive football library.

Dominic Hougham
2023

Game 1

1974 World Cup

East Germany v West Germany

22 June 1974
Volksparkstadion, Hamburg
Attendance: 60,200
Stage: First Round, Group 1

Why you should watch it

Following World War Two, the German region was divided, producing two new countries – West Germany within Europe and East Germany within the Soviet occupation zone. These were separated both ideologically and physically as the Cold War evolved, leading to the construction of the Berlin Wall, as West Germany rebuilt itself from the ashes of the war as a democratic, capitalist state while East Germany sat under the control of the Communist Soviet Union. Former neighbours were divided as travel was extremely limited between the two, and as part of this divide, both countries developed their own football sides. The two national teams became eligible for participation in World Cup qualifications, with West Germany enjoying the most success, winning the trophy in 1954 in 'The Miracle of Bern' while also reaching the final in 1966. East Germany, meanwhile, had failed to qualify for a single World Cup finals tournament since the nation's formation.

As qualification for the 1974 tournament got underway, West Germany had no need to go through the process, being the host nation. East Germany did not have this luxury and were placed into a qualification group alongside Romania, Finland, and Albania, winning five of their six games to top the group, one point ahead of the Romanians, and book their first trip to the World Cup finals. Immediately there was talk about how dramatic it would be if the two countries ended up facing one another, but first the draw had to be made.

And so, on 5 January 1974, the draw took place in Frankfurt, beamed out to a global audience. West Germany had been assigned Group 1 and as the draw developed, FIFA president Sir Stanley Rous made the historic announcement – East Germany were drawn into Group 1 alongside their western neighbours. A silence filled the room, followed by loud applause. The 1974 World Cup was set for drama even before kicking off.

The two teams had never met until this moment and so the game was full of political intrigue, especially being played in West Germany. West Germany's manager, Helmut Schön, was originally from East Germany before fleeing to the West in 1950. And there was so much more than just pride at stake – it represented socialism vs communism; a clash of ideologies. This clash meant that many East German citizens would be secretly cheering for West Germany, not wanting their unloved regime to gain positive publicity.

The West Germans went into the tournament as one of the favourites, having just won the 1972 European Championship after reaching the World Cup semi-finals in 1970, only to lose out in a classic against Italy. The team included Franz Beckenbauer at the back, playing as *libero*, along with the ace finisher Gerd Müller, *Der Bomber*, both members of the Bayern Munich squad that had just won the European Cup. There was also the emergence of Günter Netzer, a free-flowing midfielder who had played so well during the 1972 European Championship, but whose style was slightly at odds with Schön's more disciplined structure. Schön had doubts about playing Netzer, even though the German public clamoured for his inclusion.

The draw had placed West Germany against East Germany as the last group match, meaning anticipation would build over the first few days as both teams played the other group teams – Australia and Chile. On the West German side, the squad was suffering from internal strife, especially over bonuses, which saw Schön furious that his players were motivated by money instead of national pride. Although finally settled through the mediation of Beckenbauer, the team seemed a little out of sorts and, while they won their first two games, they were far from impressive. Their form was not a great omen ahead of the hyped final match.

East Germany, meanwhile, went into the tournament as a dark horse. As usual in those days, little was known about the team but there were signs that they could be dangerous. Ahead of the World Cup, FC Magdeburg had just won the Cup Winners' Cup, beating AC Milan 2-0 in the final – a Milan team containing Gianni Rivera and Romeo Benetti. Playing in attack for that FC Magdeburg side was one Jürgen Sparwasser, who would also play for the national team, and had a reputation as a clinical goalscorer.

While West Germany were winning their two opening matches, East Germany beat Australia in their first before drawing with Chile. That meant that both sides of the divide were unbeaten ahead of the final meeting and knew that they had secured the top two places and so would progress to the next round. The game would, however, determine who would top the group – but much more importantly, which of the clashing ideologies could claim the high ground. It was a game that encapsulated the political climate of the times.

What happened?

Over 60,000 fans packed the Olympiastadion in Berlin to witness the first footballing meeting between East and West. Given the East German government's reluctance for its people to witness the ways of the West, only around 1,500 'fans' were allowed to travel for the match, carefully handpicked and vetted.

The first half saw both sides playing in a cautious manner, with neither wanting to make a costly mistake. It was obvious that there was mutual respect between the two teams and that each realised the significance of the meeting. Chances were few and far between, with the more experienced West

Germans unsurprisingly dominating, their first chance falling to Heinz Flohe whose shot flew narrowly wide. Next a pass from Beckenbauer found Müller in the penalty area, *Der Bomber* turning his marker before crossing to Jürgen Grabowski inside the six-yard box. With the goal gaping, Grabowski tried to twist as the ball fell slightly behind him but could only succeed in placing it inches past the post. East Germany then carved out a chance of their own when a throw-in reached midfielder Reinhard Lauck, whose cross flew across the six-yard line where fellow midfielder Hans-Jürgen Kreische was lurking. A goal seemed inevitable until Kreische committed the cardinal sin of leaning back, sending his shot over the bar. It was an awful miss – the question was how costly would it prove?

The second half commenced in much the same vein – some long-range shooting but neither keeper seriously troubled. On 65 minutes, the East German manager Georg Buschner decided to freshen things up, bringing on midfielder Erich Hamann for Harald Irmscher. The West Germans countered with their own changes, including introducing Günter Netzer to the delight of the partisan crowd.

The East German substitution soon paid dividends when, on 77 minutes, a break saw the ball fall at the feet of Hamann who accelerated into the West German half. Seeing Sparwasser making a run through the middle, Hamann chipped it into him. Chesting it past the great Beckenbauer, Sparwasser fired the ball into the bottom corner to silence the 60,000 West German fans. Seemingly stunned by his own achievement, Sparwasser celebrated with a slightly awkward forward roll before being engulfed by team-mates. The TV cameras did successfully manage to find the handful of East German supporters, waving their flags in joy and probable disbelief.

A dumbfounded West German team, realising that they were now facing finishing second in the group, tried to retaliate, pressurising the East German goal with a series of free kicks and corners, but all to no avail. The East Germans hunkered down and, as the final whistle sounded, they faced a pitch invasion from a barrage of photographers, capturing the historic moment. East Germany had topped the group and beaten their ideological neighbours.

Final score
East Germany 1 (Sparwasser 77) West Germany 0

What was the aftermath?

This ended up being the only game between the two teams during the 41-year period of division. East Germany won the group and moved on to face another group containing the Netherlands, Brazil and Argentina – a harsh reward for coming top. Two defeats, and a draw against Argentina, followed, meaning East Germany were eliminated. West Germany's reward for losing, meanwhile, was to move on with second place to a group containing Poland, Sweden and Yugoslavia – arguably a much easier prospect. Were they Machiavellian enough to 'lose' the game with this in mind? Doubtful given the rivalry between the two nations at this time.

The defeat to East Germany caused internal navel-gazing within the West German camp, with some hard truths being aired. Rumours abounded that Helmut Schön was suffering from a nervous breakdown and locking himself in seclusion, while Franz Beckenbauer took command of the squad, even to the point of making team selections. It turned out to be a timely wake-up call as they won all their second group matches, taking them to the World Cup Final.

East Germany never qualified for another World Cup – they got close in 1990 but just missed out to Austria and then, in October 1990, Germany was reunified along with its national teams. The last competitive game played as the DDR was a friendly against Belgium in Brussels on 12 September 1990, which the East Germans won 2-0. From that time forward, there was just one German team.

Teams

West Germany: Maier, Vogts, Breitner, Schwarzenbeck (Höttges 68), Beckenbauer (c), Cullmann, Overath (Netzer 69), Hoeneß, Grabowski, Müller, Flohe
Manager: Schön
East Germany: Croy, Bransch (c), Weise, Wätzlich, Kische, Kurbjuweit, Kreische, Lauck, Irmscher (Hamann 65), Sparwasser, Hoffmann
Manager: Buschner

Iconic moment

Sparwasser's goal after 77 minutes – it earned him fame within the footballing world, but he remarked later in life, 'Rumour had it that I was richly rewarded for the goal, with a car, a house and a cash premium. But that is not true.' He also said, 'If one day my gravestone simply says "Hamburg 74", everybody will still know who is lying below.' Thankfully this has not been tested yet as Sparwasser remains alive and kicking, having defected to the West in 1988 – one year before the Berlin Wall came down.

Trivia fact

Nine of the West German team came from just two club sides – Bayern Munich and FC Köln. Bayern Munich had just won their first European Cup, and after this tournament they would continue to dominate European football, winning the European Cup again in both 1975 and 1976, making them champions for three successive years.

Game 2

1974 World Cup

Argentina v The Netherlands

26 June 1974

Parkstadion, Gelsenkirchen

Attendance: 56,548

Stage: Second Round, Group A

WORLD CUP CLASSIC

Why you should watch it

Where do you start when talking about the Netherlands in 1974? A nation which had no impact on previous tournaments suddenly produced a golden generation of players which saw Dutch clubs Feyenoord and Ajax win the European Cup from 1970 to 1973 successively; Ajax winning all the last three. And it was from that Ajax backbone that the Dutch team evolved. Football aficionados will go misty-eyed over such names as Ruud Krol, Arie Haan, Willem van Hanegem, Johan Neeskens, Rob Rensenbrink, Johnny Rep, and the undisputed genius himself, Johan Cruyff. Then throw a revolutionary coach on top of that, who had also managed Ajax during their glory days, Rinus Michels. This was a man who had developed Total Football with Ajax and then brought it over into the national team. In a nutshell, the concept of Total Football was that each player should be comfortable wherever he found himself on the pitch and should not be afraid to interchange positions with team-mates. That, combined with an early version of the high press, made the Netherlands the team to watch during the 1974 World Cup.

Placed into Group 3 in the first round, the Netherlands finished top with relative ease. Rep scored twice as they first saw off Uruguay before a goalless draw against Sweden. Then they moved up a gear, thrashing Bulgaria 4-1, including a brace of penalties converted by Neeskens. That took them on to the second round and Group A, where they were pitted in a tough group against Brazil, Argentina, and East Germany, with the opener being against the Argentinians.

The Argentinians had struggled to get through the first round, drawn into Group 4 alongside two strong teams in Italy and Poland, along with first-timers Haiti. Things had started poorly when they lost 3-2 to surprise package Poland, who would go on to be one of the revelations of the tournament – two of the Poles' goals scored by emerging star Grzegorz Lato. Their game against Italy ended in a draw, meaning that they needed to beat Haiti in the final match, hope that Poland could beat Italy and then score enough to overcome Italy's goal difference advantage. All this came true for them by the skin of their teeth – a 4-1 victory over Haiti, who Italy had beaten 3-1, along with the *Azzurri*'s 2-1 loss against Poland meant Argentina qualified for the second round by one goal. It was not perhaps the best preparation for facing the mighty Dutch. Could Argentina recover and produce an upset or would Cruyff and company roll over them?

What happened?

The Netherlands proceeded to give the Argentinians and the watching world a display of football at its purest. It was a glimpse into the future – a future where players flowed, and the ball did the work. A future of loving possession. From the very first whistle, the Netherlands took the game to Argentina. Cruyff buzzed around the edge of the Argentina penalty area, playing in whatever position he felt worked for himself and throwing one-twos around with team-mates. An early chance saw Cruyff break through, only to be narrowly offside. The Netherlands had around four chances in the first ten minutes before a lofted ball to Cruyff saw him trap the ball, round the keeper and slot home the first goal all in one beautiful motion. The Dutch then had a goal-bound shot cleared off the line as the siege of the Argentinian goal continued. Another two great chances were missed before Krol crashed in a shot through a crowd of players from outside of the penalty area – the type of goal the Netherlands would perfect in both this and the subsequent tournament. The game was only 25 minutes old, and the Netherlands were 2-0 up, which could easily have been five.

As the half progressed, Argentina's frustration began to surface in some crunching tackles. What is often forgotten when people discuss the free-flowing Dutch artists is that they could dish it out as well as take it. Refusing to be bullied, players like Neeskens demonstrated that the Netherlands could not be easily intimidated.

Surprisingly, Argentina managed to limit any further damage until half-time, despite the maelstrom that they had faced so far. A chance perhaps to regroup and come up with some kind of plan to break the stranglehold?

As a heavy rain started to fall, there was the possibility that it would impact the Netherlands' smooth passing game. But almost immediately they almost scored again as a header just sailed over the bar. Cruyff remained all over the pitch – one minute crossing from the left, the next breaking up an attack and passing back to his own keeper. The Netherlands had a very strong claim for a penalty waved off and as conditions worsened, fouls from both teams increased, some of which would seem shocking to a modern viewer. Then a cross from the left from Cruyff saw Rep dive in at the far post and head in a well-deserved third. Dutch fans were singing in the rain.

With 17 minutes left, you could have forgiven the Netherlands if they had taken their feet off the gas and coasted home, but instead they kept peppering the Argentinian goal. And in the final minute, a thoroughly dominant performance was crowned by a neat one-two on the edge of the area from Van Hanegem followed by a shot saved by the keeper. The save pushed the ball to the side of the area where Cruyff, with no hesitation, volleyed in from a tight angle. A great goal to cap a great display. This was the quintessential Dutch display of Total Football and an introduction to a wider watching world of the revolution taking place.

Final score
Netherlands 4 (Cruyff 11, 90; Krol 25; Rep 73)
Argentina 0

What was the aftermath?

Following on from their demolition of Argentina, the Netherlands met East Germany and then Brazil in Group A. East Germany were seen off with a comfortable 2-0 win through goals from Neeskens and Rensenbrink before facing holders Brazil. In front of nearly 54,000 fans packed into the Westfalenstadion in Dortmund, Neeskens and Cruyff ensured that the Netherlands ended Group A with a 100 per cent record, beating both South American giants, to progress to the final and a date with the host nation, West Germany. Sadly, the Brazil game demonstrated how much the *Seleção* had changed from that magical 1970 World Cup-winning team. Instead of *o jogo bonito*, fans had to endure a Brazil of thuggery. Brazil started the game the better side but were frequently frustrated by the Netherlands' high offside trap. As half-time approached and Brazilian frustration grew, their play became more physical.

The Dutch took control of the game in the second half through a beautiful Neeskens finish after 50 minutes, followed by a sublime volley from Cruyff at full stretch in minute 65. This pushed Brazil over the edge with fouls becoming ever more blatant, although the Dutch were no angels either, giving as good as they got and increasing the tension within the game. Finally, in the 84th minute, Luís Pereira decided to remove Neeskens' legs with an agricultural 'tackle', resulting in a red. Pereira didn't go quietly, protesting with anyone within earshot and throwing direct insults at the crowd. It was a sad way for Brazil to exit and a sad reflection on how they had changed from 1970. The Netherlands, meanwhile, showed that they could match steel with steel when needed, as they moved on to a World Cup Final against West Germany.

Teams

Netherlands: Jongbloed, Jansen, Krol, Rijsbergen, Suurbier (Israël 84), Haan, Van Hanegem, Neeskens, Cruyff (c), Rensenbrink, Rep
Manager: Michels

Argentina: Carnevali, Heredia, Perfumo (c), Sá, Wolff (Glaria HT), Houseman (Kempes HT), Squeo, Telch, Ayala, Balbuena, Yazalde
Manager: Cap

Iconic moment

Cruyff's first goal – the skill to bring the ball down on a dime, shimmy past the keeper and then slot it into the net ahead of the defender scrambling back to the goal line. Balletic in nature from the undeniable star of the tournament.

Trivia fact

The Netherlands very nearly did not make the 1974 World Cup finals. Drawn in a qualifying group containing neighbours Belgium, the Dutch went into the final game needing to avoid defeat to them at home. A late goal from Belgium looked like eliminating them before it was disallowed for offside, although replays show the decision to have been extremely tight. A sliding doors moment for world football.

Game 3
1974 World Cup

West Germany v The Netherlands

7 July 1974
Olympiastadion, Munich
Attendance: 75,200
Stage: Final

Why you should watch it

The Netherlands, as described earlier, came into the World Cup Final in red-hot form, having defeated Argentina, Brazil, and East Germany in the previous group stage by an aggregate score of 8-0. Now they were just one game away from Total Football's crowning achievement following on from Ajax's European Cup treble. The only remaining obstacle – the hosts.

West Germany had a mixed route to the final. As discussed earlier, they lost to East Germany to finish second in their first-round group, which had perversely landed them in an easier second-round group. But the defeat had led to disharmony and revolt within the squad. It was said that manager Helmut Schön was close to a nervous breakdown following the defeat, shutting himself away, and that Franz Beckenbauer had expanded his captain's role to become the de facto leader.

West Germany and Poland had both won their first two second-round group games, leading to a final winner-takes-all decider. The Poles were the tournament's dark horses, including strong players such as Władysław Żmuda, Kazimeirz Deyna, Grzegorz Lato and Robert Gadocha – a base which allowed them to enjoy success during the 1970s. They played with attacking flair and a strong passing game, but unfortunately a passing game requires good playing conditions – something that was lacking in a match that is referred to as 'The Water Battle' in Germany and 'The Water Game' in Poland. Torrential rain hit Frankfurt and Germany came away with victory through a solitary Gerd Müller goal.

And so, the final pitted the tournament darlings against the host nation. The Netherlands of Neeskens, Rep and Cruyff against the Germany of Beckenbauer, Breitner and Müller, in front of 75,000 fans decked in white and orange.

What happened?

Woe betide any supporters who were late into their seats as they perhaps grabbed refreshments as the Netherlands kicked off. The Dutch stroked the ball around defence before Johan Cruyff came back to the halfway line to pick up possession. Then, with a shimmy and a burst of acceleration, Cruyff set off into the penalty area, panicking Uli Hoeneß into tripping him. Referee Jack Taylor pointed to the spot – not only was it the first penalty ever awarded in a World Cup Final but also no German had even touched the ball yet. Johan Neeskens buried the kick, and the Netherlands were 1-0 up after just a minute – a stunning start.

Hubris is defined as 'excessive pride or self-confidence'. While no team could ask for a more ideal start, it did perhaps engender a spirit of overconfidence in the Netherlands. It should be remembered that the Dutch enjoyed a tense relationship with the Germans following on from World War Two which had only ended 29 years before. Some players and fans clearly saw the final as an opportunity for payback and for rubbing German noses in it. They didn't merely want to beat West Germany but to humiliate them. The Dutch continued to dominate a stunned German team – except they forgot to score a second.

As the half progressed, West Germany regained their composure and came back into the game. And on 25 minutes, Bernd Hölzenbein, like Cruyff, went on a run into the area. A tackle from behind from Wim Jansen, a somewhat dubious fall and a second penalty decision – gratefully converted by

Paul Breitner in his home stadium. The Dutch were paying the price for overconfidence.

The game then oscillated back and forth with both sides making opportunities. Just as half-time approached, a run down the right from Rainer Bonhof resulted in a pull-back to that ace marksman, Gerd Müller. Controlling the ball with his back to goal, he spun and shot low into the corner – his 14th goal across World Cups, setting a new record. Against the odds, West Germany were ahead going into the break.

The second half saw the Dutch increase the pressure while at the same time leaving more space at the back. Breitner cleared off the line for Germany while Müller had a goal disallowed for a narrow offside. And then, as the game wound down, the Netherlands produced one last chance. A free kick into the area was met by Neeskens with a full-force volley – only for Sepp Maier to save at his near post. Johnny Rep came close and Hölzenbein had another penalty claim waved off before Jack Taylor blew for full time, making West Germany world champions, an overcome Müller dropping to his knees in joy. A nation rejoiced.

Final score
West Germany 2 (Breitner 25 pen; Müller 43)
Netherlands 1 (Neeskens 2 pen)

What was the aftermath?

While the defeat was devastating to the Dutch at that moment, over time they have evolved as the heralded ones. A glorious team who failed at the last hurdle, they have gone down in folklore as one of the greatest teams not to have won the World Cup, like Hungary in 1954 and Brazil in 1982. Articles and books have been written in praise of the 1974 *Oranje* vintage, showering them with superlatives. The team decked in love beads and long hair, playing a new style of football while decked in vibrant orange. In the meantime, the victorious West Germans have generally been cast as partypoopers in the narrative. Of course, all this is harsh – West Germany were deserved winners on the day. But the 1974 Netherlands team will always hold a special place in football lovers' hearts.

Teams

West Germany: Maier, Vogts, Beckenbauer (c), Schwarzenbeck, Breitner, Bonhof, Overath, Hoeneß, Grabowski, Hölzenbein, Müller
Manager: Schön

Netherlands: Jongbloed, Suurbier, Rijsbergen (de Jong 69), Haan, Krol, Jansen, Neeskens, Van Hanegem, Rep, Rensenbrink (R. van de Kerkhof HT), Cruyff (c)
Manager: Michels

Iconic moment

The spin from Müller to score the winner – one of the deadliest marksmen that football has ever known scoring a then-record 14th World Cup goal with his trademark poaching. The man whose skill in finishing was second to none would end his career scoring an astonishing 68 goals in 62 games for *Die Mannschaft*.

Trivia fact

As referee Jack Taylor prepared to do the coin toss with Cruyff and Beckenbauer, he noticed that someone had forgotten to put corner flags out. Kick-off was delayed while the situation was rectified – it was a World Cup Final after all. Someone had just one job to do – and forgot.

Game 4

1978 World Cup

The Netherlands v Scotland

11 June 1978
Estadio Ciudad de Mendoza, Mendoza
Attendance: 35,130
Stage: First Round, Group 4

WORLD CUP CLASSIC

Why you should watch it

If any team in the world can cause their fans euphoria and despondency within a tournament, it is Scotland, and their 1978 campaign was another classic example of this. The 1974 World Cup had seen the Scots go out in the group stage without losing a game – they missed out on progressing by just one goal, due to having beaten Zaire by just 2-0 when Yugoslavia had beaten the Africans 9-0 and Brazil had collected a 3-0 win against the minnows. Coming into this tournament they had a squad that contained some of the finest players strutting their stuff within the English league, including the likes of Kenny Dalglish, Graeme Souness, Archie Gemmill and Joe Jordan. Players who played for Liverpool, Nottingham Forest, Manchester United and Leeds United at a time when English clubs dominated Europe.

In charge of the team was Ally MacLeod, a man who was not shy in front of the press. Given his squad, he had the right to feel confident, but there is a difference between feeling quietly confident and loudly confident. MacLeod was the latter, boasting how this could be Scotland's moment, hyping them up and persuading their loyal support, the Tartan Army, to dream. The squad even left Scotland on the back of a huge farewell party in an open-top bus, something normally reserved for returning teams who have earned it. The fact that arch-enemy England had failed to reach the finals just added to the joy the Scottish people felt. This was their moment to bask in the sunlight.

Scotland had been drawn in a group with Peru, Iran, and the Netherlands. The Netherlands were favourites, given their final appearance in 1974, although this time they would be without the talismanic Johan Cruyff. But Scotland were playing Peru and Iran first and so a couple of wins there and the Netherlands game would hopefully be a formality, just deciding who would top the group, with the top two qualifying. If only things were so straightforward.

Things took an ominous start when Scotland arrived in Córdoba to move into their training facility and the clutch burnt out on their coach, meaning a truck had to push it the final yards. The facility was lacking in amenities and entertainment, with no windows, no choice in food and an appalling training pitch, resulting in a bored squad squabbling over bonus money.

Ahead of the competition MacLeod had turned down the opportunity to scout the Peruvians, deeming it not necessary. And that appeared justified as Jordan gave Scotland the lead on 14 minutes. But then Scottish fans were to watch on in horror as Peru, through the magical Teófilo Cubillas, scored three times to defeat them, while Scotland also missed a penalty. After the game, things got worse as winger Willie Johnston failed a drugs test – he claimed that he had taken hayfever pills that he often used back home, but to no avail – and was sent home in disgrace. A win against Iran was now of paramount importance.

The Tartan Army again looked on in disbelief as Iran held them to a 1-1 draw, looking the better side for most of the second half. The indelible image became MacLeod looking on with his head in his hands. Captain Bruce Rioch described it as 'the worst horror show you've ever seen' and Scottish fans were seen verbally berating the players as they slunk off the field. The media back home laid into MacLeod and the team, especially the English press who, with England absent, could now mock the Scots for their pre-tournament swagger. The draw meant that the only path to qualification was to beat the mighty Netherlands by three clear goals. It appeared that the Scottish dream was in tatters.

What happened?

At least the Scots knew what they had to do, and they were facing a Netherlands team that, while still strong, were not the 1974 vintage with Cruyff absent. MacLeod finally picked Souness – a move many fans had been clamouring for. There was no need for caution and Scotland started strongly. A header from Rioch after just five minutes hit the bar following a Souness cross and then just two minutes later Tom Forsyth had the ball in the Dutch net, only for the effort to be disallowed for a very tight offside not even involving him. The Scots were flying and on 14 minutes Dalglish poked the ball past Jan Jongbloed for the opener, only for a second goal to be disallowed – this time for an apparent foul by Dalglish. It seemed luck had again deserted the Tartan Army.

Things got more infuriating for the Scots as Jordan had a strong claim for a penalty turned down after 19 minutes. Scotland could easily have been four goals up by now. The Dutch then started to settle, and the game became more even until suddenly, in minute 34, Scottish defender Stuart Kennedy got himself into a mess and allowed Johnny Rep to steal a loose ball and advance into the area. Kennedy desperately tried to atone but only succeeded in bringing Rep down – the referee pointing straight to the spot. Rob Rensenbrink placed it into the corner and Scotland now required four goals – surely game over.

As half-time approached, it seemed like Scotland would need the break to reorganise. But just before the whistle, a cross from Souness saw Jordan rise and head back across goal where Dalglish was perfectly placed to swivel and crack the ball into the top right-hand corner. Scotland went into half-time equal, although deserving more, and back to where they started in requiring three more goals.

Two minutes into the second half, a Dalglish cross was again nodded down by Jordan, who was winning everything in the area, into the path of Souness who was bundled down by Willy van de Kerkhof. Scotland had the perfect start to the second half as Gemmill converted the penalty – the miracle was suddenly an outside possibility.

Both teams then traded attacks until the moment that will forever live in Scottish folklore. With 69 minutes on the clock, Dalglish attacked on the right-hand side of the Dutch penalty box. He tried to move into the area, but a Ruud Krol tackle dispossessed him. The ball broke to little Archie Gemmill, who prodded the ball away from Wim Jansen before turning towards the 18-yard box. Jinking, he dribbled past despairing challenges from Krol and Jan Poortvliet before he opened his body and chipped it around Jongbloed for an incredible goal. A work of art that all of Scotland will never forget – and often referred to as one of the great World Cup goals of all time – and suddenly Scotland required just one more goal to advance. From despair to joy, the Tartan Army could hardly believe what they were witnessing. A team transformed from that which entertained Peru and Iran, a team that was 3-1 up against the 1974 World Cup finalists.

But this is Scotland after all, and hope is always extinguished by heartache. For three minutes they believed before Rep and Krol exchanged passes in the midfield after which Rep unleashed a screamer from 30 yards into the top-left corner. The two-goal lead lasted all of 202 seconds. With that, Scotland deflated, and the game petered out to a 3-2 victory. Although Scotland had beaten the Dutch, it was almost worse than if they had just lost. To be that close and yet so far – a recurring theme for the Scots over several tournaments.

Final score
Scotland 3 (Dalglish 45; Gemmill 46 pen, 68)
Netherlands 2 (Rensenbrink 34 pen; Rep 71)

What was the aftermath?

Scotland flew home with at least a touch of pride, although they had again failed to exit the group stage in a World Cup. The flight back to Glasgow stopped in London where allegedly many players got off, despite not living there, to just avoid the homecoming walk of shame. MacLeod tried to put a brave face on it and wave to the waiting supporters. It didn't go down too well.

MacLeod was hauled before the Scottish Football Association to discuss Scotland's failure and his part in it. The meeting lasted over four hours and ended with a vote as to whether to allow MacLeod to remain as manager. Somewhat surprisingly, he edged the vote and so left with his job, but it was short-lived – he would resign after Scotland's next match. He published his autobiography in 1979, *The Ally MacLeod Story*, in which he mused, 'I am a very good manager who just happened to have a few disastrous days, once upon a time, in Argentina.' Sadly, his managerial career would never recover from those few disastrous days back in 1978.

The Netherlands, meanwhile, overcame their wobble to move on and reach their second successive World Cup Final. They were within the width of the post of winning it in the last minute when Rob Rensenbrink's stretch saw the ball cannon back off the post, before succumbing in extra time. To this day, the Netherlands have still not won the World Cup, despite playing in three finals.

Teams

Scotland: Rough, Donachie, Buchan, Kennedy, Forsyth, Rioch (c), Dalglish, Hartford, Gemmill, Souness, Jordan
Manager: MacLeod

Netherlands: Jongbloed, Poortvliet, Krol (c), Rijsbergen (Wildschut HT), Suurbier, Jansen, R. van de Kerkhof, W. van de Kerkhof, Rensenbrink, Neeskens (Boskamp 10), Rep
Manager: Happel

Iconic moment

The second Archie Gemmill goal – the move across the edge of the area followed by the shimmy to the right, the flick past the flailing Poortvliet, the opening of the body and the calm finish sending Scotland into raptures. An extraordinary goal – for three whole minutes the dream was real.

Trivia fact

Gemmill's goal was immortalised in Danny Boyle's 1996 cult film, *Trainspotting*, when Mark 'Rent Boy' Renton says post-sex, 'Phew, I haven't felt that good since Archie Gemmill scored against Holland in 1978!'

Game 5

1978 World Cup

Austria v West Germany

21 June 1978

Estadio Chateau Carreras, Córdoba

Attendance: 38,318

Stage: Second Round, Group A

Why you should watch it

Austria and Germany border each other and share a lot of similarities, including a common language along with many other cultural parallels. In fact, during World War Two, Austria was reunited into Germany under the forced *Anschluss* – the first time since the 1870s – before being again granted independence in 1945 by the Allied Forces. So, like any close neighbours with much in common, there is a rivalry that exists, with Austria feeling like the smaller brother to the successful Germans, living in their shadow in terms of footballing success.

The initial 1978 World Cup stages had seen Austria surprisingly win their group, ahead of a strong Brazilian team, while West Germany had only finished second in their group following some uninspiring performances including two scoreless draws against Poland and Tunisia. Therefore, based on form, the Austrians could point to being the stronger side – something that could rarely be said when comparing the two teams in the past. For example, ahead of this game, Austria had failed to beat either West Germany or East Germany for 47 years. So there definitely existed an inferiority complex on their side despite their World Cup performance to date. Getting to the second round was an achievement – facing West Germany would be a whole new challenge fraught with history.

Austria did have an X-factor in the guise of striker Hans Krankl. Heading into the 1978 tournament, he had made a considerable name for himself back home, scoring 160 goals in 205 games over his eight seasons with Rapid Wien. In fact, he had been so deadly during the 1978 season that he won the European Golden Boot as leading goalscorer across the continent, banging in an impressive 41 goals, a feat that would earn him a move to Barcelona. Austria had managed just three goals in topping Group 3 in the first round – Krankl had supplied two of those. While they were by no means a one-man team, Krankl was the undoubted star and they would need him to be red hot if they were to stand any chance of vanquishing the Germans.

Unfortunately for the Austrians, the second round had also placed them with both the Netherlands and Italy, who they had to face ahead of the clash with West Germany. The Dutch laid down a masterful performance, thrashing Austria 5-1, before a solitary goal from Paolo Rossi had seen Austria eliminated. West Germany, meanwhile, had drawn both of their games, meaning that they could still qualify. Going into the game, the Germans were playing for a spot in the World Cup semi-finals while Austria were playing purely for pride and the chance to finally get one over on their bigger neighbours. Could Austria both register a famous win against the defending world champions while also depriving them of a semi-final berth? It would be a historic result for them if they could.

What happened?

True to form, the Germans took an early lead through key striker Karl-Heinz Rummenigge after just 19 minutes with the first clear chance of the game. A neat one-two saw him burst into the Austrian area and slot the ball past Austrian keeper Friedl Koncilia. The rest of the first half saw both teams create half-chances but nothing that really threatened to change the scoreline, meaning West Germany went into the break ahead by one goal.

Just two minutes into the second half came a powerful left-foot shot from Krankl that went narrowly wide, but a warning to West Germany that Krankl was beginning to find his range. At the other end Rummenigge continued to threaten, forcing a good save out of Koncilia, before Rainer Bonhof also went close. It looked likely that the next goal would be a German one.

But then, on 59 minutes, Austrian forward Walter Schachner whipped in a low cross which experienced German keeper Sepp Maier came out to intercept. But, uncharacteristically for him, he completely missed the ball, causing it to cannon off a surprised Berti Vogts into his own goal. Suddenly the Austrians were reinstalled with belief and just seven minutes later they took the lead. A long cross found Krankl on the right-hand side of the German area. With two players around him, Krankl cushioned the cross, swivelled and hit a left-footed volley into the far top corner – the ball not touching the ground during his control. It was exactly the sort of form that he had shown for Rapid Wien all year and would have the Barcelona hierarchy grinning.

Of course, West Germany were not the defending world champions for nothing and almost immediately a Bonhof free kick was powerfully headed in by Bernd Hölzenbein. After that the game seemed to be drifting towards a draw – a result that would also mean elimination for West Germany and a continuation of Austria's inability to defeat them. That was until 87 minutes came up on the clock.

Krankl received the ball wide and with a quick header he got past defender Rolf Rüssmann. Moving into the German penalty area, he faced the experienced Manni Kaltz as Rüssmann tried to catch up. While running at speed, he faked to his left just enough to fool Kaltz before switching right and poking the ball with the outside of his left foot past the onrushing Maier, leaving Kaltz in a sprawled heap. It was a beautiful moment of individualistic genius that sent the Austrian nation into raptures as Krankl rushed to celebrate with the bench. To fully appreciate this, you need to listen to the Austrian commentary at the time from

Edi Finger which translates as follows and is known by all Austrians of a certain age, 'Krankl is in the box. He shoots! Goal! Goal! Goal! Goal! Goal! Goal! I am going bonkers! Krankl has scored. It is 3-2 to Austria! Ladies and gentlemen, we are hugging each other here, Rippel, my colleague, graduate engineer Posch, we're kissing each other; 3-2 to Austria, by our Krankl's magnificent goal. He beat all of them. And just wait a minute, wait a minute and perhaps we can pour ourselves a small glass of wine. That's something you have to have seen. I think we have beaten them!'

The Germans pushed back with one final flourish and almost equalised through Rüdiger Abramczik but then it was all over. While not moving on in the competition, Austria had finally defeated their much bigger neighbours and the defending world champions, allowing Finger to tell a joyous nation, 'And now it is over! It's over, it's finished, it's done, it's over! Germany have been beaten, ladies and gentlemen, for the first time in 47 years, Austria have defeated Germany.'

Final score
Austria 3 (Vogts 59 og; Krankl 66, 87)
West Germany 2 (Rummenigge 19; Hölzenbein 68)

What was the aftermath?

As you can imagine, reactions differed greatly between the two neighbours. Austrians celebrated that they had prevented Germany progressing further and had put on an historic performance despite being eliminated from the World Cup. For German coach Helmut Schön, meanwhile, he had announced that he would step down after the competition ahead of time and so the defeat meant leaving on a low, although nothing could tarnish his legacy of having led the Germans to victory in both the 1972 European Championship and the 1974 World Cup, cementing his place as a German footballing legend.

The two reactions to the game can be summarised in how it is referred to in each nation. For the Austrians, it is *Das Wunder von Córdoba* (The Miracle of Córdoba) while to the Germans, it is *Die Schmach von Córdoba* (The Disgrace of Córdoba). The same game just seen from two different viewpoints.

Post-Schön, West Germany turned to Jupp Derwall as their next manager, with normal service swiftly resuming as they went on to win the 1980 European Championship. The two teams would then meet again in the 1982 World Cup in a game that was the polar opposite of this exciting instalment. But more about that later.

Teams

Austria: Koncilia, Sara (c), Obermayer, Pezzey, Strasser, Hickersberger, Prohaska, Krieger, Krankl, Kreuz, Schachner (Oberacher 71)

Manager: Senekowitsch

West Germany: Maier, Vogts (c), Dietz, Rüssmann, Kaltz, Bonhof, Beer (H. Müller HT), Hölzenbein, Abramczik, Rummenigge, D. Müller (Fischer 60)

Manager: Schön

Iconic moment

Krankl's winning goal and the Edi Finger commentary that accompanied it. His joy in shouting 'Tor! Tor! Tor! Tor! Tor! Tor! I wer' narrisch!' is imprinted on the brains of most Austrians and even Germans who witnessed the game on television. Forty-seven years of hurt ended in magnificent style by possibly the greatest Austrian player of all time.

Trivia fact

Finger's phrase about going bonkers ('I wer' narrisch') became the slogan of several advertising and marketing campaigns within Austria. In 2008, ahead of another Austria/Germany clash, Edi Finger Jr once again delivered his father's famous commentary during a reenactment of the 1978 game. Meanwhile, Krankl had a music career after hanging up his boots, including his single 'Lonely Boy' reaching number two in Austria in 1985.

Game 6

1978 World Cup

Argentina v Peru

21 June 1978

Estadio Gigante de Arroyito, Rosario

Attendance: 37,315

Stage: Second Round, Group B

Why you should watch it

There had been a lot of global unease ahead of the 1978 World Cup in respect to it being hosted by Argentina. Two years prior to the tournament, the country had been subject to a military coup, bringing in what was basically a dictatorship and the installation of a military junta headed by Jorge Videla. Once in power, the junta started to unlawfully detain opponents, including anyone who spoke out against the new leadership. Thousands of Argentinian citizens 'disappeared' as time went on, taken to detention camps and then never heard from again. This became the background against which the 1978 finals would be played, with a sense that hosting would provide the junta with further legitimacy in the eyes of the watching world.

Of course, the most valuable event that could occur for the junta would be to see Argentina win the World Cup and all the attention and glow that would bring. Therefore Videla, who had not shown any interest in football previously, ensured he was a public figure at Argentina's games. There was a lot of pressure on the team to succeed and a lot of pressure on Videla's staff to ensure that this was given every encouragement.

Argentina had to face a tricky first-round group, pitted with Italy and an emerging France, as well as Hungary, with two teams advancing to the next group stage. While Argentina beat both France and Hungary to ensure qualification, they were beaten 1-0 by the Italians, placing them second in the group. That meant going into Group B in the second round, containing local rivals Brazil, from which the top team would move on to play in the final.

Both Brazil and Argentina won their opening group games – Brazil 3-0 against Peru, Argentina 2-0 against Poland – before the two teams met in a 0-0 draw. That meant that they played their final games on 21 June – Brazil against Poland and Argentina against Peru. Controversially, the matches had been scheduled so that Brazil would play first, meaning that Argentina would then have the advantage of knowing exactly what they needed to do against the Peruvians to reach the final. As it was, Brazil defeated Poland 3-1, meaning that Argentina went into their evening game knowing that they had to beat Peru by at least four goals to play the Netherlands in the final.

The hope had been for Argentina to top their first group and play their subsequent group matches in Buenos Aires but by coming second, they instead moved to Rosario – for whom team striker Mario Kempes had once played for, which seemed to be bringing him to life in the competition. Kempes was a key player for *La Albiceleste*. He had initially made a name for himself in Rosario, scoring 85 goals over three seasons, which secured him a move to Spain with Valencia, for whom he scored 39 goals in 1977/78 ahead of the World Cup. Argentina preferred their players to play at home ahead of the tournament, allowing coach César Luis Menotti time with them, but an exception was made for the talented long-haired star, who became the only foreign-based player in the 1978 squad.

It is at this point that stories about the game enter speculation, conspiracy theories and rumour. Many accusations swirl around the events of that evening still to this day – and we will probably never know exactly what did and didn't transpire. One rumour exists that Peru received grain shipments from Argentina along with debt forgiveness at the time. Another claims that Peruvian dissidents held in Argentina were shipped back to Peru. Some Peruvian players stated later that they were visited ahead of kick-off in their changing room by Videla, who shared a speech with them on the Argentina-Peru relationship. The Peruvian goalkeeper, Ramón Quiroga, had been born in Argentina – a point noted by the Brazilian press. It should be stressed that nothing incriminating has ever been proved regarding all these rumours – but they have also never gone away when the game is discussed. A whole separate book could be written just about this topic, but whatever transpired, the upshot was that Argentina still had to go out and defeat Peru by at least four goals to advance in front of a watching world.

What happened?

The Peruvian team came out to a passionate Argentinian crowd packed into the relatively compact Rosario stadium. No one who watched the 1978 tournament will ever forget the ticker tape welcomes that accompanied every Argentina match – both an impressive and intimidating sight. With Argentina needing four goals, the crowd were going to do everything in their power to push the team over the line.

If Peru were motivated to throw the game, there seemed little evidence of that early on. In fact, after just 11 minutes, a break saw them almost score, instead unluckily hitting the post. During the first 20 minutes, the better chances fell to the Peruvians. But then Kempes picked up the ball outside of the Peru penalty area and made one of his trademark direct runs through the heart of the defence before slotting the ball past Quiroga. The keeper may have been born in Argentina but there was no suspicion on this goal as he had no chance of saving it.

Argentina pushed on and Leopoldo Luque, with his magnificent moustache, saw a shot rebound off the post. Shortly after that, Argentinian forward Oscar Ortiz hit the bar. The pressure was mounting, with Argentina aware that they still needed three more goals and, as half-time loomed, it looked like they would only get a quarter of the job completed. On 38 minutes Daniel Bertoni was felled in the area – and again, if the referee had been at all compromised, this would have been the perfect cover to award a penalty. But he didn't despite a fair claim and so his neutrality appeared to be intact.

But shortly before half-time, an Argentinian corner was strongly headed home by defender Alberto Tarantini, meaning that *La Albiceleste* went in with confidence regained and half the job done.

Argentina got off to the perfect start in the second half when, just three minutes in, a free kick fell to Kempes in the area. Chesting it down to a colleague, he took the return pass and smashed it into the corner; 3-0 to Argentina and nothing the Peru keeper could do about it. Almost straight from the restart, Argentina attacked again and a cross from the left reached Kempes at the far post. His header passed right across the goal where Luque was on hand to head home into the empty net. It was the key fourth goal that Argentina had been looking for, sparking off huge celebrations within the stadium.

It is at this point that Peruvian heads really seemed to drop. Argentina were full of confidence and attacking in waves, trying to put the game to bed. On 64 minutes, substitute René Houseman was brought on and just three minutes later he sealed Argentina's World Cup Final spot when another great Kempes run led to a cross that Houseman simply tapped in.

You now got the impression that Peru just wanted to get out of there as soon as possible and end the humiliation. But unfortunately for them Argentina were now in the mood and attacked relentlessly. Just five minutes after Argentina's fifth, Peru lost the ball in midfield, it was moved on to Luque and he powered home his second and Argentina's sixth. Any Brazilian hopes of meeting the Netherlands in the final evaporated at that moment.

The game then petered out to its inevitable end with Argentina having scored the four they needed, plus some more for good measure. They were in the final in front of their rabid fans; Brazil had to settle for a third-place play-off and a thousand conspiracy theories were born.

Final score
Argentina 6 (Kempes 21, 49; Tarantini 43; Luque 50, 72; Houseman 67) Peru 0

What was the aftermath?

The six-goal win placed Argentina into the final against the Netherlands, who had topped group A ahead of Italy, West Germany and Austria. This was the second consecutive final in which the Dutch had been pitted against the host nation. While the team was not as iconic as the 1974 vintage, notably missing Cruyff, it was still a strong side as discussed earlier with the Scotland v Netherlands match. The final saw Argentina take a first-half lead through Kempes once again, before substitute Dick Nanninga equalised with just eight minutes remaining. As the game went into its final moments, a Dutch cross reached the toe of a stretching Rensenbrink, whose shot hit the post, when a goal would certainly have meant victory. After that, Argentina took command of extra time and another Kempes goal followed by a third from Bertoni saw the host nation crowned as world champions. The junta had got the PR victory they had hoped for all along and the world was treated to the slightly disconcerting sight of Jorge Videla handing the trophy over to Argentinian captain Daniel Passarella.

Mario Kempes shot to worldwide fame during the tournament. While already a recognised talent within Argentina and Spain, he was now a global star. He ended the 1978 finals as the leading goalscorer with six goals – but most importantly he found his stride in the key final games. During the first-round stage, when all three Argentina matches were played in Buenos Aires, Kempes had failed to score – leading some to question his inclusion. But once in his old stomping ground of Rosario, he scored twice against Poland, twice against Peru and twice in the final back in Buenos Aires – all from open play. Unfortunately, those two goals in the final would prove to be his last for *La Albiceleste* at the age of just 23.

Teams

Argentina: Fillol, Passerella (c), Galván, Tarantini, Olguín, Gallego (Oviedo 85), Larrosa, Kempes, Bertoni (Houseman 64), Ortiz, Luque
Manager: Menotti

Peru: Quiroga, Chumpatiz (c), Manzo, Duarte, Rojas, Quesada, Velásquez (Gorriti 51), Cueto, Muñante, Oblitas, Cubillas
Manager: Calderón

Iconic moment

Kempes's second and Argentina's third goal – it was the perfect start to the second half and the chested one-two and finish was a thing of beauty. Also, the sight of Kempes celebrating, arms outstretched and luxurious locks flowing, would become an iconic image of the tournament after each of his six goals. Power and grace combined, 1978 saw Kempes win the World Cup, the Golden Boot as the leading goalscorer, and the Golden Ball as the player of the tournament – not a bad haul.

Trivia fact

At the exact moment that Argentina scored the vital fourth goal, a bomb exploded in the house of the secretary of finance, Juan Alemann. The explosion tore off the ground-floor window and destroyed part of the living room. While it was never discovered who was directly responsible for the attack, Alemann claimed that it was the work of Admiral Emilio Massera due to Alemann's criticisms of the Argentinian government's spend on hosting the tournament.

Game 7

1982 World Cup

Northern Ireland v Spain

25 June 1982
Estadio Luis Casanova, Valencia
Attendance: 49,562
Stage: First Round, Group 5

Why you should watch it

In 1982 Northern Ireland continued to suffer what was known globally as 'The Troubles'. The country's population was divided between Protestants and Catholics who had lived together for many generations, albeit with a degree of tension. It was in the late 1960s however when that tension built into something more catastrophic. The Catholic population complained of discrimination against them by predominantly Protestant organisations and companies and as antagonism built, the British Army entered the country, initially to protect the Catholics. Unfortunately, the situation evolved into open warfare between the communities with the British Army trapped in-between. The 1970s and early 1980s saw a litany of bombings, killings and rioting that turned cities such as Belfast and Derry into no-go war zones. Many living there felt trapped in a circle of violence, which offered little in the way of hope and joy in their daily lives.

Against this backdrop, the Northern Irish team were fighting to see if they could qualify for their first World Cup since 1958. A country of just one and a half million, the odds had always been stacked against them, and more so when The Troubles had caused some home games to have to be played in England for safety reasons. In fact, when they played in the 1958 World Cup, they became the least populous nation to ever reach the finals, until Trinidad & Tobago qualified for the 2006 tournament. Sadly, one of the greatest players to ever grace the game, George Best, never got the chance to play in a World Cup because of representing Northern Ireland during their barren period of the 1960s and 1970s.

They were placed in a qualifying group containing Sweden, Portugal, Israel, and a familiar foe in Scotland, where the top two would travel to Spain for the finals. A passionate Belfast crowd cheered the team on during their home games at the tight, intense Windsor Park, which yielded victories against Sweden, Portugal, and Israel. It was this home form that pushed them to the brink of qualification, but it was a surprise win by Sweden in Lisbon that got them over the line, behind Scotland. Managed by Billy Bingham, Northern Ireland and their fans were determined to get away from the turmoil back home and enjoy the Spanish sun.

When Bingham named his squad, there had been suggestions by some that George Best should be selected. But by the summer of 1982 he was 35 years old and had been bouncing around American teams in the NASL for the past few seasons. Instead, Bingham called up Norman Whiteside, a young player who had just turned 17 years old and had only ever played in two competitive matches for Manchester United. He would go on to play at the 1982 World Cup and therefore become the youngest player to appear in the finals at the time, knocking the great Pelé from that pedestal.

Drawn in a group with hosts Spain, Yugoslavia and debutants Honduras, it was felt that it would come down to the Irish and the Yugoslavs for the second spot. With many therefore viewing Northern Ireland vs Yugoslavia as the key match, it ended up being a cagey 0-0 draw. With Spain then beating Yugoslavia, things looked up for the Irish if they could defeat Honduras. But Honduras proved to be much stronger than expected and, having already drawn with Spain, they also held the Irish to a draw. That now left Northern Ireland needing to beat Spain in front of their fervent support in Valencia or go home. Almost 50,000 fans, nearly all Spanish, packed the stadium on a balmy night in expectation of a Spanish victory to place them top of the group. Northern Ireland had done fantastically well to get to Spain – but surely now the dream would end?

What happened?

The issue with being the host nation is that it brings the advantage of home support but also the heavy pressure of an expectant country. While Spain had already qualified for the next round, a win was expected, which would theoretically give them an easier next group. And so it was against this backdrop that the two teams took to the field in Valencia within an electric atmosphere – the Irish in their change strip of white shirts and green shorts.

The Irish team included the two extremes of age – Norman Whiteside and veteran 37-year-old keeper Pat Jennings. The tension immediately got to both sets of players, with the match becoming physical and no smoothness to the play. This wasn't the Spain one probably thinks of in recent times – this was a Spain where *La Furia* was seen as part of the approach to games, the theory that Spanish teams should play with steeliness as well as skill. That probably favoured the Irish in being closer to the British style of play that their players were used to.

However, it soon became clear that as the fouls built up, the referee was being lenient towards Spain, refusing to punish their digressions while admonishing Northern Ireland. Sadly, as the Spaniards realised this, they became increasingly physical, resulting in an ugly, goalless first half. An example of this was a blatant, wild kick by Spanish defender Periko Alonso on Northern Irish captain Martin O'Neill where there was zero attempt to play the ball, which did not even merit a yellow card in the eyes of Paraguayan official Héctor Ortiz. Yet Sammy McIlroy earned a yellow for retaliating after another nasty foul committed on him. It was ugly; fouls, body checks, stamping – it was all there. McIlroy recalled later,

'Spain went about it trying to bully us and they came unstuck because we had so many experienced lads in the team who could stand up for themselves. They were doing every trick under the sun – they were pulling shirts, they were spitting at you, kicking at you.'

It was right at the start of the second half that the game exploded into life. Gerry Armstrong intercepted a Spanish move just outside of his own penalty area and surged forward with the ball. His run took him into the Spain half before nudging a pass out to Billy Hamilton on the right wing. Hamilton took on his defender, beating him for pace on the outside, before firing a cross into the penalty area which Spanish keeper Luis Arconada dove out to claim. However, he could only push the ball away from the goal, where Armstrong was waiting. Hitting the ball first time, Armstrong drilled it between Arconada's legs. The stadium fell into a hush, interrupted only by a tiny pocket of cheers from around 300 brave Irish souls. Northern Ireland were ahead.

The Irish now knew that they would be facing 43 minutes of onslaught from the stung Spaniards. But to make matters worse, with 30 minutes remaining, Mal Donaghy went into a tackle with José Camacho on the touchline. After the tackle Camacho turned on Donaghy, who unwisely pushed his hand towards his face. Contact was minimal but the referee had been favouring Spain all evening and now, with the home crowd baying for blood, he showed Donaghy a straight red card. Northern Ireland were now going to have to hold their ground for half an hour with just ten men. The odds against them doing so appeared slim.

But the Irish held on in a brave rearguard action to do what had seemed impossible and beat Spain in Valencia, placing them top of the group and sending the hosts away to have to face a second-round group containing West Germany and England. The players celebrated a historic victory as Bingham distributed hugs.

Final score
Northern Ireland 1 (Armstrong 47) Spain 0

What was the aftermath?

To say that Northern Ireland celebrated would be an understatement. The win had been a colossal shock and the players knew it.

Beers were downed until the early morning as the players mixed with fans in the hotel bar. Placed into a second-round group with France and Austria, they drew 2-2 with the Austrians before then facing a must-win against a France team that was evolving into something great. It was then, in Madrid, that the Irish dream finally died, courtesy of a 4-1 defeat powered by Michel Platini, Dominique Rocheteau, Alain Giresse and Jean Tigana.

They went home to a heroes' welcome, although the Irish FA had not bothered to book an open-top bus for them. It had been a team made up of both Protestants and Catholics who had gelled together despite their differences. For a while, Catholics and Protestants celebrated together, bonding the war-torn country for a few weeks. A great story is told about how Norman Whiteside's mother, who lived in the predominantly loyalist area of the Shankill Road in Belfast, was invited over to tea on Falls Road, the predominantly republican area, by Gerry Armstrong's mother.

Northern Ireland would once again make it to the World Cup in 1986, but sadly since then they have failed to reach another tournament at the time of writing. But for a generation of fans, that night in Valencia will never be forgotten.

As for the Spanish, their second-round group placed them with West Germany and England, where a loss to West Germany and a goalless draw with England saw them exit. The host nation had played five games during the World Cup, winning just once, and scoring only four goals. As they had done so often in the past, and would do for several more years to come, they failed to live up to their full potential on the biggest stage.

Teams

Northern Ireland: Jennings, J. Nicholl, C. Nicholl, McClelland, Donaghy, O'Neill (c), McIlroy (Cassidy 50), McCreery, Armstrong, Whiteside (Nelson 73), Hamilton
Manager: Bingham

Spain: Arconada (c), Alexanko, Camacho, Tendillo, Gordillo, Alonso, Sánchez, Saura, Juanito, Satrústegui (Quini HT), Ufarte (Gallego 78)
Manager: Santamaría

Iconic moment

Manager Billy Bingham hugging goalscorer Gerry Armstrong on the pitch after the final whistle. Armstrong has a smile as wide as Belfast plastered on to his face. It is an image that captured the joy and togetherness of that tight-knit squad, looking more like a proud father joyously congratulating his son.

Trivia fact

After celebrating into the early hours in their hotel, the Northern Irish team discovered that they would have to move as the Irish FA had not bothered to book the hotel beyond the Spain game under the supposition that it would not be required. They had also made sure that flights home were booked – flights that could now be gleefully cancelled. Scrambling for new accommodation, the Irish had to make do with the hotel that the Yugoslavs had booked, presuming they would advance, which unfortunately lay next to an airport runway.

Game 8

1982 World Cup

Brazil v Italy

5 July 1982

Estadio de Sarriá, Barcelona

Attendance: 44,000

Stage: Group C, Second Round

WORLD CUP CLASSIC

Why you should watch it

Without wanting to get into stereotypes, there is an argument that Italy and Brazil have often represented opposite approaches to the beautiful game. Neither approach is 'the right way' to play football – they are just different sides to the coin.

On the Italian side, clubs enjoyed success in the 1960s through *catenaccio* – a setup with a strong emphasis on defence that stifled opponents before hitting them on the break. Games often ended 1-0 as chances were scarce and Italian defenders were viewed as the gold standard. The late Annibale Frossi, one of the fathers of *catenaccio*, said that the perfect game should end 0-0 as that shows a total balance between attack and defence.

In Brazil, meanwhile, there has always been a view that the game should be an expression of joy. It is mirrored in their description of the game as *o jogo bonito*, the beautiful game. The team that won the 1970 World Cup was the definition of this, but set a high bar for all subsequent selections. The Brazilian public adored that side, but it meant that a free-flowing game was then expected even as football evolved in the 1970s to new styles, such as the Dutch Total Football. The 1970 team was also a very special set of players – few could play in a comparable manner.

But as the 1982 World Cup approached, it seemed that Brazil had unearthed another special generation of players. The 1978 finals had seen a more functional team eliminated by Argentina, but the qualification tournament for 1982 had seen Brazil win all four of their games, scoring 11 goals in the process, admittedly against Venezuela and Bolivia. What really put the team on the map and drew international attention to them was a European tour in 1981. The *Seleção* played England, France and West Germany in three friendlies on European soil and won all three games: 1-0, 3-1 and 2-1, all in the space of just eight days. These were three of the best teams in Europe, and all had been defeated by this Brazilian vintage.

It should be remembered that back in those days, many of the Brazilians played in their home leagues and so were little known outside. It was not until the European tour that much of the world saw the likes of Zico, Sócrates and Éder. There had been tales of their greatness but now it was unveiled in its full glory. It was the aperitif to what was to come in Spain.

June 1982 saw the world marvel at this edition of Brazil. They were placed into a group alongside a dangerous Soviet Union side, a Scotland team that contained players who had enjoyed great success with Liverpool and Nottingham Forest in Europe, and newcomers New Zealand. The opening game against the Soviets did provide Brazil with a scare – they were a goal down with 15 minutes left. Then two fantastic goals by Sócrates and Éder turned it in their favour. Scotland then also had the nerve to take the lead against the *Seleção* before being hammered 4-1, meaning Brazil could cruise in their last game against New Zealand, although cruising still meant a 4-0 victory, with a Zico double. Three wins, ten goals and some memorable moments – this was a Brazil that brought back memories of 1970.

Group 1, meanwhile, saw a dull Italy side scrape through to the next round. Placed with Poland, Cameroon and Peru, the Italians drew all three games, scoring just two goals and only advancing because they had scored one more goal than Cameroon. Up front, the Italian manager, Enzo Bearzot, had placed his faith in Paolo Rossi, the Juventus striker who had enjoyed a good 1978 World Cup but had then become embroiled in the 1980 betting scandal known as *Totonero.* Rossi struggled in the three group games, being described as 'a ghost aimlessly wandering over the field'. Bearzot's selection was under great scrutiny by the obsessive Italian press.

The second round saw both teams placed into an extremely tough group with world champions Argentina in a three-way round robin. Italy started to show signs of life, defeating Argentina 2-1, although Rossi was substituted late on after again failing to impress. Argentina were then eliminated as Brazil put three past them before a late consolation goal – a game which also saw a young Diego Maradona sent off for violent conduct. That meant that Brazil just needed a draw against Italy to move on to the semi-finals. The world tuned in to watch the relentless march of the *Seleção* and enjoy another captivating display. They got one of the two.

What happened?

A crowd of 44,000 packed the Estadio de Sarriá in Barcelona – one of the smaller venues but one that created an intense atmosphere with its tightness to the pitch. The Brazilian fans were in great voice, the sound of samba drowning out the Italian *tifosi.* If anyone was expecting Brazil to play safe and aim for a draw, the team sheet starting Sócrates, Éder, Falcão, Zico and Serginho suggested otherwise. Serginho was the weak link within this attacking formation – designated as the number nine striker, he was not quite in the same league as the other four. But it remained a team full of attacking potential.

After just five minutes Italy shocked Brazil by taking an early lead. A cross from Antonio Cabrini found Rossi stealing in at the back post and he finally opened his World Cup account with a close-range header. It was exactly the start the *Azzurri* had hoped for as well as forcing Brazil to attack, making the game entertaining for the neutral. Just five minutes later, Serginho found himself through on goal, only to fluff his lines. But two minutes later the Brazilians were level.

Sócrates picked the ball up at the halfway line and advanced forward. Spotting Zico tightly marked, he rolled the ball to him anyway. With a deft back-heel spin, Zico escaped two Italian defenders while Sócrates continued his run forward. A neat pass from Zico put Sócrates through on the edge of the area where, with Dino Zoff probably expecting a low cross, he instead rifled it in at the near post. It was a beautiful move and Italy were back to square one, having led for just seven minutes.

As Brazil continued to dominate, renowned hard man Claudio Gentile gave Zico a little reminder of his no-nonsense reputation with a tackle from behind, earning a yellow card. The game continued to flow until a rush of blood from Toninho Cerezo after 24 minutes saw him play a square pass across the defence. Quick as a whippet, Rossi seized on the chance, intercepting the ball, moving to the edge of the area, and hitting a swift first-time shot past Waldir Peres. In the blink of an eye, the *Azzurri* were ahead again, Rossi repaying Bearzot's faith in him.

With Brazil again needing a goal, Sócrates and Zico both came close as the action became concentrated in the Italian half. Zico's effort saw him left with a torn shirt as he remonstrated with the referee about being held while shooting, but to no avail. The Brazilian attacks came in waves but the resolute Italian defence held strong.

The second half started as the first half had ended, with Falcão coming close right after kick-off. Italy seemed content to sit back and defend their lead, making few forays into the Brazilian half. It was a dangerous gamble to take – letting a team with such attacking talent have free rein with such a slim margin. Chance after chance came and went and it felt like no team could withstand such pressure for 45 minutes.

The breakthrough finally came after 68 minutes. A run from Zico saw him pass over to Falcão to the right of the area. Cerezo ran behind him, drawing the Italian defence towards the left, and Falcão used that to instead cut inside, before unleashing an unstoppable left-footed shot. Brazil were level and 22 minutes away from the semi-final. All they had to do now was to shut up shop.

But that wasn't the Brazilian way. While others might have thought of digging in, the *Seleção* still wanted to win, deciding that attack was the best form of defence. They continued to push forward until conceding a corner after 75 minutes during a rare Italian excursion. The ball fell to Marco Tardelli whose shot looked harmless until a toe poked out and deflected the ball in. Paolo Rossi wheeled away in delight, a hat-trick to his name.

At first the Brazilians seemed genuinely stunned before shaking off the shock and attacking once more. Sócrates had the ball in the Italian net but was called offside. Gaps opened in the Brazilian defence as they pushed forward, allowing midfielder Giancarlo Antognoni to score with three minutes left, but he too was deprived by the linesman's flag. Then, in the dying moments, Éder swung a free kick into the area which defender Oscar met with a powerful header, low to Zoff's left. Zoff saved brilliantly on the line, as the Brazilians appealed that the ball had crossed, but the referee was having none of it. Brazil continued to throw everything at Italy but, shortly after, the final whistle blew. As the Italians celebrated, the world looked on in shock. Brazil were out of the 1982 World Cup.

Final score
Italy 3 (Rossi 5, 25, 74) Brazil 2 (Sócrates 12; Falcão 68)

What was the aftermath?

Whenever I think of this game, Don McLean's famous 'American Pie' comes to mind, especially two lines:

'But something touched me deep inside
The day the music died'

To many around the world, it felt as if the music had died that day and that football needed to mourn. Shocked Brazilian fans and media immediately labelled the game as the *Tragédia do Sarriá* (Sarriá Tragedy), becoming another infamous day in the vein of the 1950 *Maracanazo* following their World Cup defeat to Uruguay. To this day, more has probably been written about this game than almost any other, with most books and articles highlighting the beauty of the Brazilian team and sadness at their elimination.

It is however completely unfair to Italy that they get so reviled for beating the team in front of them. They deservedly won 3-2 and would go on to win the World Cup while Paolo Rossi would end the tournament with the Golden Boot. The Italians did a thoroughly professional job yet all they ever hear is how they broke the hearts of football fans everywhere. But, especially with the passing of time, the Brazil team has entered the pantheon of legend. They are now viewed as one of the greatest teams to have never won the World Cup, along with the likes of Hungary 1954, Netherlands 1974, and Denmark 1986. I worship the 1982 Brazil team but there must be some perspective – they were naive to keep attacking when the game was 2-2. Having great attacking players does not necessarily mean having a reliable system and they lost to a team that ended up world champions.

Both teams should be praised, principally for producing one of the greatest World Cup games ever. The swinging back and forth between Italy leading and Brazil equalising, the poaching skills of Rossi, the teams resplendent in their classic kits, shimmering in the Spanish sun – it was all part of the overall spectacle played out in a tight stadium full of passionate fans. There is an old boxing expression that is perfect for this game, styles make fights, and it was the clash of differing styles that made this such a memorable match.

Some of the 1982 Boys of Brazil did return for another outing in 1986, but by then the likes of Sócrates and Zico were starting to age. It was time for a new set of heroes to emerge – the likes of Careca, Müller and Romário – along with a less swashbuckling approach. A team's system was becoming increasingly important, with less focus on individual brilliance, and Brazil would have to adapt accordingly to evolve and compete.

But the Sarriá Tragedy – oh, it still hurts.

Teams

Italy: Zoff (c), Cabrini, Collovati (Bergomi 34), Gentile, Scirea, Antognoni, Oriali, Tardelli (Marini 75), Conti, Graziani, Rossi

Manager: Bearzot

Brazil: Peres, Leandro, Oscar, Luizinho, Júnior, Cerezo, Sócrates, Éder, Falcão, Zico, Serginho (Isidoro 69)

Manager: Santana

Iconic moment

That moment when the final whistle blew, and everybody was hit by the realisation that Brazil really were out. There had been a sense throughout the game that they would not actually lose and even after falling behind 3-2 they threw everything at the *Azzurri* and you felt a goal had to come. And then it started to sink in that you would not get another chance to watch this team during the tournament. Unless you were Italian, a depression began to creep through your bones, a malaise overcoming your body. Football can be a cruel game.

Trivia fact

Hat-trick hero Paolo Rossi should not really have even been playing at the 1982 World Cup. Two years earlier he had been embroiled in the Italian betting scandal known as *Totonero*, leading to a three-year ban from the game, meaning that he missed the 1980 European Championship. But, conveniently for the *Azzurri*, his ban was later reduced from three years to two, allowing him to participate in 1982. Enzo Bearzot took a risk including him in the squad, and the rest, as they say, is history.

Game 9

1982 World Cup

France v West Germany

8 July 1982

Ramón Sánchez Pizjuán Stadium, Seville

Attendance: 70,000

Stage: Semi-Final

WORLD CUP CLASSIC

Why you should watch it

This game had absolutely everything that you would want in a classic – drama, action, goals, controversy, a hero, and a villain. From the first minute to the last it was gripping stuff. It is one of those reasons we sit through so many average matches – because you never know when an occasion like this may suddenly arise. I remember being mentally and emotionally exhausted at the end of this – and I wasn't even from either nation. Although, in a few more minutes, you will be able to guess where my allegiance lay and why.

Starting with France, this was a golden generation team that played with verve and panache. The famed *Carré Magique* (Magic Square) was already three-quarters in place with Michel Platini, Alain Giresse and Jean Tigana controlling the midfield, while Dominique Rocheteau and Didier Six were exciting players. But they had looked shaky during the initial group stage. They had been shocked in their opening game by conceding to England after just 27 seconds, eventually losing 3-1 to get off to a poor start. They were then involved in a bizarre incident during their second match against Kuwait when the Kuwaiti Emir's brother intervened to prevent his team from playing further until the referee disallowed a French goal against them, which he duly did, although it mattered little as France romped to a 4-1 win.

Finishing second in their group behind England, they had been rewarded with a relatively straightforward second-round group due to Northern Ireland shocking Spain. The French looked much improved during this second group stage, defeating both Northern Ireland and Austria as they grew into the tournament, playing attractive football and winning plaudits along the way.

West Germany, meanwhile, had been involved in one of the World Cup's most infamous games during their first group stage. They had opened their tournament with a shocking 2-1 loss to Algeria – a match that saw an African team defeat a European one for the first time during a World Cup. They then beat Chile to set up a final clash against neighbours Austria. Because FIFA had decided to schedule final group games on different days, Algeria played first, beating Chile, which left Germany and Austria both aware of what they needed to do to both qualify ahead of the Algerians. A one- or two-goal German win would mean both teams would progress. What followed became known as 'The Disgrace of Gijón'.

Pages could be written about the shambolic performance put on by both sides on that day. West Germany scored after ten minutes through Horst Hrubesch – and that was pretty much it. With 1-0 being enough for both teams to move on, West Germany and Austria – neighbours who share a common language – decided to pass the ball around innocuously for 80 minutes. There didn't even seem any effort to try and at least make it look competitive. Instead, the paying public were insulted by the audacity of their indifference. Even Germans and Austrians were appalled, with West German commentator Eberhard Stanjek refusing to continue describing the match, while his Austrian counterpart Robert Seeger asked viewers to switch off. The Algerian fans present could only watch in fury, waving banknotes at the players in frustration. A Spanish newspaper published the match report in its crime section. But while unsporting, it was not illegal under FIFA rules to play in that manner, and so the game stood, both teams progressed, and FIFA subsequently made sure that final group matches were played simultaneously in future tournaments.

West Germany then progressed through their second-round group by eliminating Spain and England, making them still further unpopular with the locals. And so, going into this semi-final, for all neutrals there was clearly already a feeling that the French were the Resistance while the Germans were the Evil Empire. This would only be heightened during the drama to follow.

What happened?

The game kicked off in the evening in Seville to avoid the southern Spanish midday heat before 70,000 expectant fans, although the temperature was still high with significant humidity. Overseeing the clash was referee Charles Corver from the Netherlands, who would have a major part to play in the unfolding drama. The good news for the French was that prolific German striker Karl-Heinz Rummenigge was starting on the bench with a hamstring issue, while *Les Bleus* included defender Patrick Battiston among their substitutes. Two European superpowers kicked off for a place in the 1982 World Cup Final.

The first scare for the Germans saw a chip shot from Alain Giresse go just wide of German keeper Harald Schumacher's post, before a free kick from Pierre Littbarski rattled off the French crossbar in retaliation. Then the first breakthrough occurred on 17 minutes as Klaus Fischer broke through before France keeper Jean-Luc Ettori rushed out to deflect the ball from him. The ball broke to Littbarski on the edge of the area and his first-time shot went through Ettori's legs to put West Germany into an early lead.

France struck back quickly when Platini headed across the face of the goal and Rocheteau moved in to convert. It looked as if he was held by defender Karlheinz Förster as they tangled, and Corver pointed straight to the spot. If you ever wanted a player to take a penalty in a huge game, Platini would be that person, and he stepped up and coolly equalised. Just 27 minutes gone, and the game had already seen two goals.

The rest of the first half saw some speculative long-range shots but neither goal was truly threatened. But just before the break, there was an interesting incident that was a sign of things to come. A pass into the area was intended for Manuel Amoros but Schumacher came out to claim it successfully. As he grabbed the ball just in time, he threw a shoulder at Amoros before running on, bringing jeers from the large French contingent of fans. Schumacher was showing that he had no hesitation in being physical if threatened by the French.

As the second half started, it became apparent that French midfielder Bernard Genghini had been unable to shake off a first-half knock and so five minutes in, manager Michel Hidalgo decided to replace him with Battiston. Shortly afterwards, Rocheteau managed to get the ball into the net, but the goal was disallowed for a push on Bernd Förster. Then, on the hour mark, came the moment that shocked the onlooking world.

Platini received the ball just within the German half and hit a beautiful pass forward for Battiston to run on to. He had found space and was clean through as Schumacher rushed out of his area to narrow the angle. Getting to the ball first, Battiston prodded it past Schumacher, only to see his attempt go narrowly wide. Except that he didn't see it. As he prodded the ball, Schumacher launched himself into the air at Battiston, turning his hip as he did so, hitting him at full speed. The blow left Battiston pole-axed on the ground. It was immediately obvious that this was very serious – Battiston twitched slightly while on the floor but otherwise looked completely knocked out.

The French players rushed around their stricken colleague before urgently indicating for a stretcher. As he was taken from the pitch still out cold, all eyes turned to Corver to see whether Schumacher would receive a red card. But to the amazement of everyone, he did not even award a free kick to France. Instead, it was a German goal kick and France needed to bring on their second and final substitute, which would have implications if the game went beyond 90 minutes.

Shortly afterwards, receiving jeers from the French fans, Schumacher faked to throw the ball at them. Platini appeared visibly angered by the gesture and the game took on an ominous tension. If any viewers had been neutral before the match, they were now likely swinging the way of *Les Bleus*. The second half continued with the French dominating. Platini hit a cheeky overhead kick that went narrowly over the bar. Ettori saved well from Hans-Peter Briegel before Amoros hit a great shot from distance that cannoned off the crossbar and out. Then Ettori parried a shot into the path of the onrushing Fischer. Throwing himself across, the keeper managed to just flick the ball away for a corner moments before Fischer could hit it into an empty net. Both sides were making chances but neither could get the all-important winner.

The game moved on into extra time in the humidity of Seville, and just two minutes in France were awarded a free kick on the edge of the area. A chip in found Marius Trésor completely unmarked in the middle, and he volleyed it sweetly past a stationary Schumacher – France had gone into the lead for the first time during the match. Both sides now went into attack mode – Littbarski went close before Tigana's effort went wide. Germany manager Jupp Derwall decided it was time to play his final card, bringing on fresh legs in the shape of Rummenigge, a luxury of which Battiston's injury had deprived the French. Rummenigge's first action was to watch Giresse drill in a shot from the edge of the area that cannoned in off the inside of the post. In the space of just eight minutes, France had grabbed a two-goal lead and Giresse ran off in an iconic celebration as the World Cup Final loomed in sight. It appeared the French would get justice for Schumacher's cynical foul after all.

But this was West Germany – a team famous for never giving up or knowing when it was beaten. While French fans were still absorbing their advantage, Fischer scored from a header but saw it disallowed for offside. Almost immediately, Littbarski hit a low ball into the area and Rummenigge flicked it into the goal just ahead of Ettori. France's two-goal lead had lasted just four minutes before being halved by the substitute.

Half-time came and the players paused to take on water during what was now a breathless game, then just three minutes after retaking the field the Germans were level. A ball to the back post was headed back by Hrubesch where Fischer scored with a magnificent bicycle kick, a trademark finish of his for years. The French appeared shell-shocked as the Germans poured forward looking for a winner. Fischer came close again but the exhausted players in blue held on. The final whistle blew, and penalties would decide the fate of both.

The French went first, and the first five penalties were scored, before Ettori saved Uli Stielike's tame effort, meaning it was advantage *Les Bleus*. Unfortunately, the advantage was short-lived as Six missed the fourth French kick. The fifth kicks saw the reliable Platini and Rummenigge both convert, moving it into sudden death. First up was Maxime Bossis and Schumacher guessed correctly, meaning if Hrubesch scored, the Germans were into the World Cup Final. It was West Germany – of course he scored. The world had to look on as Schumacher celebrated with his team-mates, hero of the penalty shoot-out. It was a sickening sight to most.

Final score
West Germany 3 (Littbarski 17; Rummenigge 102; Fischer 108) France 3 (Platini 27 pen; Tresor 92; Giresse 98)
After extra time: West Germany win 5-4 on penalties

What was the aftermath?

While the world had witnessed a breathless game, which had seen two sides battle right to the end, there was only going to be one major talking point after this – the foul by Schumacher on Battiston. News soon filtered through from the hospital as to the extent of the Frenchman's injuries – it transpired that he had lost two teeth, broken three ribs, and suffered back damage. On hearing this news, Schumacher reportedly stated, 'If that's all that's wrong, tell him I'll pay for the crowns.' He was fast turning into a pantomime villain regarding the whole affair.

And that was the summary narrative for many – Schumacher had got away with a 'near-assault' on Battiston, he had shown no concern when the player was unconscious, and he ended up saving a penalty to put West Germany into the final. All of which was true but did overshadow the fact that the Germans had shown great resilience in coming back from two goals down during extra time. As manager Derwall said post-match, 'You must give my players the credit they deserve. They showed such strength of character.' And he was right, they had. But the actions of Schumacher were never going to allow that to be the story – in neutrals' eyes, West Germany had now committed two major sins during the tournament, 'The Disgrace of Gijón' and the foul on Battiston.

They moved on to play Italy in the final, where many felt justice was served in the *Azzurri* running out 3-1 winners to lift the trophy – the game that contained Marco Tardelli's famous goal celebration, racing around the field, arms outstretched, eyes bulging in sheer ecstasy. France, meanwhile, were left to lick their wounds and regroup. Two years later, their moment would come as they won the 1984 European Championship in their own country, powered by the genius of Platini and his amazing nine goals in just five matches.

Thankfully Patrick Battiston recovered to continue playing for another nine years, finishing with 56 caps.

Schumacher went on to play for West Germany for another four years when, ironically, they would again play France at the 1986 World Cup, again at the semi-final stage, and would again be victorious. Both Battiston and Schumacher played in that match, Battiston gracefully stating before kick-off that the incident was 'forgiven and forgotten'. But to all those who witnessed the infamous 1982 clash, they will never forget that moment of footballing infamy.

Teams

West Germany: Schumacher, Kaltz (c), K. Förster, Stielike, B. Förster, Briegel (Rummenigge 97), Dremmler, Breitner, Fischer, Littbarski, Magath (Hrubesch 73)
Manager: Derwall
France: Ettori, Amoros, Janvion, Trésor, Bossis, Tigana, Giresse, Platini (c), Genghini (Battiston 50 [Lopez 60]), Rocheteau, Six
Manager: Hidalgo

Iconic moment

The image of Battiston being stretchered off unconscious with captain Platini holding his hand as they left the field, showing concern for his team-mate who he later said he feared could have died, while at the same time Schumacher leaned nonchalantly leaning against the goalpost, impatient to take the goal kick as if he could not understand what all the fuss was about. It was not a good look.

Trivia fact

The penalty shoot-out was the first seen during a World Cup finals. It had been used before in qualifying when Tunisia beat Morocco in 1977 but the French and German fans were the first to have to suffer watching penalties during a high-profile World Cup semi-final.

Game 10

1986 World Cup

Denmark v Uruguay

8 June 1986

Estadio Neza 86, Nezahualcóyotl

Attendance: 26,500

Stage: First Round, Group E

WORLD CUP CLASSIC

Why you should watch it

To many people of a certain age, the mention of the words 'Danish Dynamite' will cause them to look far into the distance with misty eyes. And those aren't people who are even Danish; mention it to someone who is from Denmark, and they will sit you down for a long evening of reminiscing. The reason is the Denmark team that played in the 1984 European Championship and the 1986 World Cup – a once-in-a-lifetime generational burst of talent. A team that many fans throughout the world took to their hearts – and who were nicknamed Danish Dynamite.

The story of this great team all started in 1982 when Denmark were drawn in the same 1984 European Championship qualifying group as England. Bobby Robson's team travelled over to Copenhagen and were met by a whirlwind of red, leading to a back-and-forth battle that it seemed as if England had won, until Jesper Olsen scored a late equaliser, swerving through the Three Lions' defence. At the time the English press were shocked that England had failed to win, but Robson was astute enough to realise that he had faced a formidable team. This was not the Denmark of old.

A year later Denmark travelled to Wembley and went one step further, beating England 1-0 through an Allan Simonsen penalty. It was this result that the Danes attributed to building their confidence – they had beaten a top team at their own famous stadium.

The team continued to evolve during the 1984 European Championship, thrashing Yugoslavia 5-0 and coming back from two goals down to defeat Belgium before narrowly losing to Spain on penalties in the semi-final. Their performances were full of verve and panache with the likes of captain Morten Olsen, Frank Arnesen, Søren Lerby, Michael Laudrup, Preben Elkjær and Jesper Olsen spinning their magic under the guidance of manager Sepp Piontek.

Denmark continued their brilliance in qualifying for the 1986 World Cup where they headed up a group containing the Soviet Union side described later under Valeriy Lobanovskyi. The two teams met in Copenhagen on Danish Constitution Day, 5 June 1985. What followed was probably the most famous game in Danish history – a 4-2 win over the Soviets which has often been described as one of the greatest qualification matches of all time. Elkjær and Laudrup both scored twice in a pulsating game that flowed from end to end before an ecstatic crowd. Laudrup, a man who played in many great games during his vaunted career, observed afterwards, 'For me this will always be the game. A lovely sunny afternoon, a packed national stadium and then the game itself: six goals – which could easily have been ten – one amazing opponent and a match where nothing was decided even when at 4-1 after 67 minutes. I haven't had that feeling before or after.'

It was with this reputation that Denmark arrived in Mexico, in their first World Cup finals, drawn into what was the 'group of death' along with West Germany, Uruguay and Scotland. Pundits and experts mused about how the Danes could be the dark horse of the tournament. Denmark kicked off slowly, defeating Scotland 1-0 while modelling a cool new concept of a kit – red-and-white-halved shirts with pinstripes. It was not vintage stuff but did mean that Denmark could relax a little more, having won their first venture into a World Cup, as they prepared for their next game against Uruguay.

Uruguay, meanwhile, had opened their 1986 World Cup with a creditable draw against West Germany – and had in fact been six minutes from winning before Klaus Allofs equalised for *Die Mannschaft.* As usual, Uruguay were tough opponents, both in terms of talent and physicality, but now they also had the emerging Enzo Francescoli within their midfield. This was a player who, while still early in his career, had scored five goals for *La Celeste* during 1985; he would end up a Uruguay legend.

The question on everyone's lips was, following their narrow win over the Scots, would Denmark now come out of their shell and demonstrate what many in Europe had witnessed during the last four years? Because if they did, then a global audience would be in for a treat.

What happened?

Right from the start, Denmark pushed forward, and it only took 11 minutes for them to break through. Laudrup picked up the ball just outside the area and beat a couple of defenders before laying it off to Elkjær on the left, whose first-time shot beat Uruguay keeper Fernando Álvez. It represented Elkjær's 35th goal in just his 58th appearance, a remarkable rate of success. Uruguayan frustration began to simmer in the face of this early onslaught, and it was not long before Miguel Bossio picked up a yellow card and then shortly afterwards he felled Frank Arnesen with a bad challenge. The referee was left with little choice and Bossio saw red after just 19 minutes, leaving Uruguay to have to face the powerful Danes a man short.

However, the expected Uruguay collapse did not immediately occur. Star player Francescoli represented *La Celeste*'s main threat and continued to create problems, while in the meantime Elkjær scored a second only to see it chalked off for offside. Laudrup began to run at the defence, causing panic every time. But eventually the Danes broke through again, with Elkjær this time turning provider, laying a cross over for Lerby to convert from close range. The speed of the whole move from defence to attack was impressive, a trait they had shown for the past few years.

As half-time approached, Francescoli picked up the ball just outside the penalty box and turned to face the Danish defenders. Moving into the area, he was barged off the ball and the referee pointed towards the spot. Francescoli took responsibility himself and tucked the ball away – the perfect time to score. The half-time whistle blew shortly afterwards and despite their man disadvantage, Uruguay could feel that being only one goal behind was not too deep a hole. Perhaps they could weather this storm and maybe come out with a draw.

The second half started well for Uruguay but then seven minutes in came a piece of pure Danish Dynamite courtesy of the silky skills of Laudrup. The Danes moved the ball nicely outside of the area before it came to the forward. Immediately spinning, he beat one defender before squaring up in front of two more. Racing between the two, he took the ball past the keeper in one smooth movement before slotting the ball home. As the English commentator put it at the time, 'The boy's a genius ... Michael Laudrup has scored one of the finest goals you could ever wish to see.'

Uruguay continued to make chances, especially from free kicks, but just as hope flickered for them it was extinguished again by some more Laudrup magic. He again picked up the ball outside the area and again ran straight at the defence, bursting through before attempting to poke past Álvez. The keeper managed to deflect the ball up as they collided and Elkjær followed up to tap in. Denmark were now 4-1 up and Uruguay's heads finally fell. Laudrup was tearing their defence to pieces and Elkjær was converting any chances falling his way.

Not taking their feet off the gas, the Danes continued to push forward at every opportunity. Elkjær came close again with a strong header before another Laudrup run created a chance for Arnesen whose header also just cleared the bar. It was wave after wave and eventually a quick ball from defence set Elkjær clean through at the halfway line. Sprinting forward, he calmly took the ball past the keeper to complete his hat-trick and register his 37th goal on the international stage. The speed of the Danish attacks was just too much for the Uruguayans.

As the game entered its final minutes, Denmark decided to bring Laudrup off ahead of the next game and replace him with Jesper Olsen. Seven minutes later another lightning-fast move on the Danish right again released Elkjaer who crossed over to Olsen, who almost stopped running as the ball came to him before calmly slotting it into the corner, bringing Denmark's goal tally up to six.

Finally, the referee ended Uruguay's agony – Denmark had shown the world just what they were capable of as they posted a 6-1 victory to make it two wins out of two. Elkjær had scored a hat-trick while Laudrup had repeatedly cut through the Uruguay defence and scored one of the World Cup great goals. If anyone was not previously aware of the Danish potential before this game, they were now – Danish Dynamite had exploded in a spectacular display.

Final score
Denmark 6 (Elkjær 11, 67, 80; Lerby 41; Laudrup 52; J. Olsen 88) Uruguay 1 (Francescoli 45 pen)

What was the aftermath?

While many who followed football closely had known of Denmark's potential ahead of the tournament, this game now brought this knowledge to the wider world. Now everyone was aware of their ability and a whole generation were transfixed by this beautiful team. They had launched themselves into the public consciousness and there was no more putting the genie back into the bottle. Two wins had already ensured their passage into the knockout stages, but they still went ahead and beat West Germany 2-0 to end the group with a 100 per cent record. Winning the group meant a last-16 clash with Spain – another classic that is covered soon.

As for Uruguay, they continued to sully their reputation during their final match against Scotland. Having had to play for 71 minutes with ten men against Denmark after Bossio's early dismissal, they went one further when José Batista was sent off in the very first minute against the Scots. Yes, you read that correctly – he was sent off after one minute for going through the back of Gordon Strachan. To their credit, they did then manage to earn a goalless draw, which saw them into the round of 16 as one of the third-placed entries, albeit without having won a game, where they were duly eliminated by Argentina. But their performance against Scotland caused great anger – defender Arthur Albiston recalled, 'They used every trick in the book to waste time because they only needed a draw to go through. It was a real eye-opener to how the game was played in South America. We had no experience of it whatsoever. Players came over to console you – or so they wanted the referee to believe – if you had been hurt in a tackle and then stood on your ankle or nipped you or pulled your hair.' The secretary of the Scottish Football Association, Ernie Walker, was more succinct, simply describing Uruguay as the 'scum of world football'. Not too pleased then, I take it.

Teams

Denmark: Rasmussen, Busk, M. Olsen (c), Nielsen, Andersen, Bertelsen (Mølby 57), Lerby, Arnesen, Laudrup (J. Olsen 81), Berggreen, Elkjær

Manager: Piontek

Uruguay: Álvez, Gutiérrez, Acevedo (c), Diogo, Batista, Bossio, Saralegui, Santin (Zalazar 57), Francescoli, Da Silva, Alzamendi (Ramos 57)

Manager: Borrás

Iconic moment

Michael Laudrup's goal – the way in which he just ghosted through the Uruguay defence and past the keeper showed the skill which would see him enjoy a successful career after the tournament with Juventus, Barcelona, and Real Madrid, three of Europe's superpower teams, leading to him being eventually named the best Danish footballer of all time in November 2006.

Trivia fact

Denmark's Group E, which saw them matched with West Germany, Scotland, and Uruguay, was described as the 'group of death' by Uruguay's manager Omar Borrás to the English-language press. The phrase had been used before in Spanish during the 1970 World Cup, but this was the first time it had been heard in English. Of course, no World Cup since would be complete without much discussion about which is, in each case, the 'group of death'. But you heard it here first, folks.

Game 11
1986 World Cup

Belgium v Soviet Union

15 June 1986
Estadio Nou Camp, León
Attendance: 32,277
Stage: Round of 16

Why you should watch it

Talk about coaching greats within a group and eventually someone will throw out the name Valeriy Lobanovskyi and his scientific approach to the game. Born in Kyiv, which now falls under Ukraine but at the time was part of the larger Soviet Union, he played for local team Dynamo Kyiv between 1957 and 1964, scoring 42 goals for them. He finally ended his playing career aged 29 and almost immediately moved into coaching, starting with another Ukrainian team – Dnipro Dnipropetrovsk. Following on from a successful four years there, he moved back to his first love, Dynamo, where he would be the head coach for an initial nine years before returning back and forth to them all the way until his death in 2002.

It was at Dynamo that Lobanovskyi teamed up with a former team-mate, Oleh Bazylevych, and between them they began to develop a scientific approach to coaching. Bringing in the expertise of a physical education scientist from the Kiev State Institute of Physical Education, they developed statistical analysis of players and workloads that was way ahead of its time. This led to Lobanovskyi instituting a pressing game into his team, with a focus on interchangeability of players similar to what Rinus Michels was doing over in the Netherlands.

Their approach immediately began paying dividends, with Dynamo winning the league and cup double in 1974 before then becoming the first Soviet club to win a major European trophy – the Cup Winners' Cup – in 1975, winning eight of their nine games during the tournament. Success continued through the 1970s and on into the 1980s, with Dynamo reaching the European Cup semi-finals in 1977 as well as the European Cup quarter-finals in both 1982 and 1983.

In 1986 Dynamo won the Cup Winners' Cup for a second time and so, after two brief stints before as Soviet coach, Lobanovskyi was appointed for a third time just three weeks ahead of the 1986 World Cup. With Dynamo being such a strong domestic force and the strong bond that Lobanovskyi had developed with the players over the years, who knew his playing system inside out, it was no surprise that a large proportion of the Soviet squad that he took to Mexico was from his Kyiv team. Going into their opening game against Hungary, Lobanovskyi included eight Dynamo players in his starting 11. The other three players were goalkeeper Rinat Dasayev (Spartak Moscow), defender Nikolay Larionov (Zenit Leningrad) and midfielder Sergei Aleinikov (Dinamo Minsk).

You often hear complaints from national coaches that they have insufficient time with players to properly develop a coherent team and a set pattern of play. For the Soviet Union in 1986, that most definitely was not the case. They were entering the World Cup with a well-drilled club team who had enjoyed considerable success and knew both what was required by their manager and each other's skills and weaknesses thoroughly. Many were curious to see how they would do as they entered their opening game of Group C against fellow eastern Europeans Hungary.

The answer to the question above was not long in coming. After scoring two goals in the first four minutes, the Soviets continued to overpower the poor Hungarians, running out 6-0 victors while also missing a penalty. It was an awesome display that grabbed everyone's attention. They then tied with an extremely good France team (more of them later) before defeating Canada 2-0 to top the group with nine goals scored and only one conceded. They had certainly earned their place in the last 16.

Their opponents would be Belgium, who had a useful team but hadn't really shone recently. They earned a place in Mexico by coming second in their qualification group, thanks to winning all three of their home games at the crumbling Heysel Stadium, before then eliminating arch-rivals Netherlands in a two-legged play-off, thanks to an 85th-minute goal from Georges Grün in Rotterdam. Once at the World Cup, they had been placed in Group B and only advanced by being one of the best third-placed teams, having lost to Mexico, narrowly beating Iraq by one goal, and finally drawing with Paraguay. Limping into the knockout rounds, they could boast players such as Franky Vercauteren, Enzo Scifo and Jan Ceulemans – they had a team that could potentially give anyone a scare. Belgian side Anderlecht had won the UEFA Cup in 1983, while also reaching the 1984 final, and seven of the 1986 World Cup squad came from that club.

Ahead of the match, the Soviets were favourites, given their powerful performances to date. But the beauty of the knockout stages is that past form can often count for nothing. Would the Soviets continue their dominant run, or would Belgium finally play to their full potential?

What happened?

The two teams lined up on a hot Mexican afternoon, the Soviets resplendent in those iconic white shirts with CCCP emblazoned across the front in large red writing while the Belgians were in all-red. It would be interesting to see how the sides paced themselves given the heat, which neither were used to playing in. Straight away, it looked as if the Soviet Union were unconcerned by the conditions as they dominated the early play, starting quickly as they had done so successfully against Hungary.

After just four minutes, Soviet defender Vasiliy Rats broke into the area and went down under a challenge from Enzo Scifo, the referee deciding not to award a penalty. Almost immediately afterwards, Oleh Kuznetsov got to the byline before turning a Belgian defender inside out to tee up Ihor Belanov who sliced wide when he should really have scored the opener. What was interesting was that both Rats and Kuznetsov were defenders who were penetrating deep into the Belgian defence. It was an onslaught – Pavel Yakovenko next hitting a vicious low shot from outside the area that Belgian keeper Jean-Marie Pfaff did well to divert past the post. From the resulting corner, the ball found its way again to Yakovenko, whose goal-bound shot was deflected away by a lunging defensive tackle. It had been a brutal first seven minutes – but somehow remained goalless.

After weathering that initial storm, Belgium began to feel their way into the game. A rare foray forward after 15 minutes saw a cross reach Franky Vercauteren whose powerful header hit the side-netting. But the Soviets were still in control and after 27 minutes came their breakthrough. A ball forward reached Belanov, a few yards outside the area. Cutting across, he made space before unleashing a piledriver past Pfaff which lasered into the top corner. It was a fantastic drive – Pfaff could only stand rooted and turn his head to watch the ball arrow in. The Soviets had the lead their play had merited.

The remainder of the first half saw the game flow back and forth, with both sides trying their luck unsuccessfully from range, Scifo coming closest. Watching games back now, you notice how, compared to modern football, there was so much more shooting from distance which, given how many ended up over or wide, seems wasteful. When they did go in though, it did make for great viewing.

The referee's whistle finally put an end to the mutual shooting practice as the Soviets took their slim lead into the break. Eight minutes into the second half, that lead was almost doubled. A cross to the near post saw Aleksandr

Zavarov's header come back off the post, Pfaff nowhere near, before a follow-up drive beat Pfaff but was cleared off the line. It was a lucky escape for Belgium, who immediately took full advantage, a cross to the far post falling to an unmarked Scifo who took one touch to control before slipping past Rinat Dasayev from close range. Belgium were level.

Some more long-distance shooting followed until, with 20 minutes remaining, Belgium were caught napping on the ball in midfield. Stealing possession, Zavarov quickly moved the ball out to Belanov to the right of the area, who slotted it over Pfaff and into the corner. It was once again advantage USSR.

But the Belgians just wouldn't go away. A long punt from defence was neatly chested down by Ceulemans just inside the Soviet penalty area before he rifled it into the corner. Viewing it now from one angle on replay, it looks offside, but the linesman's flag stayed down and, with 13 minutes remaining, we were once again all square.

The Soviet Union pushed forward in search of a winner, and with nine minutes left, Belanov set up Yaremchuk who blasted the ball, only to see it strike the top of the crossbar. Belgium then almost got a winner themselves when Scifo stole in at the far post, his header bundled out by Dasayev before he collided painfully with the upright.

And so, we had the first extra time of World Cup 1986. In those days of just two substitutions, the heat was going to become a factor for the next 30 minutes. Eleven minutes in, Belgium finally took the lead for the first time. A cross from Eric Gerets after a short corner found Stéphane Demol stealing in unmarked, whose powerful header gave Dasayev no chance. Once again, Belgium had profited from poor Soviet marking at the back post.

Moving into the second period of extra time, the game opened and Belgium could have sealed it when Daniel Veyt found himself open in the Soviet penalty area, only to send his header over. But shortly after, they did get their fourth – a header dropping to Nico Claesen who struck a sweet volley into the corner. With ten minutes remaining, a team finally had that crucial two-goal lead.

But straight away Belanov went down in the Belgian area while challenging for a cross and the referee immediately pointed to the spot. Belanov himself took it and there was no slow run-up, shuffle or feint – he just ran up and absolutely blasted the ball into the roof of the net. With Belgium's advantage back to one, you would have expected them to drop deep and defend, but instead they went on the attack, looking for a fifth. And by doing so, they held on to register a famous victory. The Soviets had looked like possible contenders during the group stage but were now on their way back home. The Red Devils had vanquished the Red Machine.

Final score
Belgium 4 (Scifo 56; Ceulemans 77; Demol 102; Claesen 110) Soviet Union 3 (Belanov 27, 70, 111 pen)
After extra time

What was the aftermath?

While Belgium had fully deserved their win, there were many neutrals who were sad to see the Soviets exit the competition. At times, especially during the group stage, they had been stunning to watch, and the fact that most of the team played for the same club side just added to their allure. But with defenders who weren't afraid to venture forward, they had often left themselves open, especially at the back post, and Belgium had punished them for that.

Following this elimination, the Soviet Union reached the final of the 1988 European Championship, where they were defeated by the Netherlands and that famous Marco van Basten volley. Russian football then took a long time to reach such heights again. Italy 1990 saw the final hurrah for a team marked as the Soviet Union, finishing bottom of their group, before switching to become Russia for USA 1994 when they were again eliminated in the group stage. They failed to reach the 1998, 2006 and 2010 tournaments, while never getting past the group stage in 2002 and 2014. It would only be 2018, when Russia hosted the competition, that they would next reach the knockout stages – the first time since that great side of 1986.

As for Belgium, they had finally put in a performance that matched the calibre of their squad. They ended up reaching the semi-finals, but if I discuss their route there or who they played, it will spoil the next few classic games that I am moving on to next. They ended up coming fourth in the 1986 World Cup overall, a fantastic performance for a country of its population, which would only be bettered in one later tournament, but again I wish to avoid spoilers. Both keeper Jean-Marie Pfaff and captain Jan Ceulemans went on to be selected in the All-Star team of the finals, while Enzo Scifo was named the best young player of the tournament, a reflection of this great generation of players.

Teams

Belgium: Pfaff, Gerets (L. Van Der Elst 112), Renquin, Grün (Clijsters 99), Vervoort, Demol, Vercauteren, Scifo, Ceulemans (c), Veyt, Claesen
Manager: Thys

Soviet Union: Dasayev, Bezsonov, Demyanenko (c), Kuznetsov, Rats, Bal, Yaremchuk, Yakovenko (Yevtushenko 79), Zavarov (Rodionov 72), Aleinikov, Belanov
Manager: Lobanovskyi

Iconic moment

Belanov's opening goal – as mentioned earlier, the amount of long-range shooting in this game, and many others from this era, seems incomprehensible to modern eyes. Did they really think they were going to score from 30 yards and more? Modern managers would tear their hair out at such a sight. But there were a handful of players who were dangerous from that range, Johnny Rep for example, and Belanov was another of those. The boy could shoot – and his team-mate Vasiliy Rats wasn't too bad either.

Trivia fact

Belanov's performance at this tournament, along with Dynamo Kyiv's Cup Winners' Cup success, earned him the 1986 Ballon D'Or award, making him only the third Russian at that time to win the prodigious honour after Lev Yashin (1963) and Oleg Blokhin (1975). Incredibly, Blokhin was still part of the Soviet Union squad 11 years after his award, one of three unused substitutes in the Belgium game.

Game 12

1986 World Cup

Denmark v Spain

18 June 1986
Estadio La Corregidora, Querétaro
Attendance: 38,500
Stage: Round of 16

WORLD CUP CLASSIC

Why you should watch it

As discussed earlier, Denmark had progressed to the round of 16 with a 100 per cent record, defeating West Germany, Scotland and thrashing Uruguay in the 'group of death' and so announcing to the wider world what Europe had been witnessing for the past couple of years – here was a team, nicknamed Danish Dynamite, with a golden generation who played exciting and effective football. However, during their final group game against West Germany, there was a key moment at the end that would influence their round of 16 fixture. With the game practically done and both teams happy, Denmark's key midfielder Frank Arnesen got entangled with West Germany's Lothar Matthäus. As they both fell, Arnesen flicked out a boot at the German, who reacted as if he had just been shot by a sniper with several rolls. But it was enough to convince the referee to show Arnesen, who had already been booked, a second yellow card, sending him off. Arnesen immediately realised what a stupid mistake it was, dropping to his knees in the knowledge that he would miss the next game. He sportingly shook Matthäus's hand as he departed but would be sorely missed in their upcoming knockout tie.

Denmark's reward for winning the group would be to play Spain, who had come second behind Brazil in theirs, beating both Northern Ireland and Algeria and only losing 1-0 to Brazil. One of their goals had been scored by a relatively new striker in the Spanish team – a striker by the name of Emilio Butragueño, otherwise known as *El Buitre* (The Vulture).

Butragueño was a product of the Real Madrid youth system, La Fabrica, and was one of five homegrown players who helped Real to dominate Spanish football in the 1980s. It was a Spanish journalist who, when writing about the five youths, first coined the phrase *La Quinta del Buitre* (Vulture's Cohort) in relation to them – a nickname that stuck over time. The other four of the five were Manolo Sanchís, Rafael Vázquez, Míchel and Miguel Pardeza. Both Butragueño and Míchel made it to the Spanish squad for the 1986 World Cup and both started all three group games as part of an exciting young team. But while all five were fantastic players, it was Butragueño who was the standout star.

He made his debut for Real Madrid in 1984, where he would play for the next 11 years, earning himself legendary status with 123 goals in 341 appearances. His first two full seasons had seen him register 28 goals, meaning that his talent was quickly recognised by the Spanish national team manager Miguel Muñoz, earning Butragueño his first international call-up in October 1984 against Wales in a World Cup qualifier. As the game against Denmark came around, he was still only 22 years old.

For a country the size of Spain, with such a love of the game, they had generally disappointed at previous World Cups. Since coming fourth in 1950, the furthest they had gone was the second group stage in 1982 when they had hosted the event. They were therefore hoping to impress for once – a tough ask though given they were having to play the red-hot Danes. They would be needing all their skills and Butragueño's clinical finishing if they were to stand a chance of progressing further.

What happened?

The match kicked off with Denmark in their change strip of all white while Spain wore their traditional red and blue. Right from the start, as expected by many, Denmark took the game to the Spaniards, with an Elkjær shot from outside the area missing narrowly. It came to life in the 33rd minute when a run by Klaus Berggreen into the penalty area saw him felled by Ricardo Gallego, resulting in the award of a penalty despite vehement Spanish protests. The replay clearly showed that the penalty was the correct decision and so up stepped Jesper Olsen to calmly roll the ball past Andoni Zubizarreta for his third goal of the tournament. First blood to Danish Dynamite.

Spain looked to answer back before half-time, with a half-chance falling to Julio Alberto, while Laudrup and Elkjær continued to cause the Spanish defence problems. It looked as if Denmark would go into the break ahead but then came an infamous moment in the country's football history – one still remembered by a whole generation.

As half-time approached, Danish keeper Lars Høgh set up for a goal kick. However, instead of powering the ball upfield, he noticed that Jesper Olsen had come short and so passed it out to him. With a Spanish forward closing in, Olsen calmly turned away from trouble and started moving up the line. So far, so good. But it was then that he inexplicably decided to play a no-look pass across the area back to Høgh, rather than just moving the ball further forward.

Unfortunately for Olsen, Høgh had not moved up in his area and was still near his six-yard box. As the ball rolled into no-man's-land, Butrageuño swooped in to place it through a scrambling Høgh's legs. Spain had been given a lifeline. In the words of the English commentator at the time, 'Jesper Olsen puts his head in his hands – made to pay for overconfidence. A totally unnecessary ball and Butragueño was very happy to accept the gift.'

The Danish commentator's take became much more famous, especially to the watching Danish public, which translated as, 'But Jesper, Jesper, Jesper, that's lethal.'

The second half started all square and immediately saw a fantastic run from Elkjær, beating three Spaniards including holding one off with a hand to the face before seeing his shot saved. It appeared as if the Olsen moment had not phased the Danes and that manager Depp Piontek had clearly told them to just keep pushing forward – the only way it often seemed the Danes knew how to play. Another Elkjær shot sliced wide, and it looked as if there was only one team likely to score next. But then, on 56 minutes, a low corner from Víctor was headed across goal by José Camacho where Butragueño was on hand to head in his second goal of the game.

Denmark responded in the only way they knew how – a Laudrup run opened a chance for substitute John Eriksen, but his shot was well saved. But as the Danes pushed forward, gaps opened behind them and a pass into one such gap sent Butragueño away towards goal, chased by Søren Busk. The two jostled in the area, Butragueño went down, and the referee pointed to the spot. Andoni Goikoetxea, the infamous 'Butcher of Bilbao', blasted the penalty home and suddenly the Danes were 3-1 down.

Denmark continued to try to force their way back into the game but now it felt like Spain could just score at will, their confidence being so high and Denmark playing a high line. With ten minutes remaining, a fast move saw Míchel release substitute Eloy whose cross was slotted in by Butragueño for his hat-trick. Spain were on their way to the quarter-finals and the poor Danes looked simply stunned.

The Spanish were now in full flow and with two minutes left, Butragueño picked up a ball in the area before a clever turn forced Morten Olsen into a clumsy challenge and resulted in a second penalty for *La Roja*. Given that they were 4-1 up – and given that Butragueño already had three goals and had been fouled – Goikoetxea classily handed him the ball. He made no mistake and became only the sixth player ever to score four goals in a World Cup finals game, alongside greats such as Just Fontaine and Eusébio.

And hence the Danish dream died – a side who had brought such joy to the competition were maybe a touch naive against the clinical finishing of Butragueño. The vulture had felled the Vikings and hipsters were left to cry into one of the coolest shirts to ever be worn by a national side.

Final score
Spain 5 (Butragueño 43, 56, 80, 88 pen; Goikoetxea 68 pen) Denmark 1 (J. Olsen 33 pen)

What was the aftermath?

Sadly, the beautiful Danish team was out while Spain would move on to then be beaten by Belgium on penalties and so continue their poor record of not passing the quarter-finals since 36 years prior. Unlike the Danes, their golden generation was still to come with the emergence of the likes of Andrés Iniesta and Xavi. But the saddest aspect of all was how Jesper Olsen, a fantastic player, had to live with his mistake recalled by all who saw it. After his career ended, Olsen kept a low public profile and ended up moving to Brighton in Australia, where he has remained ever since. He thankfully continued to work within football there, becoming involved in a training programme called Football Star Academy, helping to link talented Australian players to European club opportunities.

The 1986 World Cup was the Danish Dynamite swansong – they had sparkled during the 1984 European Championship, were breathtaking during the 1986 World Cup qualification campaign, especially in defeating the Soviet Union, and lit up the 1986 finals with their demolition of Uruguay. And rather like Brazil in 1982, their legacy would live on long after other more successful teams had faded from memory. Denmark would return to prominence when winning the 1992 European Championship, but despite that success it is still the unsuccessful 1984/86 team that is more fondly remembered.

There is a wonderful quote from Sepp Piontek, 'We showed that football can be played in a way which is fun, but which ultimately is not always effective.' And as defender Jens Bertelsen said, 'Both in France and in Mexico the championship was within reach. We could have been European champions; we could have been … world champions.'

Teams

Spain: Zubizarreta, Tomás, Camacho (c), Víctor, Goikoetxea, Gallego, Alberto, Calderé, Míchel (Francisco 83), Salinas (Eloy HT), Butragueño

Manager: Muñoz

Denmark: Høgh, Busk, M. Olsen (c), Nielsen, Andersen (Eriksen 60), Bertelsen, J. Olsen (Mølby 71), Lerby, M. Laudrup, Berggreen, Elkjær

Manager: Piontek

Iconic moment

Jesper Olsen's crossfield pass – a great player who made one mistake, unfortunately in Denmark's biggest game to date. 'I shouldn't have played that pass,' Olsen would say ten years later. 'It's just one of those things you can't change. If it had happened in the group stages, we would have played another game, and it could all have been forgotten. Of course, it's unfair that I will be remembered for such a thing, but that's how it is. It's mainly in Denmark people still talk about it so maybe it's good that I don't live there.'

Trivia fact

Some players have achieved immortality through certain plays, such as the Cruyff turn or the Panenka penalty. Unfortunately for Jesper Olsen, his crossfield pass that led to Spain's first goal has also achieved immortality within Denmark. There, an expression sometimes used to describe another person's blunder or gaffe is to call it *en rigtig Jesper Olsen* ('a real Jesper Olsen'). Football can indeed be a cruel game.

Game 13
1986 World Cup

Brazil v France

21 June 1986
Estadio Jalisco, Guadalajara
Attendance: 65,000
Stage: Quarter-Finals

WORLD CUP CLASSIC

Why you should watch it

As discussed, when reviewing the 1982 World Cup, two of the best, and most heartbreaking, games of that tournament involved Brazil and France. Both had great sides and both had a claim to be the best team there with a high chance of taking home the trophy. But as we saw, the beautiful Brazilian team were eliminated in a thriller against Italy while the fantastic French were eliminated in controversial circumstances by West Germany. Both had therefore been waiting four years to once again stake a claim to become world champions.

During that time, France had enjoyed success when hosting the European Championship in 1984. Led by talismanic captain Michel Platini's incredible nine goals from five games – remembering also that strictly speaking he was a midfielder – France lifted the trophy following a final victory over Spain. The team became famous for its midfield, known as the *Carré Magique* (Magic Square) for its formation of Platini, Luis Fernández, Alain Giresse and Jean Tigana. They qualified for the 1986 World Cup top of their group, advancing unbeaten with the same number of points as the Soviet Union, eliminating Hungary and Canada. They then faced a tough match against defending champions Italy but an early goal by Platini followed by another by Yannick Stopyra saw them overcome that hurdle and enter the quarter-finals as one of the favourites – but facing another tough tie, this time against Brazil.

Brazil, meanwhile, had begun to recover from the shock and disappointment of their loss to Italy in 1982. While a nation and most of the world mourned the defeat as pragmatic football overcoming free-flowing football, Brazil did realise that a team could no longer hope to win a World Cup any more by just employing attacking tactics. A more nuanced approach was required, blending the elements that made Brazil unique with a touch of steel and discipline. Sócrates and Zico remained part of the team from 1982, while Telê Santana was still manager, also adding young strikers such as Careca and Müller. They qualified unbeaten from CONMEBOL and then won all three of their group-stage games, defeating Spain, Northern Ireland, and Algeria, before thrashing Poland 4-0 in the round of 16. Up to this point, they had yet to concede a single goal across their four matches.

Therefore, this was a highly anticipated match-up between two teams who both still loved to attack. The question was, as it always is before such games, could it possibly live up to the hype? Like hell it could!

What happened?

Kick-off was at noon under a burning midday sun in Guadalajara with both teams resplendent in their traditional kits – the yellow and blue of Brazil opposite the blue and white of France. The French started off the more positive, Platini causing early problems with neat one-twos around the edge of the box and Manuel Amoros coming close. France continued to enjoy most of the possession, with Brazil using the speed of Careca and Müller on fast breaks. But Brazil started to get into their rhythm and, after 15 minutes, Sócrates broke through but saw his shot well saved.

It was then that the first breakthrough occurred. A ball from Josimar into Müller saw him roll his marker and head towards the area. A little flick off to Júnior saw him immediately also touch it on to Careca who blasted a first-time shot into the roof of the net. Seventeen minutes into the game and Brazil held an early lead.

After going in front, Brazil started to slow the game right down, playing at a pace they were enjoying. But every now and then they would suddenly up the tempo, a perfect example of which was after 32 minutes when Careca again caused problems, getting to the byline and sending a cross over that Müller struck against the post.

As half-time approached, France were building in confidence, with Platini, Giresse and Tigana starting to dominate the midfield battle. With four minutes left of the first period, some neat passing in the midfield between Tigana, Giresse and Amoros saw Dominique Rocheteau played through on the right wing. His low cross took a deflection which allowed Stopyra to try a diving header, which he missed but, by putting off goalkeeper Carlos, allowed Platini to sneak in at the back post and slide the ball home. The perfect time to grab an equaliser, just before half-time, and a suitable gift for birthday boy Platini. A perfectly balanced game was level at the break.

Both teams seemed conscious of the heat and were trying to play at a pace that would conserve energy, and the first 15 minutes of the second half saw the two sides continue to probe without making any real clear chances. A sudden beautiful one-two from Tigana put him through but the keeper saved well, after which Brazil went straight up to the other end and Júnior also had a shot well saved. The game was starting to open more and Careca saw his header hit the bar on 70 minutes.

Just one minute later saw a huge cheer arose from the Brazilian contingent as Müller was replaced by the iconic number ten, Zico. A hero of the legendary 1982 World Cup team, he was still held in high regard by all and now he would once again take the field with fellow 1982 hero Sócrates. A minute after Zico stepped on to the pitch, defender Branco broke up a French attack and strode forward with the ball. Playing a one-two with Zico, he went for the return pass and was brought down by French keeper Joël Bats. A penalty was awarded, and Branco celebrated as if he had just scored.

Recent games had seen both Sócrates and Careca take spot-kicks, and both were now on the field, but Zico pulled rank as he looked to make a dramatic entrance. To the despair of the watching Brazilian fans, his shot was weak, and Bats saved before France cleared the rebound – Brazil's gamble on Zico had backfired. Brazil continued to push on after that but couldn't find a way through, and so the game went into extra time.

The first action of extra time saw a fantastic run from Rocheteau, who found himself weaving his way towards goal before his shot was blocked by a defender. Both sides began to show signs of fatigue under the blazing sun, with cramp starting to become an issue. Then, with just five minutes left, came a hugely controversial moment. Brazil had been dominating possession, with France playing more on the break. And it was another swift break that saw Platini play a marvellous ball from the centre circle to put substitute Bruno Bellone clean through on goal. Carlos rushed to the edge of his area to face him and Bellone took the ball to his left. Making no effort to go for the ball, the keeper threw himself at Bellone, causing him to stumble as he chased the ball. As he tried to regain his balance, a Brazilian defender came over to cover and ran the ball away from the Frenchman.

Everybody waited for the referee's whistle – but it never came. For some inexplicable reason Romanian official Ioan Igna simply waved play on and Brazil counterattacked. The ball came to Careca who fired a great low ball across the six-yard box where Sócrates was coming in. Just needing a side-foot to score, a falling Sócrates couldn't quite sort out his legs and the ball passed him by – an open goal gaping before him. In the space of a minute, both sides could have had a winner.

The game went into a penalty shoot-out – two sets of exhausted players trying to finally settle this titanic battle. Brazil went first and up stepped Sócrates. Cool as you like, he shot with a two-step run-up, only to see Bats save his attempt. First blood to the French. The next three penalties were all converted before Zico returned to take Brazil's third, having already missed one in regular time. This time he made no mistake, opting to hit it hard down the middle.

Bellone and Branco then each scored to maintain France's advantage before Platini stepped up to take their fourth. Michel Platini – one of the greatest strikers of a penalty or free kick in the world at that time, and a man to whom free kicks outside the area were almost like penalties given his conversion rate.

With his trademark socks around his ankles and shirt unfurled, the French captain skied his effort over the bar to the amazement of all. Suddenly it was all square with just one kick left each.

Júlio César stepped up for Brazil as their fans continued to cheer the Platini miss. Hitting it hard, it looked a perfect strike before cannoning back off the post and out. Brazilian joy immediately turned back to shock as Luis Fernández came up with the chance to seal a semi-final place. As a nation held its breath, he slotted it into the corner and France had won. An outpouring of joy erupted on the pitch – the exorcism of the shoot-out loss four years ago against West Germany. Like then they had again been victims of cynical play by the opposing keeper which had gone unpunished by the referee – but this time justice had been dispensed. Two superpower teams had gone toe to toe for 120 minutes in scalding heat before ending with the drama of penalties.

Final score
France 1 (Platini 40) Brazil 1 (Careca 17)
After extra time; France win 4-3 on penalties

What was the aftermath?

The semi-finals would see France once again thrown up against their recent nemesis, West Germany. And once again, the Germans would prevail, although this time without the controversies that had marred the 1982 meeting and without penalty drama. Instead, an early goal from Andreas Brehme and a late goal from Rudi Völler saw the French again pipped just before the final. They did clinch third place in an exciting 4-2 defeat of Belgium after extra time but that did little to heal the scars of losing in two consecutive semi-finals.

Having done so well in the 1982 and 1986 World Cups, and having won the European Championship in between, this great French vintage faded over the next few years, failing to qualify for both 1990 and 1994. They would have to wait until 1998 and the emergence of Zinedine Zidane for their star to rise again.

As for Brazil, it was an end of an era as the likes of Zico and Sócrates moved off the world stage. The iconic boys of 1982 were disbanded to be replaced by a more pragmatic version of the *Seleção*. Müller and Careca would go on to again lead the line in 1990 while two substitutes during that tournament – Romário and Bebeto – would represent a brighter future to come.

Teams

France: Bats, Amoros, Bossis, Battiston, Tusseau, Fernández, Giresse (Ferreri 84), Tigana, Platini (c), Rocheteau (Bellone 99), Stopyra
Manager: Michel

Brazil: Carlos, Josimar, Edinho (c), César, Branco, Elzo, Alemão, Sócrates, Júnior (Silas 91), Müller (Zico 71), Careca
Manager: Santana

Iconic moment

The foul on Bellone so close to the end which immediately threw up memories of how France had been robbed by a similar cynical ploy and an unexplainable refereeing decision against West Germany in 1982, albeit with Bellone not losing any teeth or damaging vertebrae. French supporters must have felt a sinking feeling at that moment of déjà vu.

Trivia fact

Bellone, the player who had been denied a winning goal by Carlos's cynical and unpunished foul, took the third penalty for France in the shoot-out. His kick hit the post, flew back into the play, hit the diving Carlos on the back and went into the goal. The referee let it stand but it did throw up the question of whether that should count as a goal or not. By hitting the post, he had technically missed – but by then going in off the keeper, the ball had gone in all on the same play. Even the commentators weren't exactly sure. FIFA later clarified the ruling to state, 'A kick is successful if, having been touched once by the kicker, the ball crosses the goal line between the goal posts and under the crossbar, without touching any player, official, or outside agent other than the defending goalkeeper. The ball may touch the goalkeeper, goal posts, or crossbar any number of times before going into the goal as long as the referee believes the ball's motion is the result of the initial kick.'

Game 14

1986 World Cup

Argentina v England

22 June 1986

Estadio Azteca, Mexico City

Attendance: 114,580

Stage: Quarter-Finals

WORLD CUP CLASSIC

Why you should watch it

Any game between Argentina and England comes with a lot of baggage. A rivalry between the two countries can be traced back to the 1966 World Cup held in England. The two teams met during the quarter-finals in a violent encounter won 1-0 by England, where the Argentinian captain, Antonio Rattín, was sent off after 35 minutes in controversial circumstances. After a team-mate was booked, Rattín claimed he tried to approach the referee to discuss the reasoning, but that with a language barrier between him and the West German official, something was lost in translation, resulting in Rattín being dismissed. Angered, he refused to leave the pitch for several minutes. After the match ended, England manager Sir Alf Ramsey refused to allow his players to swap shirts with the Argentinians and then branded them as 'animals'. Unfortunately, the British press took the 'animals' quote much further in their editorials, creating heightened animosity, leading to the Argentinian president saying, 'First they stole the Malvinas, and now the World Cup from us.'

It is the subject of the Malvinas that ramped up the existing tension between these nations. Known to the English as the Falkland Islands, these tiny islands sit just 300 miles east of Argentina. In 1833 the British took control of them, despite Argentinian protests, and ever since it has been a bone of contention. 1982 saw Argentinian forces invade, partially as a distraction from economic woes at home, and British prime minister Margaret Thatcher sent a task force to reclaim the territory – the subsequent conflict saw just over 900 soldiers lose their lives before Argentina surrendered. So, when this World Cup quarter-final came around, only four years had passed and memories were still fresh in everybody's minds.

Therefore, the lead-up to the game was marked by simmering hostility, not helped by jingoistic journalism from both nations' media. While representatives from both teams tried to diffuse the rhetoric, it was the proverbial 'elephant in the room' that could not be ignored. The Azteca was going to be full of Argentinian and English fans who, like it or not, were not going to let the matter rest.

The other big talking point ahead of the game was the form of Diego Armando Maradona. An undoubted talent, Maradona had missed the 1978 World Cup as manager César Luis Menotti felt he was still too young at 17, before playing in the 1982 finals where his tournament ended in shame as he was sent off for a violent foul towards the end of Argentina's last game against Brazil. At club level he had moved over to Europe to play for Barcelona where, despite flashes of brilliance, he had not yet fully lived up to the hype, not helped by suffering a broken ankle. Again, his departure was marred by violence during the 1984 Copa del Rey Final, before he moved on to Napoli for a world record fee, where he led them to third place in the 1985/86 Serie A season ahead of the World Cup, scoring 13 goals.

There was therefore pressure on Maradona to show his true talents when coming into World Cup 1986. During the group stage and round of 16, he showed his full range of gifts, indicating the claim of possibly being the best player in the world. But the question now was, as Argentina entered the business end of the tournament, could Maradona deliver when it mattered most.

Oh yes, he could.

What happened?

In deciding whether to class this game as a World Cup Classic, I had to weigh up two factors. If you were to watch 85 of the 90 minutes, it would not fall into this category. In general, the game was cagey, with Argentina mainly dominating early on before England took charge towards the end. For those 85 minutes it was a stalemate which could easily have gone down as forgettable.

But there were five minutes that make this game one of the most famous, or infamous, ever, as well as one of the best known. And so, in describing the match, it is that period which has to take precedence. There has probably never been a five-minute period of World Cup play known to so many around the world as this and many people who have little interest in football may well know what happened during that period. But, like any great story, it is always worth retelling.

The game kicked off in the midday heat at a packed Estadio Azteca holding over 100,000 fans. In charge was Tunisian referee Ali Bin Nasser along with his two assistants, one of whom was Bogdan Dotchev of Bulgaria. Both men will become important players in the unfolding drama. Early on, Maradona showed signs of things to come with a mazy dribble before being chopped down by Terry Fenwick – England obviously planned to keep Maradona on a tight leash. A mistake by Argentinian keeper Nery Pumpido after 12 minutes gave Peter Beardsley a half-chance which narrowly missed. Both keepers remained largely untroubled as the half progressed, with Maradona going on another twisting run before again being fouled by Steve Hodge. England seemed determined to stop any Maradona runs before they caused too much damage. The main highlights of an uneventful first half were Maradona's attempted dribbles along with an ongoing feud between himself and Fenwick. As fans got half-time refreshments, few would have predicted how this game would shortly explode.

With 51 minutes on the clock, Argentina took possession of the ball in their own half. Bringing it forward to midfield, they spread the play from one side of the pitch to the other, before Maradona picked it up just within the English half. Ghosting past Glenn Hoddle, Maradona accelerated towards the penalty area before flicking the ball to Jorge Valdano. Hodge intercepted the pass but could only manage to hook the ball high towards the English goal. Maradona had continued his run into the area and, as England keeper Peter Shilton dashed out to punch the ball clear, Diego leapt up to challenge for the dropping ball.

And then occurred one of the most infamous and talked about moments in all of footballing history.

As both leapt for the ball, it seemed that 5ft 5in high Maradona had outjumped 6ft Shilton as the ball trundled into the net – a magnificent leap and header indeed. Maradona wheeled away in celebration, calling his team-mates over to join him. It was then that viewers could see several England players protesting vehemently, pointing to their arms. Chasing the referee, they seemed to be telling him that Maradona had used his arm, despite no flag from the linesman, Fenwick leading the charge, incandescent with rage. Although hard to see from the initial TV angle, something seemed out of place.

The TV replay from the side revealed why England were furious – it was clear that, in jumping for the ball, Maradona had sneaked up his hand to punch the ball into the net. It was also for that reason that he called his team-mates over so quickly to celebrate, to maintain the illusion of a goal. This is 35 years before the advent of VAR. Bogdan Dotchev had not flagged for any infringement, Ali Bin Nasser had not spotted the handball, Argentina were 1-0 ahead. The hardest thing for English fans to stomach was the sight of Maradona continuing to celebrate while all knew that his goal was a fraud. The game had sparked into life.

As viewers around the world discussed this incident, Maradona re-entered the narrative just four minutes later.

Receiving the ball in his own half, there seemed little danger for England. A beautiful little spin move saw him bamboozle both Peter Reid and Beardsley and take off over the halfway line. Terry Butcher came over to cover but Maradona jinked inside of him, still running towards the penalty area. Next, he beat Fenwick as he entered the area and Shilton came out to narrow the angle. Faking a shot, Maradona glided past the outside of Shilton while Butcher came in from behind to attempt a tackle. But just in time Maradona poked the ball into the empty net before wheeling away in celebration.

The best way to really appreciate the greatness of this goal, and its immediate impact, is to listen to the various commentators at that moment.

Barry Davies (English TV), 'Ohhh, you have to say that's magnificent. There is no debate about that goal.'

Bryon Butler (English radio), 'Maradona, turns like a little eel, he comes away from trouble, little squat man, comes inside Butcher, leaves him for dead, outside Fenwick, leaves him for dead and puts the ball away and that is why Maradona is the greatest player in the world.'

Jimmy Magee (Irish TV), 'Different class, DIFFERENT CLASS, when they talk about the great players of world championship football this man will be on a pedestal.'

And most famously, Victor Hugo Morales's translated Argentinian commentary, 'He's going to pass it to Diego, there's Maradona with it, two men on him, Maradona steps on the ball, there goes down the right flank the genius of world football, he leaves the wing and he's going to pass it to Burruchaga. Still Maradona! Genius! Genius! Genius! There, there, there, there, there, there! Goaaaaaaaal! Goaaaaaaal! I want to cry, oh holy God, long live football! What a goal! Diegoal! Maradona! It is to cry for, excuse me! Maradona, in a memorable run, in the best play of all time! Cosmic kite, what planet did you come from, to leave so many Englishmen behind, for the country to be a clenched fist crying for Argentina? Argentina 2, England 0! Diegoal, Diegoal, Diego

Armando Maradona! Thank you, God, for football, for Maradona, for these tears, for this Argentina 2, England 0.'

So, a pretty good goal then, I suppose. And you should hear the Morales commentary in Spanish – it will give you goosebumps.

From then on, the key highlights were that England were spurred into life and realised that they needed some width to their play. On came Chris Waddle and John Barnes, the latter immediately starting to make an impact on the left. With nine minutes left, Barnes got down to the byline and his cross was headed home by Gary Lineker. A glimmer of hope now appeared, and England kept pressing down the left with Barnes. As the 90-minute mark approached, Barnes set off on another trademark run and sent a beautiful cross to the back post. Lineker dived in bravely but couldn't quite stretch enough, leaving him sprawled in the net, and with that England's final chance had gone.

Final score
Argentina 2 (Maradona 51; 55) England 1 (Lineker 81)

What was the aftermath?

Not surprisingly, the handball goal became the big talking point. Interviewed after the game, Maradona explained that the goal was 'a little with the head of Maradona and a little with the hand of God'. And that gave birth to the phrase 'The Hand of God' which is now how the goal is described the world over. Looking back, if Maradona had only scored that goal, his legacy may have been different, but the fact that he scored one of the greatest goals ever just four minutes later seems to have lessened the impact. In fact, FIFA voted his second as its Goal of the Century in 2002.

The fallout from the goal would continue to rumble for decades after. Peter Shilton, famously, never forgave him. Referee Ali Bin Nasser and assistant Bogdan Dotchev had a simmering dispute over whose fault the decision was. A whole book could be devoted to the subject alone. But at the end of the day, Argentina had won 2-1 and moved on to a semi-final against Belgium, in which Maradona put in another magical performance, scoring both goals in a 2-0 win, before then inspiring Argentina to win the tournament. His legacy in footballing history was assured, making him a deity back home. From that moment on, his life wheeled from the highs of Napoli to the lows of drug addiction in spectacular fashion until his sad death in 2020. But on this day, he demonstrated why the Argentinian people loved him so much – the perfect mix of the football genius and the roguish scamp.

Teams

Argentina: Pumpido, Brown, Cuciuffo, Ruggeri, Giusti, Olarticoechea, Batista, Burruchaga (Tapia 75), Enrique, Maradona (c), Valdano

Manager: Bilardo

England: Shilton, Stevens, Fenwick, Butcher, Sansom, Hoddle, Reid (Waddle 69), Steven (Barnes 74), Hodge, Beardsley, Lineker

Manager: Robson

Iconic moment

The four minutes when Maradona wrote himself into football legend. From the deceitful to the sublime, Maradona lived up to his Argentinian nickname of *El Pibe de Oro*, where a *pibe*, while hard to translate, means an anti-establishment rogue, street smart and full of guile.

Trivia fact

At the end of the game, the smartest England player out there was Steve Hodge, who wisely made sure to exchange shirts with Maradona. After holding on to it for many years, he loaned it to the National Football Museum in Manchester. After Maradona passed away in 2020, the shirt went up for auction in 2022 with expectations of perhaps raising £4m. It sold for £7.1m, setting a record for a piece of sports memorabilia. The irony is that the shirts worn by Argentina on that day were bought hastily from a Mexican shop as the Argentinian manager wanted something more lightweight for the heat. So, Maradona's shirt wasn't even an official Argentinian jersey. Not that it mattered to the anonymous buyer.

Game 15

1990 World Cup

Argentina v Cameroon

8 June 1990

San Siro, Milan

Attendance: 73,780

Stage: Group B, Round 1

Why you should watch it

Up to 1990, African World Cup finals qualification had been dominated by the Saharan region, with Morocco playing in the 1970 and 1986 tournaments, Algeria in 1982 and 1986 and Tunisia in 1978. The only sub-Saharan country to have reached the finals since 1974 had been Cameroon, who qualified for 1982 and acquitted themselves well, drawing all three games including against Italy, who went on to win the trophy, and only failing to get out of the first group on goal difference. But it did mean that no sub-Saharan African team had ever won a World Cup finals game to date.

The qualification from the African region for 1990 was again dominated by the Saharan countries, with the final four pitting Algeria against Egypt and Tunisia against Cameroon for two places in Italy. Egypt took one spot while Cameroon beat Tunisia by three goals to zero to claim the other, placing them in their second World Cup. The leading goalscorer for the whole African qualification process was Cameroon's François Omam-Biyik with four goals.

Most of the Cameroon players plied their trade in the French lower leagues and were generally unknown throughout Europe. They were managed by a Russian – Valery Nepomnyashchy – who had previously managed a little-known Turkmenistani club in the Russian third division for one season. He applied for the job in 1988 and got it despite speaking no French. Coming into the tournament, his position had been under threat due to a poor performance in the Africa Cup of Nations.

Just before the 1990 World Cup, Paul Biya, president of Cameroon, requested that retired player Roger Milla come back to the team. Milla had played in all three of Cameroon's games in the 1982 World Cup and was rumoured to be 38 years old. Despite not having played for the past two years, he answered Biya's call, which unfortunately led to unrest ahead of the tournament among the other players, along with bonus disputes. The main instigator of the arguments was keeper Joseph-Antoine Bell and it cost him his starting place, with back-up Thomas N'Kono – who, like Milla, had played throughout the 1982 tournament – called up at the last moment.

Argentina, meanwhile, were the defending world champions, captained by Diego Maradona who had just enjoyed his greatest success at club level with Napoli as he led them to their first *Scudetti* in 1987 and 1990. The remainder of the Argentina team was not as strong as in 1986 but still boasted the likes of Oscar Ruggeri, Jorge Burruchaga and Claudio Caniggia, while being overseen by 1986 manager Carlos Bilardo. Bilardo was not overly concerned by Cameroon, stating after the draw, 'The Soviet Union is a tough opponent, but I'm generally pleased. Our group is not the easiest but we should have no problems in qualifying for the second round.'

As the game kicked off in Milan, Cameroon were ranked 500/1 outsiders to win the World Cup. An easy win for the world champions and Maradona was widely expected. The opening game of Italia '90 would get the tournament off to a cracking start.

What happened?

As expected, Argentina controlled the game early on while it soon became apparent that Cameroon were going to tightly mark Maradona and ensure no long runs from him, often with tackles that bordered on rough and usually led to a free kick. They were not dirty as such, but definitely on the physical side, which helped to unsettle any Argentinian rhythm. As the game settled, Cameroon started to create chances, with an early opportunity falling to Cyrille Makanaky who prodded the ball past Argentinian keeper Nery Pumpido only to see the ball cleared off the line by defender Néstor Lorenzo. Meanwhile, yellow cards began to appear for the repeated fouls on Maradona. Some of the Cameroon challenges were becoming slightly wild and, after around 30 minutes, Maradona had already been fouled six times.

The game settled into Argentinian attacks countered by Cameroon breakaways with few clear chances and as both teams went into the half-time break goalless, the Africans could feel satisfied that they had grown into the match comfortably and not been overawed by the world champions. Starting the second half, Cameroon continued to smother Maradona both fairly and unfairly, determined not to let him play by any means. The foul count against him was soon up to 11.

Then, on 61 minutes, came the first flashpoint. Caniggia had come on for the second half and while on a run down the right wing, he was clipped from behind by André Kana-Biyik. Referees had been asked ahead of the tournament to award red cards for fouls on players who were deemed to be clearly through on goal but in this case, there looked to be covering defenders. But despite that, French referee Michel Vautrot issued a straight red to Kana-Biyik and so Cameroon now faced 30 minutes of having to hold on against the champions a man short. The game had taken a turn for the worse for the Indomitable Lions.

But six minutes later the world was turned on its head. Awarded a free kick near the touchline, Cameroon sent in a low hopeful cross that was deflected upwards in a slow arc. As Argentinian defender Roberto Sensini casually watched the ball drop, Omam-Biyik cut in front of him and jumped to head the ball towards goal. The header appeared harmless and Pumpido had it covered but inexplicably spilled it through his hands into the goal. Ten-man Cameroon had taken the lead against the Maradona-led holders of the World Cup.

Suddenly the famous San Siro was awash with red, green, and yellow as the Cameroon fans celebrated wildly. It was a terrible goal for Argentina to concede from a defensive standpoint, with poor marking and goalkeeping. Argentina pushed forward seeking an equaliser but still had difficulty creating any clear chances. With nine minutes left, a Cameroon substitution saw the entrance of Milla to the field. Argentina seemed bereft of ideas of how to penetrate Cameroon, with Caniggia being the main threat.

As the match entered the final couple of minutes, a Cameroon attack broke down close to the Argentina area and Caniggia picked up the ball. Heading forwards at full steam, his long blond locks flowing, he hurdled a first challenge to burst across the halfway line. He then managed to avoid an attempted foul, although it caused him to start to lose his balance while running, before Benjamin Massing came across and completely wiped him out with a wild tackle. It was so dreadful that Massing lost his shoe and, as he put it back on, he was awarded a red card, taking Cameroon down to nine.

A few minutes later and it was all over – Cameroon had beaten the defending champions. Argentinian fans looked on in disbelief as the African supporters celebrated a historic day.

Final score
Cameroon 1 (Omam-Biyik 67) Argentina 0

What was the aftermath?

This was the moment when African football, which had so often been looked down upon by European and South American countries, showed its true potential. Huge celebrations kicked off both in Cameroon and across a lot of the rest of the continent. When interviewed, goalscorer Oyam-Biyik, remarked, 'No one thought we could do anything here against Maradona, but we knew what we could do. We hate it when European reporters ask us if we eat monkeys and have a witch doctor. We are real football players and we proved this tonight.'

The Cameroon team became media darlings after this opening victory – none more so than Roger Milla. Their next game against Romania saw Milla score twice in a 2-1 victory and unleash his hip-swivelling corner flag celebration on to the watching world. Cameroon were then beaten 4-0 by the Soviet Union but still topped the group. The round of 16 saw their game against Colombia go to extra time, only for Milla to again score twice and take them to a quarter-final date with England.

Argentina, meanwhile, scraped through the group stage as one of the best third-placed finishers, to then go on and reach the World Cup Final, albeit with generally bland performances, beating Brazil 1-0 after being under the cosh for most of the game, defeating Yugoslavia on penalties after a goalless draw and eliminating Italy again on penalties after a 1-1 draw. They are widely regarded as one of the weakest teams to ever to reach a World Cup Final. As for who they met there, that will become unfurled in the next three chapters.

Teams

Cameroon: N'Kono, N'Dip, Tataw (c), Kundé, Massing, Ebwellé, M'Bouh, Kana-Biyik, M'Fédé (Libiih 66), Omam-Biyik, Makanaky (Milla 81)
Manager: Nepomnyashchy

Argentina: Pumpido, Simón, Fabbri, Ruggeri (Caniggia HT), Lorenzo, Sensini (Calderón 69), Basualdo, Batista, Burruchaga, Balbo, Maradona (c)
Manager: Bilardo

Iconic moment

Although the goal from Omam-Biyik is the key moment of the game, most people's overriding memory is the foul by

Massing on Caniggia towards the end. A perfect summary of it was penned by Pete Davis in his wonderful book on Italia '90, *All Played Out*: 'A kind of full-pelt, waist-high, horizontal flying bodycheck. The general intention seemed to be not so much to break Caniggia's legs, as actually to separate them from the rest of his body.'

I honestly could not describe it any better – one of the leading contenders in the pantheon of all-time classic fouls.

Trivia fact

Roger Milla played again for the Indomitable Lions in the 1994 World Cup in the US, scoring during their 6-1 defeat to the Soviet Union, which made him the World Cup's oldest ever goalscorer at the age of 42. Or was that really his age? No one really knows.

Game 16

1990 World Cup

The Netherlands v West Germany

24 June 1990
San Siro, Milan
Attendance: 74,559
Stage: Round of 16

Why you should watch it

One of the great moments of any World Cup is when the draw throws up a game between two intense rivals, especially during the knockout phase. Who can resist watching Argentina v Brazil or England v Scotland? And one of the most intense rivalries in football exists between neighbours Germany and the Netherlands. When I was younger, I had a Dutch friend who would explain how, to him, the most important game for them to win was against the Germans.

The reasons for the rivalry go back in time all the way to World War Two. The Netherlands suffered a five-year occupation by the Germans, resulting in around a quarter of a million deaths. As time proceeds, these events fade into the distance for each subsequent generation, but, for the Dutch, it is where it all began.

In footballing terms, the rivalry then developed during the 1974 World Cup, where West Germany vanquished a groundbreaking Dutch side in the final. To many in the Netherlands, the result was a tragedy, being referred to locally as *De moeder aller nederlagen* (The mother of all defeats). The two sides met again during the 1978 World Cup, sharing a thrilling 2-2 draw that resulted in the Netherlands topping the group and moving on to their second successive World Cup Final, against Argentina. And then, more infamously, they were paired together in the following 1980 European Championship when another goal fest saw the Germans take a three-goal lead courtesy of a Klaus Allofs hat-trick before the Dutch struck back twice during the final 11 minutes but could not muster an equaliser, putting West Germany into the final and on the path to a championship win. The 1980 game saw Harald Schumacher and Huub Stevens fight on the pitch, as well as the Netherlands' René van de Kerkhof punching Germany's Bernd Schuster in the eye. Karl-Heinz Förster, Germany's midfielder, summed up the situation: 'Before the game we knew that it was going to be tense. We had sworn to win because that victory was so important to our sense of pride. To them, beating us is the best thing there is. They hate us so much more than we hate them.'

The rivalry developed further just two years before the 1990 World Cup as West Germany and the Netherlands met in the semi-final of the 1988 European Championship. This time the Dutch finally got past their old foes as a late Marco van Basten winner saw them reach the final and ultimately claim their first major trophy. Even sweeter, they beat the Germans in Hamburg. But just to increase the tension between both nations, Ronald Koeman decided to pretend to wipe his backside with Olaf Thon's shirt during the post-match celebrations. The sides then met during World Cup 1990 qualification when Dutch fans unfurled a huge banner comparing German captain Lothar Matthäus to Adolf Hitler. The rivalry was getting out of hand.

So, when these two met each other in the round of 16 in Italy, everyone prepared for the next instalment of the conflict. What made this game even more fascinating was that the San Siro is the home of both AC Milan and Inter Milan and, with Italian football being at its apex, many of the top players in the world plied their trade there. The season just ended had seen AC Milan win the European Cup, spurred on by their Dutch trio of Frank Rijkaard, Ruud Gullit and Marco van Basten, all of whom were in the Netherlands' starting 11. Inter Milan, meanwhile, had just won the Supercoppa Italiana, driven by their German trio of Andreas Brehme, Lothar Matthäus and

Jürgen Klinsmann, all of whom were in the West Germany starting 11. And hence there was an AC Milan versus Inter Milan rivalry also at play within the San Siro itself.

Would the game contain the same level of drama as past meetings? Well, it certainly did as one of the most infamous incidents in World Cup history occurred.

What happened?

A crowd of almost 75,000 packed the iconic stadium for the showdown. As usual, Dutch fans were bedecked in orange, bringing expressive colour to the proceedings. Naturally both sets of rival supporters tried to drown out the other's national anthem as the atmosphere swelled. Almost immediately after kick-off the tone was set as Adri van Tiggelen clattered into Pierre Littbarski – there was to be no love lost as usual.

A tense start then exploded into life after 21 minutes, creating a series of events that would live in infamy. It began with Germany's Rudi Völler being hacked down by Rijkaard in midfield. It was a badly timed challenge that led to a well-deserved yellow card, although Völler did throw in some extra rolling for good measure. Then, as Rijkaard ran back towards the penalty area, it appeared as if he spat at Völler's curly mullet while passing him. The camera footage was not conclusive but both players then started sparring verbally as it was obvious something had upset Völler. Or, as the English commentator so nicely put it, 'The two of them are exchanging unpleasantries.' As West Germany prepared to take the free kick, the referee called Völler over and showed him a yellow card even though it looked obvious that Völler was indicating to him that he had been spat at by Rijkaard, but to no avail. It seemed that something suspect had occurred between the AC Milan and Roma stars.

The free kick was swung into the area and Völler went up for the header, looping it harmlessly towards Hans van Breukelen. As the keeper came out to collect, Völler decided to challenge for the ball anyway but Van Breukelen got there first, causing the striker to try and put the brakes on his challenge. He seemed to pull out fairly, but as he got up from the ground Rijkaard was there again. Pulling Völler up by his ear, he stamped on his foot as both he and Van Bruekelen squared off against the German, who had to be rescued by Klinsmann.

The referee had no hesitation in showing first Rijkaard and then Völler red cards. As Völler stood in amazement at the injustice of the decision, Rijkaard walked by, and this time could be seen clearly spitting at the German. Both players trudged off to the sound of whistles, Völler wiping the back of his hair as the offensive spittle hung there. To be fair to Völler, he did well not to react to the spitting – a disgusting act within any game – and he deserves huge credit for being so stoic in the heat of battle.

And so, after 22 minutes, both teams were down to ten men. The Dutch initially reacted better, with Gullit coming close to opening the scoring. Then a terrible attempted back-pass from Jan Wouters was intercepted by Littbarski, whose cross was volleyed by Thomas Berthold but well saved by Van Breukelen. Neither team could break the deadlock as the half-time whistle sounded.

That was to change just six minutes into the second half. A cross from the byline saw Klinsmann strike at the near post to open the scoring. Wouters then had a great chance to equalise but his shot went narrowly wide. The Dutch continued to press but without making many clear opportunities, Gullit looking like the most likely to create something. The normally cool Van Basten even got caught up in the tension, earning a yellow card for a cynical challenge on Matthäus, although the subsequent four rolls were a little over the top.

Then, as the game started to approach the end, Klinsmann saw a great shot cannon back off the post. Van Breukelen then saved in a one-on-one from Littbarski as the Netherlands pushed forward in search of an equaliser. Finally, with just five minutes left, Brehme received the ball on the corner of the penalty area. Looking up, he curled a beautiful shot past Van Breukelen – West Germany appeared home and dry. But as German fans celebrated, the Dutch got a last-minute penalty following a somewhat soft challenge on Van Basten, which Koeman coolly converted. But it was too little, too late – West Germany had once again inflicted defeat upon the Netherlands. German coverage immediately went to an interview with Völler in the stands as it became obvious what would be the post-match topic of discussion.

Final score
West Germany 2 (Klinsmann 51; Brehme 85)
Netherlands 1 (Koeman 89 pen)

What was the aftermath?

Inevitably the aftermath focused on the Völler-Rijkaard incident. It is one of those unwritten codes within sport that spitting at an opponent is a cowardly, disgusting act and so much was penned about this topic. The photographs became iconic and an early edition of Simon Kuper's excellent *Football Against The Enemy* included one on its cover – something that was later changed. The surprising thing to most onlookers was that it was Rijkaard who had been the instigator of such an offence. He was generally viewed as a mild-mannered, stylish player and so it seemed totally out of character. Within the German media he earned himself the nickname 'Llama', for obvious reasons. To be fair, Rijkaard did later apologise to Völler for his actions, which the German gracefully accepted, leading them to eventually film a commercial together with their fees being donated to charity.

West Germany would move on to next knock out Czechoslovakia by a solitary Matthäus penalty in the quarter-finals before a classic semi-final which we will focus on soon. But first we will have to see who would earn a place to play them.

Teams

West Germany: Illgner, Augenthaler, Reuter, Kohler, Berthold, Brehme, Littbarski, Matthäus (c), Buchwald, Völler, Klinsmann (Riedle 77)
Manager: Beckenbauer

Netherlands: Van Breukelen, Van Aerle (Kieft 66), Koeman, Rijkaard, Van Tiggelen, van't Schip, Wouters, Winter, Richard Witschge (Gillhaus 78), Van Basten, Gullit (c)
Manager: Beenhakker

Iconic moment

Unfortunately, there is no getting away from the spitting incident as the moment for which the game will always be remembered. While the camera footage at the time was not crystal clear, German photographer Martina Hellmann was at pitch-side during the game. It was her camera that caught the iconic image showing the spittle in mid-flight towards the back of Völler. She had accompanied the team during the tournament and grown to respect Völler, who she described as 'just decent, he was just a really good guy'. She recalled in an interview the tension within the stadium during the game and that as the incident developed, she 'actually thought Rijkaard was about to punch Völler in the neck'. So, she trained her camera on both and caught the moment for posterity. She recalled later giving Völler a blown-up colour print of the picture – one wonders where, if at all, it hangs in his house.

Trivia fact

The Irish coverage of the game was enriched by pundit Eamon Dunphy using a pen to mark out the action on a VR screen at half-time. His analysis of the incident included the following classic commentary: 'Rijkaard launches the spit from here, now stop it there. There it is, Bill. It's hitting his head there and that's bad news for Rudi Völler and even worse news for his hairdresser!'

Game 17

1990 World Cup

Cameroon v England

1 July 1990
Stadio San Paolo, Naples
Attendance: 55,205
Stage: Quarter-Finals

Why you should watch it

Having shocked Argentina in the opening game of the tournament, Cameroon next played Romania and came away with a 2-1 win, their second successive victory. The recalled Roger Milla, after his late cameo against Argentina, was again named among the substitutes. This time he entered after 58 minutes (under the name 'Miller', which Italian TV insisted on calling him within their coverage) and would have a huge impact upon both the game and the World Cup. After 76 minutes, a long hopeful punt upfield saw Milla challenge for the ball and suddenly find himself one-on-one with the keeper before giving Cameroon the lead. That led to one of the iconic images of the World Cup as Milla raced to the corner flag and did a hip-swivel celebration. Four minutes from the end, he repeated the feat and, despite a consolation goal for the Romanians, Cameroon were two from two and into the knockout rounds.

Their opponents in the round of 16 were Colombia in Naples – a side that included stars such as René Higuita, Andrés Escobar, Carlos Valderrama and Freddy Rincón. Milla again started on the bench and again came on, this time after 54 minutes with the game goalless. It remained goalless after 90 minutes and so moved into extra time. Neither team could break the deadlock during the first 15 minutes but then it became Milla time yet again. Just as the last period of extra time commenced, Milla picked up the ball just outside the area, skipped past a defender and then blasted his shot into the roof of the net, before unleashing his trademark corner flag dance again. The 38-year-old had struck once more. And he was not finished – next came a moment of madness from goalkeeper Higuita.

For context, Higuita was one of the most colourful goalkeepers ever to play the game. Probably the first stopper to define the role 'sweeper-keeper', he also took penalties and free kicks from outside the area for Colombia, often with success, earning him the nickname *El Loco.* Unfortunately, that spark of craziness could occasionally backfire, and just two minutes after Milla opened the scoring, exactly that happened. A long ball into the Colombian half saw Higuita control it comfortably way outside of his area. Playing a one-two with a colleague, Milla closed in, and Higuita decided to try and flick it around him. It failed of course and Milla ran through on to an open goal to double the lead and take his tally to four goals in two games, both coming off the bench.

Cameroon became the first African nation ever to reach a World Cup quarter-final. Their opponents were England, who had been less than impressive to date. A dire group stage had seen the Three Lions draw 1-1 with the Republic of Ireland and 0-0 with the Netherlands before narrowly beating Egypt 1-0. The round of 16 saw England progress against Belgium with a David Platt stunner in the last minute of extra time, meaning England had reached the quarter-finals despite scoring just three goals in four games. But naturally much of the English media were excited to be playing Cameroon – after all, how many problems could a team from West Africa, who had never played at this stage and relied on a 38-year-old for goals, honestly cause? The answer would be many.

What happened?

A crowd of 55,000 packed the Stadio San Paolo in Naples, including a contingent of noisy English, to see if the Cameroon fairytale could continue. England seemed in control from the start but without mustering any real threat to the Cameroon goal. While they typically huffed and puffed, keeper Thomas N'Kono had little to do. The first real chance fell to Cameroon, with Peter Shilton saving well from François Omam-Biyik, and England suddenly appreciated that they were in a game. Another warning came as Omam-Biyik struck a long-range effort that flew narrowly wide. Then, just as Cameroon were dominating play, a Stuart Pearce cross from the left was headed in by Platt, giving England an undeserved lead, as relieved cries of 'Eng-er-land' rang around the stadium.

If anyone thought Cameroon would fold on going behind, they were soon disavowed of that notion as Thomas Libiih stole in unmarked to just head over. Minutes later he almost got in again, causing commentator Brian Moore to say, 'We are riding our luck in the most dangerous way.' Cameroon were still demonstrating some of their undisciplined tackling, gifting England several free kicks just outside the area which they failed to take advantage of. England continued to ride their luck to the half-time break, but it was obvious that manager Bobby Robson was going to have to address some issues.

The start of the second half saw the usual entrance of Roger Milla as Cameroon sought to get back into the match. A sign of things to come arose as Platt went down under a challenge from N'Kono, with the penalty claim waved away by the referee. But then finally the Cameroon pressure told as Milla was clumsily brought down in the area by Paul Gascoigne. Emmanuel Kundé calmly placed the ball past Shilton to even matters up.

Things quickly went from bad to worse for the Three Lions as Milla played a charging Eugène Ekéké through the middle to dink over the diving Shilton. In the space of just four minutes, the Indomitable Lions had flipped the script. Again, per English commentary, 'Suddenly a crisis has developed for England and a disaster is beckoning.' The stadium became awash with red, green, and yellow.

As England started to push forward, more gaps appeared at the back for Cameroon to exploit. Cyril Makanaky broke through but his effort was blocked by a defender. Platt went close before Omam-Biyik had a cheeky back-heel well saved – the game was now thrusting back and forth. Then, with just seven minutes remaining, Gary Lineker spun nicely just inside the area and went down under a challenge from Benjamin Massing. A penalty was awarded and Lineker himself coolly converted to bring England back into the game, a massive sigh of relief echoing around English bars and houses.

With the game approaching full time, Shilton was called into action again from a sharp shot from Omam-Biyik. Finally, the whistle blew, and England could count themselves lucky to earn an extra 30 minutes of opportunity.

Straight away that man Omam-Biyik again came close with Shilton saving on the line. He was now at the centre of everything for Cameroon and threatened with another long-range strike. It was all one-way traffic as Cameroon came on in waves – England desperately hanging on. It seemed to be only a matter of time before a goal and just before the break in extra time it finally came – to England. A clever ball from Gascoigne put Lineker through and he appeared to be felled by N'Kono while trying to round him. Once again Lineker took responsibility and once again he coolly converted. Somehow, inexplicably, England had a 3-2 lead.

Lineker came inches from completing a hat-trick a couple of times as Cameroon finally faded. England fans danced a conga around the stands as they reached their first World Cup semi-final for 24 years while Cameroon bowed out with heads held high. They had come so close to becoming the first African team to reach the semi-finals.

Final score
England 3 (Platt 25; Lineker 83 pen, 105 pen)
Cameroon 2 (Kundé 61 pen; Ekéké 65)
After extra time

What was the aftermath?

Cameroon may have exited the tournament, but their overall performance had helped to erase many perceived stereotypes regarding African football. Ever since Zaire's pitiful display in the 1974 finals, African presence at the World Cup had been courtesy of the sub-Saharan nations – Morocco, Egypt, Tunisia, and Algeria. Cameroon were the only nation outside of this area to make it to the finals since 1974 and had shown that, unlike Zaire, they were a thoroughly professional outfit who could give any team a scare. Let's not forget that until losing to England they had defeated the defending champions Argentina, plus Romania, and Colombia. An enormous sense of pride could be taken by the Indomitable Lions, and no one would ever again underestimate the abilities of African countries.

England, meanwhile, fully appreciated the scare they had suffered. Of course, it is always easier to be magnanimous having won, but all involved knew that they had been just seven minutes from elimination in a game many had taken for granted ahead of kick-off. Bobby Robson's immediate reaction was, 'At one time I thought we were on the plane home. They were the better team when they went ahead but it was a see-sawing saga of a match.' He later added, 'We pulled it out of the fire and I don't really know how.'

However, the best quote came from England winger Chris Waddle. Ahead of the encounter, England had sent Howard Wilkinson, who at that time was manager of Leeds United, to scout Cameroon. His analysis was that the game would be 'a practical bye to the semi-finals'. Immediately after the match, an exhausted Waddle observed, 'Some fucking bye, that.' Never have truer words been spoken.

Next up for the Three Lions would be a meeting with West Germany, which is our next match for discussion.

Teams

England: Shilton, Wright, Parker, Walker, Butcher (c) (Steven 73), Pearce, Waddle, Platt, Gascoigne, Barnes (Beardsley HT), Lineker
Manager: Robson

Cameroon: N'Kono, Kundé, Tataw (c), Massing, Ebwellé, Libiih, Maboang (Milla HT), Pagal, Mfédé (Ekéké 62), Omam-Biyik, Makanaky
Manager: Nepomnyashchy

Iconic moment

The sheer relief among English commentators and fans when Gary Lineker earned and converted the 83rd-minute penalty. Many people had already been looking forward to the England v West Germany semi-final ahead of kick-off, writing off the Africans, and suddenly there was the realisation that it may all be going wrong. A huge collective sigh of relief as England dodged a bullet.

Trivia fact

Bobby Robson suspected that Cameroon were spying on their training sessions. He therefore told Gary Lineker to hit all his practice penalties to the keeper's right – which was in fact opposite to Lineker's preference. He did so and therefore, when the spot-kick was awarded seven minutes from time, Lineker guessed that N'Kono would be expecting it to his right if someone had been feeding him training information. Lineker hit it to the left, N'Kono dived to the right – and the rest is history.

Game 18

1990 World Cup

England v West Germany

4 July 1990

Stadio delle Alpi, Turin

Attendance: 62,628

Stage: Semi-Finals

WORLD CUP CLASSIC

Why you should watch it

We have covered both West Germany's and England's routes to this semi-final, with both teams having played in significant games against the Netherlands and Cameroon respectively. Those progressions led to this meeting of the old foes. The Germans had been here many times before – to them, reaching a major tournament semi-final was almost the minimum expectation. But for the English, this was their first World Cup semi-final since winning it back in 1966. To say that the country was in a fervour ahead of this game is an understatement.

Argentina had defeated Italy in the other semi-final ahead of this match and so English fans knew that a victory would mean a final against an Argentinian team that had failed to impress. The general feeling among everyone was that this was the major hurdle – get past West Germany and the trophy was there for the taking. England manager Bobby Robson summed up the feeling of a nation, 'If we can win tonight, we're in the final, with a great chance of beating Argentina. Great chance. This is the big one. Germany's the big one.'

There was obvious trepidation among English fans about having to play West Germany. Since England had beaten them 4-2 at Wembley in 1966 to lift the Jules Rimet Trophy, the Germans had a vastly better international record. The

English had lived in the shadow of that World Cup triumph ever since. The 1970 tournament had seen an England team that was probably stronger than the 1966 edition eliminated by the Germans in a traumatic game – the Three Lions throwing away a 2-0 lead to lose 3-2 after extra time. That pain was then increased by West Germany again beating England in the 1972 European Championship. Coming to Wembley's hallowed turf, the Germans completely outclassed England, administering a footballing lesson, primarily through the genius of Günter Netzer, which revealed how far England had fallen in six years. This was followed up by West Germany winning the 1972 European Championship. England failed to qualify for the 1974 World Cup and fans had to sit at home and watch West Germany again triumph. The trend continued as the Germans reached the final of the 1976 European Championship while England failed to qualify for the finals, and then England suffered the embarrassment of again failing to qualify for the 1978 World Cup. And so it was that, from 1966 onwards, West Germany had been a dominant world force while the sun had set on England.

The 1980s weren't much better for the Three Lions. 1982 would see the two clash again during the second group stage of the World Cup – a game that ended goalless and ultimately ended up with West Germany progressing and England being eliminated due to their relative records against Spain. And so it was that England came into this match not having beaten the Germans in a significant game since 1966, a full 24 years prior. Could they break this hoodoo in the Turin heat?

What happened?

The game kicked off with England in their traditional white shirts while Germany wore their second strip of green shirts – the same colour they wore when they outclassed England at Wembley back in 1972. A lot of England's hopes rested on the precocious genius of young midfielder Paul Gascoigne and the striking boots of Gary Lineker. Early on, Gascoigne showed he was ready for the challenge with a couple of shots that were well saved by German keeper Bodo Illgner. After 38 minutes, Rudi Völler picked up an injury, meaning he had to be replaced by Karl-Heinz Riedle. Then we almost saw one of the goals of the tournament. Chris Waddle picked up a loose ball just outside the centre circle and instantly hit it towards the goal, sensing that Illgner was off his line. Illgner desperately scrambled backwards with the ball heading in and just managed to tip it on to the bar. It had been a brilliant piece of opportunism from the winger which sadly wouldn't have counted due to a late whistle for a foul – but he was not to know that.

It was left to Peter Shilton to save a Klaus Augenthaler free kick before the teams headed in for the break. The first half had been cagey with no clear chances but, encouragingly for England fans, the Three Lions were more than holding their own, playing with more confidence than they had shown in earlier rounds. It looked like they were rising to the occasion.

Fifteen minutes into the second half, Thomas Häßler was brought down by Stuart Pearce just outside the area, within shooting range. The free kick was nudged to Andreas Brehme whose shot was blocked by an onrushing Paul Parker. But, to the horror of England fans, the ball spun up and arched over a back-pedalling Shilton, dropping just beneath the bar. It was an incredibly lucky strike, but the Germans had taken control – it was now up to England to react.

England pushed forward and Waddle had a valid penalty shout denied after being brought down by Augenthaler. Then, with ten minutes remaining, England got the equaliser they deserved and, to no one's surprise, it was Lineker who again came to their rescue. A hopeful cross by Parker saw three German defenders get in a mess. The ball broke to Lineker who tidily placed it in the corner. It was all square again and remained so as the game headed into extra time.

Jürgen Klinsmann went close with a couple of chances before, nine minutes in, came the moment all English fans recall. Gascoigne received the ball in midfield and beat a couple of players before pushing it slightly too far ahead. Thomas Berthold came in to just reach the ball ahead of the stretching Gascoigne. A moment too late into the tackle, Gascoigne caught Berthold who made sure to throw a couple of rolls in going down. Immediately Gascoigne raised his hands to indicate to the referee that it was a complete accident. Desperation showed in his face.

The reason for this was because he was on a yellow card from an earlier game. World Cups at this time had a rule that two yellow cards meant missing the next match. Cruelly that applied even in the semi-final, meaning that a player could miss the biggest match of their career due to just one yellow card (a rule that has since been changed – now yellow cards are wiped ahead of the semi-finals). Gascoigne immediately knew that a yellow would mean missing the final against Argentina.

To Gascoigne's horror, the referee brandished the card. Cameras closed in on Gascoigne as he looked inconsolable. Famously, Lineker was seen checking on him and then indicating to the bench to keep an eye on him as he was clearly distraught. It was a cruel twist of fate for England's creative midfielder.

As the first half of extra time approached the end, Waddle got hold of a loose ball and saw his effort bounce back off the post, so nearly giving England the lead. Going into the final 15 minutes, Platt had the ball in the German net but was given offside, although the replay showed it to be very debatable. If England felt that luck had deserted them with Waddle's shot on to the post, balance was restored as an Augenthaler shot did likewise. It seemed destined to go to a penalty shoot-out.

And it did – after a draining, tense 120 minutes, the place in the final would come down to who could hold their nerve. England had the advantage of going first and all the first six penalties were converted. Up stepped Pearce, who hit it with his usual venom down the middle. A diving Illgner got a foot to it, and it was advantage Germany. Thon converted their fourth which left Waddle having to score to keep England in with a chance as a tearful Pearce watched on. His attempt flew over the bar – and Germany headed off to the final – while cameras showed a distraught Pearce. The English dream died on penalties – something that would become a future recurring theme.

Final score
West Germany 1 (Brehme 60) England 1 (Lineker 80)
After extra time; West Germany win 4-3 on penalties

What was the aftermath?

The game became one of the most cherished in English history. Bobby Robson had taken so much stick from the media up to this stage, with England's shoddy group-stage play and close win over Cameroon. He had been a true gentleman throughout and the English public suddenly appreciated this team. The semi-final was their strongest performance to date – they had taken the Germans to a shoot-out and narrowly lost. There was an outpouring of sympathy for Pearce and Waddle while Gascoigne was taken to the nation's hearts. It is due to this game that many English supporters look back on Italia '90 with such nostalgia, even though the tournament was actually pretty poor.

Many of the players were not fully aware at the time of the depth of affection which the English people held them in after that great night in Turin. Coming home, they were not sure what the reaction would be to their semi-final effort. But, as their plane landed at Luton Airport, they soon realised what they had created. Fans swamped the airport, climbing on roofs and road signs, to cheer their returning heroes. An open-top bus struggled to move the team through the thick throng – the streets awash with red, blue, and white. England had finally, at least for now, rejoined the elite of world football.

For the Germans, it was business as usual. Having scraped past England, they then defeated Argentina in what must be considered the worst World Cup Final of all time. A horrendous game saw Argentina reduced to ten men before, thankfully, we were spared another 30 minutes by a late penalty from Brehme, after which the Argentinians completely lost their heads. A second red card was brandished while Maradona was booked as their players surrounded the referee in a shocking display of petulance. The World Cup ended with the image of Lother Matthäus lifting the trophy in front of a tearful Maradona. Nearly all neutrals agreed that West Germany fully deserved their triumph.

Teams

West Germany: Illgner, Augenthaler, Berthold, Buchwald, Kohler, Brehme, Häßler (Reuter 66), Matthäus (c), Thon, Völler (Riedle 38), Klinsmann
Manager: Beckenbauer
England: Shilton, Wright, Parker, Walker, Butcher (c) (Steven 70), Pearce, Waddle, Platt, Gascoigne, Beardsley, Lineker
Manager: Robson

Iconic moment

There may be many German fans who disagree but for so many, the image that will always come to mind is that of Paul Gascoigne's tears. The whole country had fallen in love with the goofy man-child and when everyone realised that he would miss the final should England get through, the nation grieved along with him. To see him at that moment crying just highlighted how we often forget that footballers are human beings like the rest of us. This was a young man who would miss possibly the biggest match of his lifetime due to one mistimed tackle. Everyone just wanted to give him a hug.

Trivia fact

Chris Waddle tells a great story about Paul Gascoigne that perfectly sums up the player, who was once described by Bobby Robson as 'daft as a brush'. The night before the game, Robson was taking the players through tactics. Looking at Gascoigne, Robson told him, 'When we lose the ball in midfield, Gazza, you pick up Matthäus.' As the players walked out of the briefing, Gascoigne turned to Waddle and asked, 'Who's Matthaus?' Only the German captain who had recently won Serie A with Inter in 1989 and would soon be awarded the Ballon D'Or as best player in the world for 1990. There will only ever be one Paul Gascoigne.

Game 19

1994 World Cup

Argentina v Romania

3 July 1994

Rose Bowl, Pasadena

Attendance: 90,469

Stage: Round of 16

WORLD CUP CLASSIC

Why you should watch it

Since World War Two, Romania had only qualified for two World Cups: 1970 (in which they were eliminated in the group stage) and 1990 (where they were eliminated in the round of 16). But 1990 had seen the first signs of a golden generation team forming.

Romania had reached the 1994 tournament in some style, winning seven of their ten qualifiers and scoring 29 goals in the process. Their top scorer had been Florin Răducioiu with nine goals, while Gheorghe Hagi had contributed another five. At the time, Răducioiu was part of the dominant AC Milan squad that had just lifted the European Cup, although he rarely started that season. However, the true star was Hagi, nicknamed 'The Maradona of the Carpathians' for his outstanding creativity in midfield.

Romanian club Steaua Bucharest had stunned Europe by lifting the European Cup in 1986, beating Barcelona in the final courtesy of goalkeeper Helmuth Duckadam saving all four Barça penalties in the shoot-out. It was later that year that Hagi joined them, aged just 21. He initially signed on a one-game loan – with that game being the European Super Cup against Dynamo Kyiv – but that was soon extended to a full transfer when Hagi scored the only goal of the final from a trademark free kick. A legend was born.

Steaua were eliminated early in the 1987 European Cup before enjoying another successful run in 1988 that took them all the way to the semi-finals where they were knocked out by Benfica. Hagi ended the tournament as one of the joint top scorers with four goals, ensuring that European eyes noticed him. Steaua then went one step better the next year, reaching the final for the second time in four years. A legendary AC Milan team swept them aside 4-0, powered by Marco van Basten and Ruud Gullit, but again Hagi enhanced his reputation, scoring six tournament goals only behind Van Basten's ten and team-mate Marius Lăcătuş's seven. European clubs were now desperate to sign the Romanian, but the communist government headed by Nicolae Ceauşescu would not allow such a move.

After again impressing during the 1990 World Cup, Hagi remaining at Steaua was no longer an option. Real Madrid offered $3.5m to prise their star asset away after the tournament. His time with Madrid was not a total success – he did score 16 goals in 64 appearances but never quite lived up to his true potential. And so it was that he moved on to Italian side Brescia in 1992, where he experienced relegation before helping Brescia back up the following season, before joining the Romania squad for the 1994 World Cup.

While Hagi was the undoubted star and leader of the 1994 group, there were many other talented individuals including Dan Petrescu (Genoa), Miodrag Belodedici (Valencia), Gheorghe Popescu (PSV Eindhoven), Florin Răducioiu (AC Milan) and Ilie Dumitrescu (Steaua Bucharest). In the group phase, Romania had beaten Colombia and USA, although they were also thrashed 4-1 by Switzerland. The Colombia game included a sublime goal from Hagi, lobbing the goalkeeper from near to the touchline. That was enough to top the group, but with Argentina surprisingly coming third in their group, Romania's reward was a challenging round of 16 tie.

The big story ahead of this game was all about Diego Maradona. During their opener against Greece, he had celebrated a goal with a manic mad-eyed shout into a TV camera. After their next match against Nigeria, he was selected for a drugs test, where ephedrine, a performance-enhancing stimulant, was found in his sample. Maradona's World Cup, and for that matter his international career, was ended. Argentina would have to face Romania without their iconic talisman. The question was how would that impact their play?

What happened?

The Rose Bowl in Pasadena is so named because it is, well, a giant bowl. Originally built in 1922, it is completely open, providing no shade from the Californian sun. Over 90,000 fans packed in for the 1.30pm kick-off in 35°C/95°F heat, with Argentinian fans not surprisingly hugely outnumbering those cheering for Romania. Everyone was wondering how Argentina would cope without superstar Maradona – but their side still included the likes of Gabriel Batistuta and Ariel Ortega.

The game started at a ferocious pace despite the searing heat. Batistuta immediately showed why he would earn the nickname *Batigol* during his career with Argentina, Fiorentina, and Roma with an early shot on target as Argentina applied early pressure. But after just 11 minutes, Romania earned themselves a free kick to the left of the area. As Dumitrescu stepped up to take it, all expectations were for a cross into the area, but to everyone's surprise, including the Argentinian keeper Luis Islas, he instead went straight for goal, placing a hard-hit shot over Islas and into the top corner. It was both audacious and brilliant and gave Romania an early unexpected lead.

Just a few minutes later, Batistuta received the ball at his feet in the area. A lovely flick between his own legs saw him fool defender Daniel Prodan who then leaned on him, resulting in a penalty decision. *Batigol* himself brushed himself off and coolly converted, bringing Argentina level.

The game sat at 1-1 after just 16 minutes of play – a terrifically entertaining start.

With Argentinian cheers still resounding around the stadium, Romania launched another attack from deep as a ball out of defence found Hagi on the wing at the halfway line. A beautiful one-two saw Hagi regain possession closer to the area where, with three players close to him, he threaded a through ball right into the path of the onrushing Dumitrescu, who side-footed it past Islas. In one quick move, Romania had cut Argentina open as they regained the lead – and we had still only seen 18 minutes of action. If the players were concerned about the heat, they certainly weren't showing it – the pace was unrelenting.

Both teams continued the high tempo, creating chances at both ends – Batistuta and Abel Balbo linking well as an attacking partnership. Then, right on half-time, Dumitrescu almost completed a first-half hat-trick, breaking through on goal but seeing his goal-bound poke cleared off the line. Romania went into the break with a one-goal lead as both sides earned well-deserved rest and refreshments.

The second half started at the same pace, with Batistuta bringing a good save out of Romanian keeper Florin Prunea before having a dubious penalty appeal rejected. Just as it looked like a matter of time before Argentina would equalise, a fantastic break from Dumitrescu saw him run with the ball from his own half to the Argentine penalty area before slipping it wide to the onrushing Hagi, who drilled it into the corner. The speed of the counterattack was breathtaking, giving Romania a two-goal advantage with 30 minutes left.

Batistuta continued to be Argentina's focal point, looking dangerous on the ball as his team committed more men forward, seeking a way back into the game. Finally, the breakthrough came with 15 minutes left when Prunea failed to hold a shot from Diego Simeone, allowing Balbo to sweep in the loose ball in front of a cheering Maradona up in the stands, resplendent in dark shades.

The remaining 15 minutes saw Argentina continue to press and Romania continue to hit them on the counter until finally the referee's whistle sounded. The 1986 winners and 1990 runners-up had been eliminated by a fast, skilful Romanian team, led by the little magician himself, living up to his 'Maradona of the Carpathians' nickname.

Final score
Romania 3 (Dumitrescu 11, 18; Hagi 58) Argentina 2 (Batistuta 16 pen; Balbo 75)

What was the aftermath?

This encounter became widely acknowledged as the match of the 1994 World Cup. In the quarter-finals, the Romanians would again be involved in a thriller – this time equalising late against Sweden to take the tie to extra time, before then seeing Sweden do the same to them to take it to penalties. Unfortunately, that was where their dream ended – but not without having already stamped their mark on the tournament. To this day, they are still referenced as the 'golden generation' – a team who brought joy to a country that had only recently emerged from a brutal dictatorship. Sadly, no Romanian team since has enjoyed the same level of success.

The World Cup run would change the lives of many of the players as clubs paid attention to the talent within the squad. Tottenham Hotspur would make the double signing of Gheorghe Popescu and Ilie Dumitrescu, although both only remained at White Hart Lane for one season. Popescu moved on to captain Barcelona while Dumitrescu was less successful, going on loan to Seville before ending up at West Ham United. Dan Petrescu also moved to England, joining Sheffield Wednesday for a year before then enjoying four seasons at Chelsea. Miodrag Belodedici moved first to Valladolid and then Villarreal before ending his career back in Romania with Steaua Bucharest. Florin Răducioiu moved from AC Milan to Espanyol, before later, like Dumitrescu, also ending up for a brief spell on loan at West Ham United.

And as for star player Gheorghe Hagi, his World Cup performances earned him a move to Barcelona, although again his club form would not match his international form as he struggled under Johan Cruyff. That resulted in a move to Turkish side Galatasaray in 1996 and it was there that his club form finally blossomed; 59 goals in 132 appearances saw the Turkish fans take him to heart as they lifted four consecutive league titles with him as well as the 2000 UEFA Cup, beating Arsenal on penalties, although Hagi himself got red-carded in extra time for punching Gunners captain Tony Adams. He always had a bit of a wild streak within him.

As for Diego Maradona, one of the greatest players of all time sadly brought the curtain down on his international career with the failed drug test. This would not be the only time in his life that drugs would hurt his career. Before this tournament, his cocaine use while at Napoli had increased, resulting in a 15-month ban for testing positive. After being kicked out of the 1994 World Cup following the Nigeria drug test, Maradona would return to Argentina to play for his beloved Boca Juniors for a couple of years before retiring. Managerial stints would follow along with drug, alcohol and weight issues which resulted in frequent hospitalisations and treatment centres before his death in November 2020 from a cardiac arrest. Sadly the 1994 World Cup would be the world's last view of the great man in the blue and white of *La Albiceleste*.

Teams

Romania: Prunea, Petrescu, Mihali, Belodedici, Prodan, Selymes, Lupescu, Popescu, Munteanu, Hagi (c) (Gâlcă 86), Dumitrescu (Papură 89)
Manager: Iordănescu

Argentina: Islas, Sensini (Bello 63), Cácares, Ruggeri (c), Chamot, Simeone, Redondo, Basualdo, Ortega, Batistuta, Balbo
Manager: Basile

Iconic moment

The pass from Hagi to set up Dumitrescu's second goal was sublime. To have the vision to slot the perfect ball through two Argentinian defenders right into the path of Dumitrescu so that he did not even have to break stride to slot home was worthy of the real Maradona himself. It was at that moment that the world realised just how much talent the little midfielder possessed, before then cementing that impression with his own goal later. While Hagi never quite hit the full heights at club level, he always stepped up for his nation when needed.

Trivia fact

Although banned from playing due to his failed drug test, that did not stop Maradona from commentating on the game for Argentinian television. Typically, he still tried to apportion blame elsewhere, stating, 'Romania didn't beat us on the pitch. We were beaten off the pitch and that's what hurts.' It would be a sad trend during his life of not taking responsibility for his actions.

Game 20

1994 World Cup

Brazil v The Netherlands

9 July 1994
Cotton Bowl, Dallas
Attendance: 63,500
Stage: Quarter-Finals

Why you should watch it

Sweden 1958 – a 17-year-old Pelé had helped the *Seleção* lift the World Cup. Chile 1962 – the magic of Garrincha had helped the *Seleção* to lift the World Cup. Mexico 1970 – one of the greatest Brazilian teams of all time had lifted the World Cup. Three victories in four tournaments – and then nothing since. Going into the 1994 finals, Brazil were 24 years without victory and the population was getting restless. They had seen the beautiful 1982 side cruelly lose to Italy and were mourning the fact that it seemed that just playing fast, attacking football was no longer adequate – instead some steel and pragmatism was needed.

They turned to coach Carlos Alberto Parreira, part of the physio team back in Mexico 1970 and a devotee of a more methodical way of playing than Brazilian tradition. But he was still a fan of two strikers within a 4-4-2 formation. He built a squad that contained the likes of tough midfielders Dunga and Mauro Silva rather than a flowing playmaker in the Zico/Sócrates mould. But Brazil being Brazil, people at least expected attacking flair and were looking for a partnership that could deliver goals.

The partnership that developed paired Romário and Bebeto – two players with decidedly different temperaments and a sometimes less-than-glowing appreciation of each other. Bebeto had been brought up in a middle-class environment and eventually signed for Flamengo in 1983.

Despite being relatively small and light, he had great pace along with an ability to produce extraordinary volleys. He was not a pure striker – but rather an attacker who could link up play, sometimes dropping deep to do so. A deeply religious man, Bebeto's was a quiet lifestyle with family being his priority.

The same most certainly could not be said for Romário. If Bebeto's idea of a good night was an evening in with his wife, then Romário's was much more rock and roll. Born in one of Rio's largest favelas, his was a childhood full of poverty where learning the game meant street football with the onus on developing a tough skin and trickiness. A short, squat player, Romário ended up playing for Flamengo's biggest rivals, Vasco da Gama. Comparing himself to Bebeto, he once made the comparison, 'We are different people, Bebeto is a family type, stay at home. I'm a street cat.'

They showed their potential during the 1989 Copa América, earning the nickname 'Diabolical Duo'. The 1990 World Cup however proved frustrating for Romário, who injured himself ahead of the tournament and so was restricted to a solitary substitute appearance, with Napoli's Careca leading the line. Romário's volatility then caused him to fall out with the coach, criticising Parreira after he dropped him for a friendly against Germany, who retaliated by dropping Romário indefinitely from Brazil's World Cup qualification squad. Unfortunately, the striker was sorely missed, and Brazil found themselves needing to win their final qualification game against Uruguay to go to USA '94. Bebeto helped to persuade Parreira to bring Romário back in for the big game and he did so, resulting in two Romário goals and qualification. Unfortunately, that did not prevent him from yet more controversy. He called a press conference to announce that he would not sit next to Bebeto on the flight to the US, which just built on the tension that had also caused Romário to give Bebeto the nickname *Chorão*, translating as 'Crybaby'.

But going into the tournament, Parreira decided to risk sticking with the Romário-Bebeto partnership, relegating Müller to the bench alongside a youthful, gap-toothed teenager known as Ronaldo. Thankfully for Parreira, once in America, the two buried their differences for the good of the squad. The group stage saw them come out on top unbeaten, with Romário bagging three goals and Bebeto one, before Bebeto then scored the goal that eliminated the USA in the round of 16, setting up the quarter-final against the Dutch. Starring within a Brazilian team that was more pragmatic and rugged than previous versions, the pair were pushing the *Seleção* forward.

The Dutch had scraped through the group stage, coming top but on equal points with both Saudi Arabia and Belgium. They had needed a late winner to overcome the Saudis before losing 1-0 to their local rivals Belgium, meaning they had to win their last game against Morocco. Again, it was a late winner with just 13 minutes remaining that got them over the line. Eliminating the Republic of Ireland 2-0 in the midday heat and humidity of Orlando meant a quarter-final place against the *Seleção* and the Romário-Bebeto duo. The question was, could the partnership continue to flourish against the Netherlands?

What happened?

Both teams lined up for the match in uncharacteristic kits – Brazil in blue shirts and the Netherlands in white – but the stadium was awash with Dutch *Oranje* and Brazilian yellow, driven on by the beat of samba drums. There were absolutely no indications during the first 30 minutes that this game would be at all memorable. For two sides that were famed for their beautiful, flowing football, this was anything but, as neither keeper was remotely threatened, and it was only after 30 minutes that Brazil finally went close with a long-distance effort from Márcio Santos. The shots of colourful fans in the stadium were more interesting than the football, which the cameraman seemed to acknowledge as the game progressed, seeking out more and more characters. Pelé and Cruyff would have been less than impressed.

But luckily a game is made up of two halves, and so, while the players trudged off at half-time locked in a goalless stalemate, there was still hope that maybe the game could come to life in the second 45 minutes. As the old cliché goes, the match was just calling out for a goal and maybe then the whole tone might change.

Whatever happened during half-time, Brazil started the second half like a team possessed. Almost immediately Romário nearly broke through before a dangerous Bebeto cross was cut out by Dutch keeper Ed de Goeij. But Romário suddenly looked like a man on a mission, and another cross from Bebeto on the left saw him convert with aplomb. Just eight second-half minutes had elapsed and the game finally burst into life – the attacking partnership yielding dividends. A Mexican wave began to develop around the stadium as Brazilian flags billowed.

Brazil were now flying and, almost immediately following kick-off, Bebeto saw an effort clip the far post. Next Romário broke through only to see his effort well saved again by de Goeij. The Brazilian front pair were ripping the Dutch apart in a flurry of attacks and eventually the inevitable happened – Bebeto broke through, rounded the keeper and put Brazil two ahead. At this point the Dutch were reeling, and it seemed just a matter of how many Brazil would score. A boxing referee would have been considering whether to stop the fight.

But immediately the Netherlands struck back. A ball into Dennis Bergkamp in the area saw him beat one defender before cracking a shot into the top corner. In the blink of an eye they were back in the game – Brazil having made the cardinal sin of switching off after scoring. A match that had been sleep-inducing for the first 45 minutes had now yielded three goals in just 11 second-half minutes.

Dutch heads picked up and they started to drag themselves back into the game, mainly through long-range efforts. With 14 minutes remaining, the Dutch earned themselves a corner. Brazil keeper Cláudio Taffarel started to come and then stopped in no-man's-land, allowing Aron Winter to head in the equaliser. With the Netherlands having been under the cosh, the stadium was now awash with orange, causing Barry Davies on commentary to state, 'What a turnaround! And all credit to the Dutch ... the only question is why didn't they start like this?' Why indeed?

How the game would turn next was anyone's guess. Would the Brazilians completely crack, or could they muster a response? The momentum was all with the Netherlands. The answer came just five minutes later as a run by defender Branco saw him fouled around 30 yards from goal. With a wall in place, Branco himself ran up and rifled the ball low into the corner. It proved too much for the Dutch to come back again and so Brazil moved on to the semi-finals, having survived the scare.

A game of two halves indeed.

Final score
Brazil 3 (Romário 53; Bebeto 63; Branco 81)
Netherlands 2 (Bergkamp 64; Winter 76)

What was the aftermath?

Having survived the scare against the Dutch, Brazil were now just two games from lifting the monkey off their back of 24 years without success. Neither of these games would live up to the excitement of their earlier group and knockout games. Sweden would be beaten in the semi-final through a late Romário strike while the final, in the punishing California heat, would see them play out a goalless 120 minutes against Italy, with very few highlights to talk of. It went to penalties, where Romário would convert, while the overriding image is poor Roberto Baggio, head bowed and hands on hips, after he missed Italy's fifth to hand Brazil the trophy. This was the same Roberto Baggio who had almost single-handedly dragged Italy through the knockout stages. It is criminal that people remember the penalty miss and often forget that it was Baggio that got Italy into the final in the first place.

So, Brazil would end as 1994 champions, but it is a team that is not fondly loved within the country – there is still much more affection for the 1982 team despite their elimination. But a strong defence and the effective Romário-Bebeto partnership had delivered – Parreira had achieved the task given to him despite constant criticism and the scare of almost not even qualifying. It may not have been a vintage Brazil, but football had progressed since 1970 and 1982 – and the *Seleção* had finally moved along to reflect those changes.

Teams

Brazil: Taffarel, Jorginho, Aldair, Santos, Branco (Cafu 90), Mazinho (Raí 81), Silva, Dunga (c), Zinho, Bebeto, Romário
Manager: Parreira

Netherlands: de Goeij, Wouters, Koeman (c), Valckx, Winter, Rijkaard (R. de Boer 65), Jong, Rob Witschge, Overmars, Bergkamp, Van Vossen (Roy 54)
Manager: Advocaat

Iconic moment

Bebeto's celebration – after scoring he ran to the sideline making a cradling motion, swiftly joined by strike partner Romário and Mazinho who joined in the gesture. The inspiration – Bebeto's wife Denise had just given birth to their first child two days earlier. Bebeto himself explained, 'It was spontaneous. Nothing had been planned. But I was pleasantly surprised to see some of my team-mates joining me in celebrating that goal. At first no one outside the team knew about our son being born. But later, I explained to the world.' The celebration became iconic – and perhaps could be blamed for starting a trend of increasingly bizarre rituals that continues to this day.

Trivia fact

Maybe somewhat surprisingly, given his volatility during his playing days, Romário has since built a career in politics since retiring from the game. Elected to the Chamber of Deputies for the Brazilian Socialist Party in the 2010 general election, he was then elected to the Senate during the 2014 general election, obtaining the most votes ever received by a candidate representing the state of Rio de Janeiro. Since then, he has switched parties twice – firstly joining Podemos in 2017 and then the Liberal Party in 2021.

Game 21

1994 World Cup

Bulgaria v Germany

10 July 1994

Giants Stadium, East Rutherford

Attendance: 72,416

Stage: Quarter-Finals

Why you should watch it

They shouldn't have even been there. Going into their final qualification game away to France, Bulgaria needed to win in the Parc des Princes to reach USA '94 and deny their hosts. A first-half goal by the mercurial Eric Cantona was almost immediately cancelled out by Bulgarian striker Emil Kostadinov – and that scoreline remained as the game went into the final minute. France earned a free kick near the corner in the Bulgarian half and everyone assumed they would play short and hold it there to kill the remaining seconds, and as predicted the ball was played to David Ginola who ran to the corner – and then swung in a cross towards the far post. His delivery was overhit and picked up by a Bulgarian defender, after which some quick passing saw a through ball played to Kostadinov and, to the horror of the crowd, he drilled it into the roof of the net. Bulgaria were heading for the USA and a lifetime feud began between Ginola and Gérard Houllier, following the France coach's summary, 'He [Ginola] sent an Exocet missile through the heart of French football and committed a crime against the team.'

Five of the Bulgarian qualification goals had come from Hristo Stoichkov. If Hagi was 'The Maradona of the Carpathians' then Stoichkov was the other eastern European superstar of this era. Starting his career in Bulgaria, he scored 81 goals in 119 appearances for CSKA Sofia before earning a big-money move to Barcelona in 1990. That saw him become part of the 'Dream Team' managed by the legendary Johan Cruyff, which won La Liga in four successive seasons and the 1992 European Cup, resulting in Stoichkov being named FIFA World Player of the Year in 1992. Going into USA '94, he had built a fearsome reputation as a great attacking midfielder.

His standing did not just end with his playing ability. A volatile character on the field saw many run-ins with authority and rules. He had been involved in a fight during the 1985 Bulgarian Cup Final and was suspended for two months early at Barcelona for stamping on a referee's foot. Ironically, he was given the task at Barcelona of making sure strike partner Romário attended training on time, not simple given Romário's love of the nightlife.

Heading into the 1994 tournament, Bulgaria had never won a World Cup finals match and their opener saw them lose heavily, 3-0 to Nigeria. It looked like another disappointing outing for them but then a 4-0 thrashing of Greece, including two goals from Stoichkov, gave them hope. They would need to beat Argentina, 1990's losing finalists, to move on and did so 2-0 with another Stoichkov contribution. Surprisingly, Bulgaria had reached the knockout stages.

But no team gets so far thanks to just one player alone. While Stoichkov was the undisputed star, the squad contained plenty of other skilful players. Kostadinov had shown his talents in getting Bulgaria past France while Stoichkov was accompanied in attack by Yordan Letchkov, nicknamed 'The Magician' and known for his dribbling ability and balding pate. They were by no means a one-man team.

The round of 16 saw Bulgaria scrape past Mexico on penalties, with Stoichkov grabbing his fourth goal in four games, before lining up against Germany. The Germans had headed their group with two wins and a draw, powered by the goals of Jürgen Klinsmann, before disposing of Belgium 3-2 in the round of 16. The world champions looked like they were powering on to yet another final, what would have been their fourth in succession. It was a side containing the likes of Lothar Matthäus, Rudi Völler, Jürgen Klinsmann and Thomas Häßler, all of whom had plied their trade in the ultra-competitive Italian league. Even with the genius of Stoichkov, Bulgaria faced an uphill battle to progress any further.

What happened?

With Germany now a united nation following the collapse of communism and East Germany, they had even more resources to choose from. As always, they were a physically imposing team who often steamrollered opponents with their remorseless play. But Bulgaria showed that they were not intimidated early on, creating the first chance when Krasimir Balakov's shot rebounded off the post. That awoke the Germans, who then came close through a diving Klinsmann header, well stopped on the line by Bulgarian keeper Borislav Mihaylov. Shortly afterwards, Andreas Möller drilled a shot towards goal which was luckily blocked by a defender, hitting him in a particularly painful area. Germany were starting to take control.

Goalless at half-time, the Germans came out determined to continue where they had left off. A high ball into the area reached Klinsmann, who was tapped by Letchkov and reacted somewhat theatrically. The follicly challenged Bulgarian had caught Klinsmann but there was no doubt that the striker made a meal of it – a penalty was the decision.

Matthäus coolly sent Mihaylov the wrong way and the Germans were in front. *Die Mannschaft* had not lost a World Cup game once ahead since 1978 and so the outlook was grim for the Bulgarians. Looking to kill off the tie, Möller hit another fearsome shot which this time cannoned off the post, falling to Völler. Sweeping the ball home, it looked like game over until the linesman's flag rescued Bulgaria, but as the game reached the final 15 minutes there only looked like being one winner.

It was at that point that Stoichkov won a free kick just outside the German area. With the wall in place, Stoichkov bent the ball over and into the corner, leaving keeper Bodo Illgner rooted to the spot. Their talisman had pulled Bulgaria back into the game with his fifth tournament goal to stun the Germans. Almost immediately, a German attack broke down close to the Bulgarian area, leading to a fast counterattack that drew a corner. As green, red, and white flags waved to the beat of a Bulgarian drummer, the ball was cleared, eventually coming to Zlatko Yankov who crossed into the area. Letchkov stole in front of a defender and launched himself at the ball, his diving header perfectly directed beyond Illgner's outstretched hand, turning Letchkov from villain to hero – in the space of just three minutes, the game had turned on its head. As the Bulgarian commentator shouted 'God is Bulgarian! God is Bulgarian!' Germany had just 12 minutes to try and respond.

After seeing his star player pick up a yellow card shortly afterwards, Bulgarian manager Dimitar Penev decided to risk taking Stoichkov off to prevent any possibility of a red, hoping that extra time would not be required. Naturally the Germans pushed forward seeking the equaliser, but they never truly threatened. Bulgarian joy was unbridled as the final whistle sounded and they realised they were into the semi-finals. A team that had only once ever reached as far as the round of 16 in 1986 had just defeated the two 1990 World Cup Final participants and Stoichkov was becoming one of the players of the tournament.

Final score
Bulgaria 2 (Stoichkov 75; Letchkov 78) Germany 1 (Matthäus 47 pen)

What was the aftermath?

Following on from their historical win, Bulgaria moved on to play Italy in the semi-finals. There they were unfortunately defeated by the sublime skills of Roberto Baggio, who scored two first-half goals. Stoichkov, of course, pulled one back from the penalty spot just before half-time but this time they couldn't muster the same comeback as against Germany, despite having a strong penalty appeal waved off. When the tournament ended, Stoichkov stood as joint top scorer, along with Russia's Oleg Salenko, earning him a share of the Golden Boot as well as being named in the 1994 World Cup All-Star Team, along with team-mate Krasimir Balakov.

A golden generation team reached the height of its powers and, unfortunately, this would be as good as it would ever get for them. While they did also qualify for the 1998 finals, they only earned one point in their group and incurred a 6-1 thrashing at the hands of Spain. Since then, they have failed to reach another World Cup.

As for Stoichkov, he went on to both be named FIFA World Player of the Year and win the Ballon D'Or for 1994, in no small part due to his fine World Cup performance, which brought his skills to the attention of a global audience. He continued to play for Barcelona and Parma for a while, but he never reached the heights of his 1994 opus magnum.

Germany, meanwhile, continued their dominance in World Cups, never going out earlier than the quarter-finals until 2018. For them, it soon became business as usual. But for the people of Bulgaria, who had lived under communism until 1990, while this might have been just a fleeting moment, what a moment it was.

Teams

Bulgaria: Mihaylov (c), Kiryakov, Ivanov, Hubchev, Tsvetanov, Yankov, Letchkov, Balakov, Kostadinov (Genchev 90), Sirakov, Stoichkov (Yordanov 85)

Manager: Penev

Germany: Illgner, Helmer, Buchwald, Kohler, Berthold, Möller, Matthäus (c), Häßler (Brehme 83), Wagner (Strunz 59), Völler, Klinsmann

Manager: Vogts

Iconic moment

Letchkov's diving header became the image of the match. The way in which he stole in front of Häßler and launched himself at the ball, planting such a sublime header beyond Illgner and so eliminating Germany, momentarily even stole the limelight from the fabulous Stoichkov. It was quite the way to celebrate his birthday which had fallen the day before the match and which he had allegedly celebrated with a couple of beers.

Trivia fact

Letchkov was always recognisable on the field due to his prematurely balding head. When asked about it, he attributed his male baldness to growing up in the town of Sliven, just 500 miles from Chernobyl. Apparently, in his mind, radiation therefrom had led to his distinctive look. Later in life, Letchkov returned to Sliven where he became mayor. However, his political career was not as distinguished as his footballing one – he was eventually forced to resign after showing the middle finger to journalists as well as police officers after fleeing from a traffic violation and throwing his documents at them.

Game 22

1998 World Cup

Nigeria v Spain

13 June 1998
Stade de la Beaujoire, Nantes
Attendance: 33,257
Stage: First Round, Group D

Why you should watch it

Following on from Cameroon's fine performance at the 1990 World Cup, which changed the way that the rest of the world viewed African football, they were soon supplanted by a new power within the continent. The Indomitable Lions gave way to The Super Eagles, as Nigeria became the dominant force. It began with the 1992 Africa Cup of Nations, when Nigeria finished third under Dutch coach Clemens Westerhof with a young squad including a 20-year-old Finidi George, then playing for Sharks FC but shortly to move to Ajax. During the following 1994 Africa Cup of Nations, Nigeria went two places better, winning the tournament in Tunisia by defeating Zambia 2-1 in the final through two goals from Emmanuel Amuneke, again under the guidance of coach Westerhof. The young 1992 squad had evolved into a much more powerful team, including the likes of George, Efan Ekoku (Norwich City), Jay-Jay Okocha (Frankfurt) and Daniel Amokachi (Club Brugge).

The Super Eagles followed this early 1994 success with a trip to USA '94, their first appearance in the World Cup finals, where the same set of players topped their group ahead of Argentina and the golden generation Bulgarian side. Nigeria beat Bulgaria and Greece while only narrowly losing 2-1 to Argentina, setting up a meeting with powerhouse Italy in the round of 16. There they were two minutes from eliminating the *Azzurri* before a late Roberto Baggio equaliser and then an extra-time penalty broke Nigerian hearts.

But despite the disappointment, the squad had now gained valuable experience at the top level. And they used this experience to propel them to their greatest achievement. Playing in the 1996 Olympics, Nigeria shocked everyone by first defeating Brazil 4-3 in the semi-final and then overcoming Argentina 3-2 in the final, both thrilling games that are well worth watching, to win the gold medal. While Olympic football is not always as well noticed as other tournaments, more knowledgeable footballing pundits noted that this Nigeria squad was one to watch for the future.

1998 saw them again qualify as one of five African nations to head to France as the tournament expanded from 24 to 32 teams. The draw saw them placed into a tough group, along with Spain, Paraguay, and Bulgaria, and facing the Spaniards in the opening game in Nantes. Having played so well against Italy in 1994, they knew they could hold their own against European teams, so there was no need to be overawed. Nigeria were now being coached by the experienced and much travelled Serb, Bora Milutinović, who had managed three different countries at the last three World Cups: Mexico in 1986, Costa Rica in 1990 and the USA in 1994.

Spain, meanwhile, were hoping to remove the curse of continuous underperformance in World Cups. A country boasting two of Europe's strongest club sides in Real Madrid and Barcelona had regularly failed to deliver on the biggest stage; in fact, since 1950, the furthest they had gone was to the quarter-finals twice in 1986 and 1994. For a nation with such a strong footballing tradition, this was unacceptable. For France '98, they had placed their trust in coach Javier Clemente, who had enjoyed success managing Athletic Bilbao in the 1980s and had a reputation for a tough, defensive style of play. The Spanish were led up front by Raúl, then in his fourth season at Real Madrid where he would eventually earn legendary status with 323 goals over 16 seasons.

For both teams, getting off to a strong start to the tournament was key. Could Spain finally banish their reputation for choking or could Nigeria strike another blow for rising African talent?

What happened?

Nigeria lined up for the anthems in their traditional all-green strip, leaving Spain to sport their change strip of all white. As the Nigerian contingent in the crowd made themselves heard within a sea of green, Raúl took just four minutes to almost open the scoring, heading against the bar with keeper Peter Rufai stranded.

But Nigeria soon showed that they did not fear their more illustrious opponents, exemplified by Okocha cheekily nutmegging Albert Ferrer, before three long-distance attempts were all easily collected by Spanish keeper Andoni Zubizarreta. Then, just as Nigeria were creating the better chances, Spain got a free kick just outside the penalty area. Fernando Hierro shot it around the wall and into the corner as Rufai staggered across his goal line, resulting in a sea of red scarves being held aloft in celebration. Favourites Spain had the lead after 21 minutes.

The Super Eagles took just three minutes to react and level when a corner from the right was headed powerfully into the roof of the net by midfielder Mutiu Adepoju. Nigeria continued to hit Spain with speedy counterattacks while *La Roja* midfielder Miguel Nadal was lucky to avoid a yellow card for an outrageous dive in the Nigerian penalty area. As the half-time whistle sounded the sides went into the break tied at 1-1, the first 45 minutes showing that Nigeria were more than a match for the Spaniards.

Just two minutes into the second half, a long pass from Hierro in midfield found Raúl stealing behind the Nigerian defence, and as the ball fell over his right shoulder, he struck it on the run first time with his left foot, volleying it home. It was a fantastic finish from the Real Madrid hitman, worthy of the World Cup stage – a future international star had announced himself to the watching global audience.

Nigeria were going to have to come from behind for a second time. With half an hour remaining, Raúl hit a tamer effort that Rufai almost let slip through before bundling it out for a corner. As the clock reached 73 minutes, Nigerian winger Garba Lawal broke into the left of the Spanish area before firing in a low cross. Zubizarreta had it covered at the near post, but to the horror of onlooking Spanish fans his right hand could only parry the ball goal-wards, agonisingly crossing the line to draw the Nigerians level. A horrible moment for the Spanish captain that woke up Nigerian trumpets and dancing in the stands as he lay despondent with his face in his hands.

With both sides now looking for a winner, Raúl missed a glorious chance, slicing the ball from close range the wrong side of the post. Nigeria immediately attacked and a headed clearance fell to midfielder Sunday Oliseh around 30 yards from goal. Without any hesitation, Oliseh thumped a rocket which flew past Zubizarreta as true as an arrow, before running wide-eyed to celebrate with the Nigerian bench. If Zubizarreta had been at fault for Nigeria's second, there was absolutely nothing he could do about their third, which was a fantastic strike and, for the first time, the Super Eagles found themselves ahead with just 12 minutes remaining.

Substitute Rasheed Yekini almost settled the match with a spectacular hooked volley that narrowly flew over the bar. Then, just as the end was approaching, Sergi almost equalised as his curled effort scraped the top of the crossbar. But it wasn't to be for the Spaniards as they once again suffered a disappointing start to a World Cup campaign. Nigeria had deservedly won and showed more evidence that African nations were to be taken seriously.

Final score
Nigeria 3 (Adepoju 24; Zubizarreta 73 og; Oliseh 78)
Spain 2 (Hierro 21; Raúl 47)

What was the aftermath?

Having been eliminated by Italy in the round of 16 in 1994, this talented group of Nigerian players were hoping to progress further this time. To do so, they would need to overcome Denmark, who had finished second in their relatively weak group. But it was a Danish team that included the Laudrup brothers as well as Peter Schmeichel in goal. On the day, the Danes were simply too strong for Nigeria, overpowering them 4-1, and Nigeria again exited at the same stage.

While Nigeria remained a strong team, the squad had effectively peaked from 1994 to 1998 with the two World Cup runs and the Olympic title. After that they still were runners-up in the 2000 Africa Cup of Nations and did also qualify for the 2002 World Cup where they exited at the group stage. But they would not enjoy reaching the round of 16 in a tournament again until 2014.

Several members of the 1998 squad did go on to enjoy success at club level within Europe. Defender Taribo West, for example, played for both Milan teams, while his defensive partner Celestine Babayaro enjoyed an eight-year spell at Chelsea. Sunday Oliseh, like Finidi George, made a name for himself at Ajax. Attacking midfielder Jay-Jay Okocha went on to become a cult hero at first Paris Saint-Germain and then Bolton Wanderers, with his transfer to Paris after the World Cup for £14m making him the most expensive African footballer at the time. Striker Nwankwo Kanu moved to Arsenal in 1999 and became a member of the unbeaten 'Invincibles' of the 2003/04 Premier League season.

Spain, meanwhile, followed up their loss against Nigeria with a disappointing 0-0 draw with Paraguay before thrashing Bulgaria 6-1. However, that was not enough to take them into the knockout phase, finishing third in the group behind Nigeria and Paraguay and resulting in yet another World Cup underperformance. Their time would eventually come – but they would still have to wait a while.

Teams

Nigeria: Rufai, Oparaku (Yekini 70), Okechukwu (c), West, Babayaro, Oliseh, George, Adepoju, Okocha, Lawal (Okpara 90+3), Ikpeba (Babangida 83)

Manager: Milutinović

Spain: Zubizarreta (c), Ferrer (Amor HT), Campo, Alkorta, Sergi, Luis Enrique, Nadal (Celades 77), Hierro, Raúl, Kiko, Alfonso (Etxeberria 58)

Manager: Clemente

Iconic moment

The game will always be remembered for Sunday Oliseh's magnificent strike and wild celebration thereafter. When interviewed about it, Oliseh recalled how in training before the match, his team-mate Taribo West had asked if he wanted to practise some shots against him. Oliseh took around ten shots – nine of them went in – and then when his chance came during the game, the ball came to him similarly to how West had been rolling them out to him in training. Proudly he stated that the goal had cemented his family name in the history of world football: 'It was like a big folklore back home and people always talk about it.' And well they should.

Trivia fact

Nigerian squad member Nwankwo Kanu was later involved in one of the most famous incidents in FA Cup history. On his Arsenal debut against Sheffield United in the 1999 tournament, the game was tied with ten minutes remaining when Blades keeper Alan Kelly kicked the ball out of play so that treatment could be given to an injured team-mate. Tradition dictates that the throw-in should then be returned to the team that kicked the ball out – and Arsenal's Ray Parlour tried to do exactly that. However, maybe unaware of this convention, Kanu chased down the throw-in and crossed it for Marc Overmars to score. While it was not against the rules, Arsenal manager Arsène Wenger did accept after the game that it was unsporting and so offered a replay. Arsenal won again, this time fairly.

Game 23

1998 World Cup

Iran v USA

21 June 1998

Stade de Gerland, Lyon

Attendance: 39,100

Stage: First Round, Group F

Why you should watch it

Not since East Germany and West Germany met during the 1974 World Cup had there been a game more politically charged than this one. From the moment that the draw was made for the 1998 tournament and Iran and USA were placed together, everyone had pencilled in this match for special attention. It immediately became headline news around the world.

Ever since the Iranian Revolution in 1979, ill-feelings had been high between the two nations. The Revolution saw the overthrowing of the Pahlavi Dynasty, royalty who had ruled over Iran for many years, to be replaced by an Islamic Republic led by the Ayatollah Khomeini. With Khomeini becoming the Supreme Leader of Iran, the Shah of Iran fled to the US, with whom he had always shared a close bond as America had helped him remain in power for so many years.

One of the effects of the Revolution was the Iranian hostage crisis. November 1979 saw a group of militarised Iranian college students storm the US Embassy in Tehran and take 52 American diplomats and citizens hostage. They remained hostage for 444 days and became a nightly news item in the US, with the crisis widely believed to have caused president Jimmy Carter's defeat in the 1980 election and led to American economic sanctions on Iran, further increasing ill-feelings. Later, tensions were escalated as the US lent support to Iraq during the Iran-Iraq War in the 1980s.

While this game was occurring 18 years after these events, they still loomed large in the memory. The two countries had not met in a competitive match since. Iran had only previously qualified for one World Cup, Argentina in 1978, when they shocked the Tartan Army by drawing with Scotland but otherwise lost their other two group games. The US had not fared much better – having played in just two of the previous 11 tournaments, qualifying for 1994 automatically as hosts.

Iran qualified for the 1998 World Cup by defeating Australia over two legs on away goals. The first leg had seen 128,000 fans pack into the Azadi Stadium in Tehran, despite an official 100,000 capacity, to see the two sides draw 1-1 before the return leg in Melbourne saw Australia 2-0 ahead with 15 minutes remaining and looking like booking their ticket to France, until two quick goals sent Iran on their way instead.

As soon as the draw was complete, the president of the US Soccer Federation described it as 'the mother of all games' and immediately there arose the issue of security. The ground at Lyon could hold 42,000 and so trying to ensure that no trouble would arise was a mammoth task as thousands of fans from both nations arrived in town. There was intelligence that an Iranian terrorist organisation had bought 7,000 tickets so that they could protest at the game. TV cameramen were briefed what banners should not be aired and they complied, despite some banners being smuggled in pieces and reformed with Velcro. There were also rumours that Iranian radical groups might target the US team, resulting in high security around their training camp – a compound in the countryside. Extra security were also on hand at the stadium to ensure no one ran on to the pitch to make any political statements with 150 armed police called in on duty – an unprecedented number for a World Cup match.

As coverage started, it was apparent that, at least between fans, there was no animosity but rather a party spirit within

Two ideologies clash – East Germany stun their western neighbours before a packed Hamburg crowd

Football will never again be the same – Johan Cruyff's balletic moves torment Argentina

One of the deadliest goalscorers of all time – Der Bomber spins on a dime to defeat Total Football

As good as sex – Archie Gemmill gives the Tartan Army hope for two minutes with his wonder goal

Tor! Tor! Tor! – Hans Krankl ends 47 years of hurt as Austria get one over their illustrious neighbours

Hair flowing as he races through a sea of tickertape – Mario Kempes strikes again for the Albiceleste

Young guns having some fun – Northern Ireland's 17-year-old Norman Whiteside shows no nerves against Spain

The day the music died – Paolo Rossi breaks Brazilian and worldwide hearts with his hat-trick

Old cold – Dominique Rocheteau takes care of injured Patrick Battiston after Schumacher's knockout blow

CCCP – Ihor Belanov in that iconic Soviet Union jersey

The Vulture strikes again – Emilio Butragueño swoops four times to end the Danish dream

Rockstars with mullets in the coolest kit ever – Danish Dynamite line up in the Mexican sun

Tears of joy – Michel Platini and Luis Fernandez celebrate winning the penalty shootout against Brazil

Maradona turns like a little eel ... and that is why Maradona is the greatest player in the world

Africa rising – Oyam-Biyik leaps highest to shock Maradona and the World Champions

Caught in the act – Frank Rijkaard earns the nickname "Llama" from German media

Three Lions against Indomitable Lions – Gary Lineker leads from the front as he helps England struggle through a 'practical bye'

Who's Matthäus? – England's Paul Gascoigne finds out in their titanic semi-final battle against West Germany

The Maradona of the Carpathians – Gheorghe Hagi and Ariel Ortega fight for the ball under the scorching Californian sun

Rocking the baby – Brazil's Bebeto's iconic goal celebration against the Netherlands

God is Bulgarian! – Hristo Stoichkov hits the top corner as Yordan Letchkov looks on admiringly

I told my workplace I was sick – a Nigerian fan preserves his anonymity as he enjoys their victory over Spain

The mother of all games – Iran and USA line up pre-match to show that football can cross political divides

Down to ten men – David Beckham sees red, leaving England to battle Argentina a man short in Saint-Etienne

Dennis Bergkamp! Dennis Bergkamp! – three sublime touches of pure genius

and outside the stadium. Supporters talked about the great atmosphere and how food and drinks had been bought and shared. It was now just a matter of whether that same spirit of reconciliation would also occur on the pitch as the two teams exited the tunnel.

What happened?

No game up to that point had seen so many pitch-side photographers. The then Supreme Leader of Iran, Ali Khamenei, had ordered the team not to walk towards the Americans and engage in traditional pre-match handshakes, but, in the spirit of reconciliation, the two sides lined up for the pre-match photo together, each Iranian next to each American before exchanging flowers. It was a magnificent gesture, especially by the Iranians, that helped to diffuse the tension. An early chance saw a powerful header from US striker Brian McBride come back off the bar with Iranian keeper Ahmad Abedzadeh well beaten. Another header shortly afterwards by McBride again saw him hit the woodwork – it looked like it might not be USA's day. Iran started to gain confidence and after 20 minutes, forward Khodadad Azizi broke through the US defence. Beating the last defender, it was him against Kasey Keller and, after prodding the ball past the keeper, they collided on the edge of the area. It looked an obvious penalty – but for some reason the Swiss referee waved it off.

With half an hour gone, US midfielder Claudio Reyna struck a left-footed effort from just outside the box – and for the third time in 30 minutes the ball flew back out off the post. Lady luck had completely deserted the Americans. Tab Ramos next tried a long-distance effort that Abedzadeh covered well. But then, just as it looked like the US would break through, a fantastic header from midfielder Hamid Estili bulleted into the top corner to give Iran the lead just before half-time. An exciting first half had seen the woodwork pounded, a clear penalty denied and a great headed goal. Maybe not 'the mother of all games' but certainly exciting.

If expectations were for Iran to stubbornly defend their one goal-lead in the second half, they were to prove wrong. While the US pushed forward, Iran also attacked whenever chances presented themselves. The game was end to end but, although both sides created opportunities, there was nothing that overly troubled either keeper. Then a ball to the back post found US defender David Regis unmarked – his first time left-footed volley beat Abedzadeh at the near post – but once again the woodwork came to Iran's rescue. The US could hardly believe their continued bad luck.

The US were now in full attack mode and only a brave save from Abedzadeh at the feet of Frankie Hejduk kept Iran ahead. The game moved into the last ten minutes with USA cranking up the pressure, but then, as they committed more players forward in search of an equaliser, Iran hit them on the break. Midfielder Mehdi Mahdavikia found himself free on the left and through on goal. Breaking into the area, he fired the ball low and hard past Keller and the Iranian bench erupted in joy. The Americans had just six minutes to find a way back in.

The US defence was now wide open as they pushed forward and Iran almost snatched a third, striker Ali Daei seeing his effort cleared off the line. Straight away the ball went to the other end where McBride scrambled in a messy goal to give the US a lifeline. Three minutes remaining – could the US find one more goal to level?

They couldn't and the Iranian bench rushed on to the field in wild celebration. They had got their first win at a World Cup – and had done it against a team that many of their fans saw as 'the enemy'.

Final score
Iran 2 (Estili 40; Mahdavikia 84) USA 1 (McBride 87)

What was the aftermath?

Millions of Iranians poured out on to the streets to celebrate long into the night. A country that had seen much suffering and misery for so many years had a reason to rejoice – and rejoice they did. Although the Iranian government tried to rein in the celebrations, it was impossible, with women even joining in, refusing to wear the traditionally mandated headscarves. Funnily enough, spontaneous celebrations also broke out in Los Angeles, where a substantial Iranian diaspora resides, causing blocked traffic as horns honked and passengers waved Iranian flags, standing out of sunroofs. US residents, who at that time were still learning about football, marvelled at the outpouring of joy from their Persian neighbours. It was quite the spontaneous street party.

The general feeling was that the game had helped to mend fences between the two nations. The spirit of reconciliation continued after the tournament, with the teams playing a friendly in Pasadena, on the outskirts of Los Angeles, 18 months later, allowing the large Californian Persian diaspora to see their heroes in the flesh. The game ended in a diplomatic 1-1 tie.

With the US suffering their second defeat, their World Cup was over. Their only aim now was to at least get something from their last match against FR Yugoslavia, but an early goal by the Europeans put paid to that hope, leaving the US exiting the group stage with three defeats, having scored just one goal – against Iran. The victory over the US did however provide Iran a glimmer of hope – but just a glimmer as it would require them to get a result against Germany. Again, it wasn't to be as the Germans ran out 2-0 victors, meaning Iran joined the US on flights home. But, for the Iranians, it was a flight back to a heroes' welcome – they had won the game that mattered.

Teams

Iran: Abedzadeh (c), Khakpour, Mohammadkhani (Peyravani 75), Pashazadeh, Zarincheh (Sadavi 77), Mahdavikia, Bagheri, Estili, Minavand, Azizi (Mansourian 74), Daei
Manager: Talebi

USA: Keller, Pope, Dooley (c) (Maisonneuve 82), Regis, Hejduk, Ramos (Stewart 57), Reyna, Moore, Jones, Wegerle (Radosavljević 57), McBride
Manager: Sampson

Iconic moment

Despite all the pre-match fears, both sets of players showed that football could rise above politics. While the game had ended with a disappointing loss for the US, the teams exchanged shirts and embraced to show the world that there were no hard feelings – this was after all just a football match.

Trivia fact

The political nature of the fixture was exemplified by the fact that US president Bill Clinton recorded a specific address ahead of the game. In it he expressed this desire: 'I hope it can be another step towards ending the estrangement between our nations.' It just shows how heightened the pre-match tension was that it required such an address to the nation.

Game 24

1998 World Cup

Argentina v England

30 June 1998

Stade Geoffroy-Guichard, Saint-Étienne

Attendance: 30,600

Stage: Round of 16

WORLD CUP CLASSIC

Why you should watch it

We last met Argentina playing against England back in 1986 – a World Cup classic which featured the two famous goals by Diego Maradona that eliminated the English. Since that fateful day, resentment had festered among the English public regarding the so-called 'Hand of God', which, to the English, was victory through cheating and an example of the dark arts they felt were often employed by Argentina. As far as they were concerned, the Argentinians had behaved disgracefully against them in 1966 when captain Antonio Rattín was sent off, they had behaved disgracefully against them in 1986 when Maradona had punched the ball into the net, and payback was due. If there was one team in the world that England wanted revenge upon, it was Argentina.

The opportunity arose when they came up against each other in the round of 16 during the 1998 tournament. It was not expected to happen – it was widely assumed that both teams would top their groups and so avoid each other so early. Argentina did just that, winning all three matches against Croatia, Jamaica, and Japan. But England lost to Romania through a last-minute goal and so came second behind them, having beaten Colombia and Tunisia. First-placed Argentina would face second-placed England – and immediately all the talk was about 1986 again.

Although England had lost to Romania, there was one occurrence during that match that would have implications for the round of 16 match-up. England's squad contained a young striker by the name of Michael Owen, who was starting to make a name for himself at Liverpool. He had scored on his Premier League debut for them one year earlier, at the tender age of 17 years and 143 days, before sharing the Premier League Golden Boot in 1997/98 with 18 goals – a season in which he was also named the PFA Young Player of the Year. Throughout the campaign he demonstrated frightening speed and deadly finishing, terrorising defences around the country.

Manager Glenn Hoddle had seen Owen score in a pre-tournament friendly against Morocco, making him the youngest player ever to have scored for England at that time. It was enough to get him into the squad as backup to the established strike partnership of Alan Shearer and Teddy Sheringham. England's opening 2-0 victory over Tunisia saw Owen replace Sheringham with five minutes remaining, while the next game against Romania saw the same substitution occur – this time with 18 minutes left and England 1-0 down. After being on the field for just nine minutes, Owen pounced on to a loose ball in the area and drew England level. The teenage sensation had announced himself on the world stage.

Owen's form earned him his first World Cup start in the final match against Colombia, where he played his part in England's 2-0 victory, so Hoddle made the big call of putting him in the game against Argentina. An Argentina who had won all three group games, an Argentina whose team included Juan Sebastián Verón, Ariel Ortega, Gabriel Batistuta and Hernán Crespo, and an Argentina captained by Diego Simeone – he of Atlético Madrid managerial fame who, to put it kindly, has never been averse to practising the darker arts of the game.

The world tuned in to see if England could get revenge for the 'Hand of God' or if Argentina could once again get one over the Three Lions. Would there again be a great goal and controversy just like 1986? Oh yes there would. And more.

What happened?

Over 30,000 fanatical English and Argentine supporters packed into Saint-Étienne's stadium and right from the kick-off the game set off at lightning speed. Almost immediately, England nearly took the lead as Alan Shearer narrowly missed getting on to the end of a Graeme Le Saux cross. In reaction, Simeone broke into the England penalty area and, as goalkeeper David Seaman slid out to challenge, down went the midfielder. The game was only five minutes old, and the referee was awarding Argentina a penalty. Responsibility fell on the broad shoulders of Batistuta, aka *Batigol*, who had already scored a hat-trick in the group stage against Jamaica, making him the first player to have recorded a treble in two separate World Cups. Seaman got a hand to the ball, but the strike was too powerful – *La Albiceleste* had an early lead.

How would England respond to such an early setback? The answer came just four minutes later as Owen went on one of his trademark bursts into the Argentine penalty area. As Roberto Ayala tried to block him off, he was judged to have nudged Owen over, Danish referee Kim Milton Nielsen again pointing to the spot. Contact looked minimal, but Owen was going so fast that the slightest touch would send him down. The young teenager had made an immediate mark and now it was up to Shearer to level things up, which he did, striking the ball perfectly into the top corner, his trademark one-arm celebration bringing joy to England fans. The game was nine minutes old and already 1-1 – surely this frantic pace would have to slow down.

It didn't. Both sides continued to attack one another, and the play was breathless, whipping the crowd into an early frenzy. Then, after 16 minutes, David Beckham picked up the ball in midfield. Glancing up, he spotted Owen ahead in the centre circle and quickly played it in his direction. The ball came to Owen at an awkward height and in his peripheral vision he could see José Chamot closing in on him. Instinctively, he flicked the ball forward past the onrushing Chamot and immediately jetted full speed ahead. As the defender tried to match his speed, Owen cleverly muscled him off, despite his slight frame, before coming face-to-face with Roberto Ayala at the edge of the penalty area. Without breaking stride, Owen dipped to his right, beat Ayala for pace before then slamming the ball across the goal into the top corner. As commentator Martin Tyler put it at the time, 'Oh, what a goal! This 18-year-old has electrified the world!'

It was an incredible run and strike, showcasing the youngster's speed and cool finishing. The fact that it had been scored in a World Cup knockout game by a teenager made it even more astonishing. The pace of Owen's run gave the Argentinian defence no chance and the reaction of the English substitutes celebrating off the bench showed how everyone was speechless. While not as great as Maradona's solo run against England in 1986, it wasn't far off – and the 1998 meeting had now mirrored 1986 in providing a moment of pure genius. And it was still less than 20 minutes old.

Still both sides attacked, Paul Ince seeing a furious shot just clear the crossbar. Ariel Ortega was causing the Three Lions concerns with his sharp dribbling while Argentina looked terrified every time Owen ran at them. Paul Scholes came inches from extending England's lead but, despite the pace of the game, it looked like 2-1 would remain the score as half-time approached. But as stoppage time began, Argentina were awarded a soft free kick just outside England's area. A five-man wall stood firm as Batistuta shaped to blast the ball, only for him to run over it and instead Veron placed a clever pass to the side where Javier Zanetti stood. Spinning, he blasted it past Seaman to restore equality – a beautifully worked training-ground routine.

A frenetic first 45 minutes had resulted in four goals, including two penalties and a memorable solo effort. By this stage alone, it was already a classic match.

The game had matched 1986 with a wonderful solo goal – now it would match it for controversy. Just two minutes into the second half, Simeone charged into the back of Beckham as he received the ball in midfield, sending him sprawling. Simeone went down on to Beckham's spine, placing his weight on to his hand to effectively pin Beckham on the pitch, and as he rose to walk away, Beckham flicked out his boot in frustration, catching the back of the Inter Milan star's calf. Without hesitation, Simeone went down while looking at the referee, who was right on the spot. A hand went into a pocket and out came a card – red. It was a moment of stupidity from Beckham who had fallen right into Simeone's trap, meaning England now faced the second half with just ten men.

The complexion of the game would now change as England's structure became more defensive. Unsurprisingly, Argentina became more dominant, with England's attacks leaning more to breakaways and set pieces. Claudio López was inches from giving the Argentines the lead but otherwise the English defence held strong, absorbing the pressure, and limiting chances. Then, with ten minutes remaining, England earned themselves a corner. An inswinger from Darren Anderton was met firmly by Sol Campbell's head. With the centre-back wheeling away in delight, it looked like England had snatched a late lead, only for the goal to be overturned for an apparent Shearer push. The decision looked harsh and what almost made it worse was that, while England were celebrating, Argentina took the free kick quickly and sped upfield. Crespo looked like he might score before being robbed by a last-ditch tackle from Anderton, who had raced back from taking the corner to save the Three Lions. It was frantic stuff.

Eventually the final whistle sounded and while England could feel proud of having stood firm with ten men for 43 minutes, they now faced an additional 30. The question was whether the exhausted team could continue to hold out and perhaps get to a penalty shoot-out.

Almost immediately England had a penalty shout ignored when it looked like Chamot had handled above Shearer's head. An increasingly tired-looking England brought on midfielder David Batty to replace Anderton as Argentina dominated but found it hard to create any clear-cut chances, while Owen still managed to find enough speed to trouble them. The ten men of England survived another 30 minutes – the game would be decided on penalties. For England, it had been a great achievement to get that far, but they were exhausted from the effort.

Argentina went first and Sergio Berti converted, followed by Shearer levelling. Next up was striker Hernán Crespo, who saw his effort well saved by Seaman. Advantage England, but only momentarily – Ince had his shot saved too. Verón, Paul Merson, Marcelo Gallardo and Owen all proceeded to score, taking it to 4-4 as the last of the initial penalty takers stepped up. Ayala rolled his kick in, which left David Batty to take the shoot-out to sudden death. Keeper Carlos Roa guessed correctly, saved Batty's shot, and an exhausted England team slumped to the ground in disappointment and tears, while a jubilant Argentina celebrated. An incredible game that had it all – great goals, drama, controversy, a penalty shoot-out – had gone all the way to the last penalty kick, and England were left to rue Beckham's red card.

Final score
Argentina 2 (Batistuta 5 pen; Zanetti 45+1) England 2 (Shearer 9 pen; Owen 16)
After extra time; Argentina win 4-3 on penalties

What was the aftermath?

It took everyone who watched the game a few days to process – it had been a rollercoaster. But as the English went through the first stages of grief, denial unfortunately soon turned to anger. The notorious British press wanted a scapegoat and so it was that they turned their ire on David Beckham, whipping the public into a frenzy concerning his red card.

Beckham had been accused by Glenn Hoddle of not being fully focused coming into the tournament and the emerging golden boy of English football was dropped for the first two group matches. The loss to Romania saw his recall to the starting 11 against Colombia, taking his place in midfield and scoring England's second goal – his first for his country. For that reason, he kept his place against Argentina.

There is no doubt that Simeone overreacted to Beckham's kick – he admitted so later in his career – but it was a foolish and petulant kick-out. However, the press vilification of Beckham was spectacularly harsh. The *Daily Mirror* printed the headline '10 Heroic Lions, One Stupid Boy' and then provided readers with a pull-out dartboard, with Beckham's face in the centre.

As the 1998/99 season commenced, Beckham was subject to vile hatred when playing in away fixtures, including objects thrown at him, death threats posted and an effigy of him hung erected outside a pub. Thankfully his Manchester United manager, Alex Ferguson, and team-mates supported him throughout the ordeal.

Redemption came quickly to Beckham as United went on to win the treble in 1998/99 – the Champions League, the Premier League and the FA Cup – writing his name into United folklore. England fans also soon embraced him again when he scored a last-minute free kick against Greece to take the Three Lions to the 2002 World Cup finals. He ended his international career with 115 caps and maybe, most sweetly of all, he was part of the England team that beat Argentina in the 2002 World Cup, obtaining some revenge by scoring the only goal of the game from the penalty spot after Owen went down rather easily, perhaps learning from Simeone's 1998 theatrics.

As for Argentina, they progressed on to meet the Netherlands in the next round, which just happens to be the next game covered. So, no spoilers.

Teams

Argentina: Roa, Zanetti, Vivas, Ayala, Chamot, Almeyda, Simeone (c) (Berti 91), Verón, Ortega, López (Crespo 68), Batistuta (Gallardo 68)
Manager: Passarella

England: Seaman, Neville, Adams, Campbell, Anderton (Batty 97), Beckham, Ince, Le Saux (Southgate 71), Scholes (Merson 78), Owen, Shearer (c)
Manager: Hoddle

Iconic moment

In a game that contained many incidents of excitement and drama, including Beckham's sending off, the iconic moment must be Owen's wonder goal. As he recalled years later, 'That was the one moment that probably changed my life. I didn't know it at the time, but I quickly found out.' Respected magazine *World Soccer* named it one of the 13 greatest World Cup goals of all time in 2018.

Trivia fact

When later asked about his penalty miss, David Batty admitted it was the first time he had ever taken a penalty in a competitive match. He quickly shook off the disappointment – no tears for him, just a walk back to his team-mates, head held high. After showering, he phoned his wife before boarding the team bus, still calm. When his agent asked him if everything was all right, Batty coolly replied, 'I'm fine. I'm more annoyed at Argentina and the way they're celebrating the win and mocking us.' Unlike others, he never let that moment define his life – he just moved on.

Game 25

1998 World Cup

Argentina v The Netherlands

4 July 1998
Stade Vélodrome, Marseille
Attendance: 55,000
Stage: Quarter-Finals

Why you should watch it

Coming out of their classic encounter against England, the Argentinians focused on their next opponents. The day before the England game had seen the Netherlands defeat Yugoslavia courtesy of a stoppage-time winner from Edgar Davids, meaning that they would play *La Albiceleste* in the quarter-finals. It was a mouthwatering prospect.

The two sides had met twice during the 1970s at World Cups, with both games great encounters. 1974 had seen Johan Cruyff lead Rinus Michels' glorious Total Football side to a 4-0 thrashing of Argentina described earlier in this book. Argentina got their revenge in the 1978 final, beating the Netherlands 3-1 in Buenos Aires after extra time, having survived a last-minute scare where Rob Rensenbrink was inches from becoming a Dutch legend. Since those great two games, the nations had avoided each other on the football pitch – the world was due a third instalment of this classic match-up.

The Netherlands had come into the 1998 tournament with an exciting young side, rooted in Ajax-developed talent. Up front, they could boast the skills of Dennis Bergkamp, who was building a considerable reputation within Europe. He had come up through the Ajax youth system before breaking into the first team in the 1986/87 season after which he soon made an impact, with Ajax winning the Eredivisie in 1989/90, while Bergkamp led the league in scoring in 1990/91, 1991/92 and 1992/93, netting 103 goals in 185 appearances for the Amsterdam side, before Italian eyes became covetous. A move to Inter Milan followed, which proved a somewhat frustrating experience, before Bruce Rioch brought him over to Arsenal, shortly before being replaced by Arsène Wenger. It was a match made in heaven as Bergkamp scored 22 goals in their 1997/98 season, helping them win the Premier League and FA Cup double. He was entering the World Cup a striker in form.

Bergkamp was accompanied by other Ajax alumni. After Bergkamp departed for Inter Milan, Ajax manager Louis van Gaal re-signed past hero Frank Rijkaard and brought in academy graduates such as Edwin van der Sar, brothers Frank and Ronald de Boer, Clarence Seedorf, Edgar Davids, Marc Overmars and Michael Reiziger. The young team went on to win the Dutch league for three successive years, including going one season unbeaten, and crowned their prominence by winning the 1995 European Cup, defeating AC Milan, before again reaching the final in 1996 only to lose to Juventus. It was a golden generation on which the Netherlands leaned heavily for the 1998 World Cup with the starting line-up against Argentina containing seven Ajax graduates plus Patrick Kluivert, who had started there, and Bergkamp. Leading them through the tournament was Guus Hiddink, who had enjoyed managerial success at PSV Eindhoven in the 1980s, winning three league titles and the 1988 European Cup.

While Argentina had won all three of their group games, the Netherlands had drawn with both old rivals Belgium and Mexico, while also thumping South Korea 5-0, before then overcoming Yugoslavia with their late, dramatic winner. Argentina came into the tie just four days after their 120-minute battle with England while the Dutch squad had enjoyed an extra day's rest.

Would we see another marathon match like Argentina vs England, or would we get late excitement like the Netherlands vs Yugoslavia?

What happened?

As the two teams lined up under a baking Mediterranean sun, the stadium was awash with colour – the Dutch fans resplendent in orange opposite the blue and white Argentinian hordes. The Netherlands went on the offensive and almost took an early lead as midfielder Wim Jonk saw his shot strike the post after just five minutes. It seemed as if they were ignoring the heat, playing at a fast pace. The main Argentine threat was Ariel Ortega who, buzzing around the midfield, caused Dutch defender Jaap Stam to go into a rash challenge, picking up an early yellow card.

With just 12 minutes on the clock, Ronald de Boer advanced through the midfield before hitting a crossfield pass to Bergkamp, whose beautifully cushioned header fell perfectly into the path of the onrushing Kluivert who calmly finished. Argentina had been cut apart by the swift movement of the Dutch and their Ajax telepathy.

Ortega took the game by the scruff of the neck, again causing a defender to take a yellow card for a mistimed challenge, this time Arthur Numan. He then threaded a ball through to the Argentine midfield, where a first-time pass caught the Dutch defence completely square as Claudio López found himself clean through on goal. It was one of those camera illusions where he looked a mile offside, except when viewed slowly on replay his timing proved perfect. He faced up to Van der Saar, and they eyeballed each other – before López coolly passed it through the keeper's legs. Seventeen minutes gone and we were all level again; Mediterranean heat be damned.

Davids next burst into the Argentinian box, his shot just missing the post – a typical powerful run by the Dutch player nicknamed 'The Pitbull'. He followed that with another effort, swerving nastily before being beaten out by Argentine keeper Carlos Roa. Next up was Wim Jong, whose vicious shot was again kept out by Roa, but Argentina were rocking as the Dutch attacks now came in waves.

But they did still have Ortega, and once again the little magician smashed a long-range effort towards goal only to see it cannon back off the post before, on the stroke of half-time, Simeone's shot fizzed narrowly wide. The match was all square after 45 minutes, but both sides had hit the woodwork. It was anyone's guess what might happen next.

The first 15 minutes of the second period saw the Dutch again dominate, but with no end product. But, just like earlier with Ortega, an Argentinian break finished with Batistuta whose ferocious shot rebounded back off the post. It was textbook *Batigol* and so nearly the lead for *La Albiceleste*. The Netherlands came back again, Roa making a spectacular save to deny Kluivert's header. It was breathless stuff.

Then came a possible turning point, as Simeone burst through the midfield, colliding with Numan. It was the England game all over again – Simeone rolled in 'pain' as the inevitable second yellow card was produced, and Numan took the long walk to the changing rooms. Stretchered off, Simeone quickly managed to rejoin the action. The game had 14 minutes of regular time left and once again Argentina faced ten men – could they break through this time after failing to do so against the Three Lions?

Unsurprisingly the game now swung towards Argentina who pushed forward for a winner – efforts from Batistuta and Veron not really threatening too much. Then, with three minutes remaining, a moment of madness from Ortega saw him also see red. Firstly he went down in the area under a challenge from Stam which the referee judged to be a dive worthy of a yellow card. Then, as Van der Sar confronted him about the dive, Ortega contacted the keeper's chin with his head. Seeing the incident, the referee gave a second yellow and Ortega was off.

It now appeared that Argentina were once again heading for extra time but this time with ten men apiece, Ortega having matched Beckham's show of petulance. But as 90 minutes elapsed, Frank de Boer brought the ball out of defence. He slowed and seemed to weigh up his options before almost casually hitting a 70-yard diagonal laser-accurate pass towards Bergkamp, who was entering the area marked by Ayala. Flicking out his right boot while in the air, Bergkamp brought the ball under control in an instant, while still on the move. He then flicked it inside, completely fooling Ayala who couldn't possibly turn in time to follow, before toe-poking it into the net with the outside of his right foot.

In the space of a couple of seconds, Bergkamp had produced three sublime touches with his right foot, resulting in one of the all-time great World Cup goals. The pass from de Boer had been perfection and he did the rest. It was Dutch football at its most beautiful, delivered at just the right time, leaving Argentina crushed – they had no time to react before the final whistle – and even Bergkamp looked close to tears when celebrating, his hands held to his face in wonder after prostrating himself on the ground, mobbed by his team-mates. Johan Cruyff himself would have been proud. It was 1978 and Rob Rensenbrink but with a happy ending.

Final score
Netherlands 2 (Kluivert 12; Bergkamp 90) Argentina 1 (López 17)

What was the aftermath?

Every post-match discussion was dominated by praise for Bergkamp's skill. Ironically, he had only really contributed two pieces of quality throughout the game – but one was to set up Davids' goal and the second was to score the winner. The Dutch now had a shot at a third World Cup Final to exorcise the 1974 and 1978 disasters – but they would first have to overcome Brazil in the semi-final. For the third match running, the Netherlands produced a late goal – this time Kluivert equalising in the 87th minute – the tie eventually going to penalties. Bergkamp converted his effort before misses by Philip Cocu and Ronald de Boer meant elimination.

The young Ajax lions had finally fallen but had shown that once again the small country of the Netherlands could punch above its weight on the world stage.

Bergkamp was named in the All-Star team of the tournament alongside team-mates Frank de Boer and Edgar Davids. It was to be his final World Cup appearance for the *Oranje* – he retired from international football after Euro 2000 having scored 37 goals in 79 appearances. Many of them were great, and many of them were important – but none so great and important as his three touches against Argentina.

Teams

Netherlands: Van der Sar, Reiziger, Stam, F. de Boer (c), Numan, Jonk, Davids, R. de Boer (Overmars 64), Cocu, Bergkamp, Kluivert
Manager: Hiddink

Argentina: Roa, Zanetti, Ayala, Chamot (Balbo 89), Sensini, Almeyda (Pineda 68), Simeone (c), Verón, Ortega, López, Batistuta
Manager: Passarella

Iconic moment

It can only be one – the sublime last-minute goal from Bergkamp. Past Dutch master Ruud Gullit described it as 'perfect' during ITV's match coverage. Bergkamp also employed a similar description, saying, 'You never play the perfect game but the moment itself was, I think, perfect.' The goal was balletic and appreciation of it has only grown over the years with repeat viewing; it still sends shivers to watch the Dutch coverage, with commentator Jack Van Gelder repeatedly crying 'Dennis Bergkamp!' To this day, Bergkamp claims not to have rewatched the goal, saying, 'I don't really need to see it on television, I know exactly how it went.' Come on, Dennis. You've never had a sneaky look on YouTube? Really?

Trivia fact

Bergkamp could have easily missed this game. During the Netherlands' round of 16 victory over Yugoslavia, he had appeared to stamp on Siniša Mihajlović, which if seen would almost certainly have drawn a red card and a suspension. He was extremely lucky that Spanish referee José María García-Aranda, for whatever reason, decided to let the incident go unpunished. Even Bergkamp himself later admitted, 'I haven't the faintest idea why I did that. I was startled by my own behaviour.' He avoided the red, he played against Argentina and the rest is now World Cup folklore.

Game 26

1998 World Cup

Brazil v France

12 July 1998

Stade de France, Saint-Denis

Attendance: 75,000

Stage: Final

WORLD CUP CLASSIC

Why you should watch it

World Cup Finals are often tense, tight affairs and not always great games, but 1998 matched perennial favourites Brazil against hosts France – a final most neutrals wanted. It was a mouthwatering prospect that 75,000 lucky people would be witnessing inside the stadium.

France had ridden a wave of home-nation emotion to get this far. Sweeping through the group phase with three wins out of three, they scored nine goals in overcoming South Africa, Saudi Arabia, and Denmark, including three from Thierry Henry. A tight match against Paraguay in the round of 16 needed an extra-time golden goal from Laurent Blanc to decide the affair followed by a quarter-final victory over Italy on penalties. The semi-final saw an early scare as Croatia took the lead before unlikely hero Lilian Thuram, a defender by trade, scored twice to put France into their first final. Unfortunately, the semi-final was soured by a red card for Blanc, following an overreaction by Slaven Bilić, which meant the French defender would miss the final.

The French public embraced the team as a representation of the new multicultural France. There were players of colour, such as Thuram, Henry and Marcel Desailly, as well as players with North African heritage, including Youri Djorkaeff and talisman Zinedine Zidane.

Brazil also topped their group, beating Scotland and Morocco but suffering defeat to Norway. Chile were easily dealt with in the round of 16 as César Sampaio and Ronaldo scored two each before they then eliminated Denmark 3-2 courtesy of two goals from Rivaldo. A tense semi-final saw the *Seleção* win on penalties against the Netherlands, setting up their date of destiny against the host nation.

While both teams were strong, each had a particular standout player who had enjoyed a strong tournament as they became global superstars. For France, that player was Zidane. Growing up in Marseille, Zidane was of Algerian descent, of which he was fiercely proud. His career commenced in a strong Bordeaux team, earning him a move to Juventus in 1996, where the two seasons there ahead of the World Cup would see him win two Serie A titles and play in two Champions League Finals, as well as be named Serie A Foreign Footballer of the Year in 1997. He had become a key part of one of the strongest club sides in world football.

Brazil, meanwhile, had Ronaldo. A teenage sensation at Brazilian club Cruzeiro, he was part of the nation's 1994 World Cup-winning squad, although he did not play any games, still being just 17. Following the advice of team-mate Romário, he next moved to PSV Eindhoven where he terrorised defences for two years, scoring 42 league goals in 46 appearances. His outstanding skills earned him the 1996 FIFA World Footballer of the Year, making him the youngest ever recipient at just 20. Barcelona swooped in with a world record transfer fee, where his one season at the Camp Nou saw him score another 34 league goals. A global superstar at 21, he was awarded the Ballon d'Or before again breaking the transfer world record in joining Inter Milan.

So, while the French had Zidane, Brazil had the biggest name around at that time in Ronaldo. The hype surrounding him and the *Seleção* was summed up in an iconic ad run by Nike ahead of the tournament, showing Ronaldo instigating an impromptu kick-around in an airport between the whole team before finishing with him narrowly missing the 'goal' at the end.

With both teams in the final, all eyes were on both superstars. Both would have huge impacts upon the final, albeit for very different reasons.

What happened?

So normally we would jump straight into the match and go through all the action. But this game is an exception to the rule, in that half of the story exists in the lead-up. As the world tuned in ahead of the final, the two managers turned in their team sheets to FIFA around 72 minutes before kick-off. A stunned media learned that the Brazil line-up had one glaring omission – Ronaldo. Instead, manager Mário Zagallo had pencilled in striker Edmundo, nicknamed 'The Animal'. The news spread like wildfire around fans and viewers – where was Ronaldo? As BBC commentator John Motson recalled, 'The team sheets were handed around by the stewards as usual; lo and behold, Ronaldo's name was not there and everybody looking at their handout had the same reaction. There were people standing up and waving and asking what was going on? We sat there in an absolute ferment for quite a long time.'

Half an hour later, Brazil turned in an amended team sheet, with Ronaldo now back in the starting 11. Confusion reigned again – what had happened during those 30 minutes? Was the original sheet a mistake, a typo – or maybe the Brazilians were playing mind games on the French? But there was also the fact that the Brazilian team had failed to come out for the usual pre-match warm-up. Something seemed to have happened that was causing panic within their dressing room – but what exactly? The full story would only come out several years later as discussed in the aftermath.

Eventually the *Seleção* emerged on to the field, hands held together in solidarity, including a subdued-looking Ronaldo. Media attention could now finally turn to the game.

France looked the sharper early on with Zidane setting up a great chance for Stéphane Guivarc'h. Shortly afterwards Zidane whipped in a free kick that saw Djorkaeff head wide, with the French talisman already pulling the strings from midfield. It was not until 20 minutes in that Ronaldo made his first impact on the match – a cross from the left that floated towards the goal, needing to be smartly saved by Fabien Barthez. Meanwhile, Zidane was still twisting and turning Brazilians around in the midfield.

Twenty-seven minutes in, France won a corner which was swung in towards the near post, where Zidane stole in front of Leonardo to powerfully head his team into the lead, sending the home crowd into delirium.

Ronaldo's struggles continued as he raced on to a through ball, only to be flattened by the onrushing Barthez. It looked serious for a moment, a stretcher being brought out, until to the relief of Brazilian fans, Ronaldo was able to continue unaided. As half-time approached, Emmanuel Petit saw his deflected shot hit the side-netting before Guivarc'h spurned a great chance when through on goal. It looked like listless Brazil would get into the break just the one behind – but another corner in stoppage time again saw Zidane power into the area and grab his second headed goal; perfect timing for the French psychologically. The first half had belonged to one man: Zinedane Zidane.

Unsurprisingly Brazil picked up the pace at the start of the second half, although not threatening until Ronaldo controlled a cross in the area only to see his shot well saved by Barthez. Barthez then gave the French a scare, flapping at a cross that fell to Bebeto, whose shot was cleared off the line. More trouble was to come as a sliding tackle by Marcel Desailly on Cafu saw a second yellow produced – France now faced the final 22 minutes a man down.

It was France, however, who produced the next chance, substitute Christophe Dugarry dragging his shot wide when through on goal with just eight minutes remaining. Brazil struggled to make their one-man advantage count, although Cafu did hit the bar as the game entered stoppage time. But as a smiling Michel Platini looked on, Petit iced the cake with a last-minute third for France, allowing the players to finally celebrate as *Les Bleus* won their first World Cup in front of a jubilant nation. A fully deserved win – but why had Brazil looked so flat?

Final score
France 3 (Zidane 27, 45+1; Petit 90+3) Brazil 0

What was the aftermath?

France broke out into celebrations reminiscent of VE Day. It was estimated that over one million people poured on to the Champs-Élysées of all creeds – Muslim and Christian, black and white, a representation of the French melting pot. Tricolour flags were proudly waved against a cacophony of car horns and renditions of 'La Marseillaise'. It was exactly the tonic needed against a rising right-wing element within the country – a celebration of a racially diverse team led by a star of Algerian origin. At the head of the avenue, the Arc de Triomphe's arch was lit up with blue lasers spelling out 'Merci, Les Bleus'.

The team took on the nickname *Black, Blanc, Beur* ('Black, White, Arab'), a play on the tricolour's blue, white and red. In an interview, Thuram proudly declared, 'The World Cup victory was a defining moment for questioning what we are, as French people. The French team was composed of players of different colours and different religions; can we also accept this in our society, outside of sports?'

But there remained the mystery of Ronaldo and the changed team sheet. Slowly the facts began to emerge of what exactly had occurred that fateful day. And it was a shocking story.

According to Ronaldo himself, he had decided to rest after lunch before the game and went to lie down. Room-mate

Roberto Carlos then found him experiencing convulsions, his mouth frothing, leading to several minutes of unconsciousness. His tongue was unravelled by Edmundo to prevent him from swallowing it, before the team doctor arrived. Ronaldo then simply fell back to sleep. Colleagues watched over him until he awoke, when it was decided to transport him to hospital where he undertook three hours of medical tests – but nothing untoward was identified.

Meanwhile, the shocked Brazilian team set out for the final – their coach silent, devoid of the usual samba beat. Edmundo was added into the starting 11 and the necessary team sheet submitted.

Then Ronaldo arrived, saying he had been cleared to play and was willing to do so. Manager Zagallo had little time to decide – be prudent and play Edmundo or take a risk on the world's best striker. He gambled on Ronaldo, resubmitted a fresh team sheet and rolled the dice. Unfortunately, Ronaldo was a shadow of his usual self on the field, surrounded by team-mates still in shock.

As the story developed, so too did the wild theories. Nike, Brazil's sponsors, had supposedly pressured the CBF, Brazil's football federation, into playing Ronaldo before a global audience. Ronaldo had supposedly suffered a nervous breakdown. Brazil supposedly let France win to appease new FIFA head Sepp Blatter. It seemed nothing was too crazy to postulate. In 2000, a Parliamentary Inquiry Commission was held in Brazil to investigate the contract between Nike and the team, but nothing suspicious was discovered.

Happily, for Ronaldo, this would not be his last World Cup and redemption would soon be forthcoming.

Teams

France: Barthez, Thuram, Leboeuf, Desailly, Lizarazu, Deschamps (c), Karembeu (Boghossian 57), Petit, Zidane, Djorkaeff (Vieira 74), Guivarc'h (Dugarry 66)
Manager: Jacquet

Brazil: Taffarel, Cafu, Baiano, Aldair, Roberto Carlos, Dunga (c), Sampaio (Edmundo 73), Leonardo (Denílson HT), Rivaldo, Bebeto, Ronaldo
Manager: Zagallo

Iconic moment

The sight of French captain Didier Deschamps lifting the World Cup in front of a jubilant nation – the French had never won the trophy and now they had done so on home soil. The team would always hold a vaunted spot in French memories.

Trivia fact

Zidane's career saw periods in French, Italian and Spanish football but he never played for an English team. But it could have been so different. While Zidane was playing for Bordeaux in 1995, Blackburn Rovers manager Kenny Dalglish recommended him to club owner Jack Walker, who had the wealth to afford him. His reported reply was, 'Why do you want to sign Zidane when we have Tim Sherwood?'

Sherwood went on to win three England caps, while enjoying a seven-year career with Blackburn. Zidane earned 108 caps for France and was named FIFA World Player of the Year three times. Enough said.

Game 27
2002 World Cup

France v Senegal

31 May 2002
Seoul World Cup Stadium, Seoul
Attendance: 62,561
Stage: First Round, Group A

Why you should watch it

The opening game of the World Cup always used to involve the defending champions – and so the 2002 tournament opener showcased France. *Les Bleus* had gone from strength to strength after winning their first World Cup on home turf and 2000 saw them enter the European Championship, hosted in both the Netherlands and Belgium, looking to build on their status as world champions. Finishing runners-up in their group, they beat both Spain and Portugal to reach the final, where they faced Italy.

Despite France dominating the game, the Italians were ahead entering stoppage time before French substitute Sylvain Wiltord scored a last-gasp equaliser to take the match into extra time. The golden goal rule was in place, meaning any goal would immediately end the game, and 13 minutes in, another substitute, David Trezegeut, gave France their second major trophy in two years. There was no doubt that the French were the dominant international nation ahead of the 2002 World Cup.

The Confederation of African Football had been granted five spots in the 2002 tournament, for which 51 nations competed. Four of the five qualifiers had previous World Cup finals experience – Cameroon, Nigeria, Tunisia, and South Africa. That left Senegal as the only African team qualifying for the first time, having just beaten out Morocco on goal difference.

The Lions of *Teranga* came into the finals having been narrowly beaten in the 2002 Africa Cup of Nations Final on penalties by Cameroon – their best performance. Led by a French manager, Bruno Metsu, their starting 11 for the game against France all played for French club sides. Senegal was once part of French West Africa, held under French colonial rule until earning its independence in 1960, and that past connection meant that French was still the official language and accounted for the attraction of French clubs to Senegalese players. It would add to the spice of the opening game – an ex-colony against their former colonisers – as well as ensuring that the Senegalese and French players knew each other well.

Naturally, France were clear favourites to win. They were the number two-ranked team in the world heading into the tournament, having lost just six times between 1998 and the 2002 opener. Their players represented teams including Juventus, Arsenal and Chelsea, unlike the Senegalese who frequented lower-level French sides. Talisman and global superstar Zinedine Zidane would miss the game due to a thigh injury but that still left a wealth of talent and big-match experience. But Senegal did have one standout player – African Footballer of the Year El Hadji Diouf. Interviewed about the game later, he recalled, 'The night before, we'd noticed that the French squad hadn't come and trained on the pitch where the match was going to take place. It seemed like they'd decided that they didn't need to do that if all they had to do was beat Senegal. According to the French papers, they were going to win 8-0. We'd heard so many things along those lines that we said to ourselves, "Hey, lads, we're lions, after all; we're not cockerels!" How could a cockerel eat a lion? That's impossible!'

As the teams prepared to walk out into the Seoul World Cup Stadium, Metsu gave his final speech to his players: 'What can I possibly say to you today? We've been together for a long time now. I know you all so well. You're a crazy bunch. I know that tonight, after the match is finished, people will be talking about you right across the world. Up you get and show me what you're capable of.'

Fighting words indeed – but this was the defending world and European champions that Senegal were facing. It would need a colossal performance from the Lions of Teranga to avoid a mauling.

What happened?

The game kicked off with France in their traditional blue, white and red, while Senegal adopted a more brightly coloured white, green, yellow, and red mix to mirror their national flag. Early on, El Hadji Diouf showed a taste of the problems he would cause the French, comfortably beating Marcel Desailly out wide before his cross was weakly struck by Khalilou Fadiga. Diouf's bleached blond hair made him easy to track for spectators. Another cute flick from him opened up France, but Diouf strayed offside for the return pass. The French were finding him a handful to deal with.

After 22 minutes, France created their first chance when a clever pass from Thierry Henry set up strike partner David Trezeguet for a shot which came back off the post. France began to control the game, particularly through Emmanuel Petit whose incisive passes forward from midfield were finding openings. But then, with half an hour gone, defender Omar Daf caught Youri Djorkaeff napping on the ball in midfield, dispossessing him and quickly passing to Diouf. Frank Leboeuf rashly committed himself, sliding in on Diouf who skipped past him. Heading for the byline, he looked up before cutting the ball across goal where Petit's block struck keeper Fabien Barthez before a sliding Papa Bouba Diop tapped the ball home.

The stadium exploded in a sea of red, yellow, and green as Diop headed for the corner flag, before taking off his shirt, placing it on the turf and encouraging his team-mates to dance around it. Many shirts were removed, and much joyous dancing ensued – it was unorthodox but then so was the fact that Senegal were ahead against the world champions.

The shock goal pushed the French into increased attacking, but they failed to create any threatening chances for the rest of the first half. Diouf later admitted, 'We went into the changing rooms … with big smiles on our faces. We were giving each other high fives. Bruno [Metsu] came in and he was annoyed. He proceeded to tear strips off us. "Lads, it's not done yet!"'

The second half started in the same vein with French attacks being comfortably handled by a well-organised Senegal defence. Ten minutes in, *Les Bleus* finally created a great chance for Henry, but the Arsenal legend headed over from close range. Almost immediately afterwards, Djorkaeff came close, his shot well saved with Trezeguet just failing to reach the rebound. Patrick Vieira came close next – his header calmly handled by Senegal keeper Tony Sylva. The game was threatening to become one-way traffic, until Fadiga was played through. Squaring up to Leboeuf, Fadiga sold him a step-over before blasting a shot against the crossbar. French fans could breathe again.

The crossbar was again involved shortly afterwards when a curled effort from Henry struck the woodwork with Sylva beaten. The French pressure continued while Diouf buzzed around on breakaways. Then, as full time approached, Henry got free again, only to see his shot saved. The camera caught him in a semi-shrug as if to say, 'What do I have to do to score today?'

As the final whistle sounded, the Senegalese bench rushed on to the pitch to celebrate a historic victory. Just like Cameroon had in 1990, an African nation had once again shocked the reigning champions in a World Cup opener. Seoul was to experience quite the street party that night.

Final score
Senegal 1 (Diop 30) France 0

What was the aftermath?

Suddenly Senegal could see a way out of a group that contained France, Denmark, and Uruguay. They had won the toughest game on paper and so faced Denmark in confident mood. A draw was only marred by the sending off for Salif Diao, meaning that if they could avoid defeat against Uruguay, they would progress to the knockout stage. With Uruguay needing a win, the stakes were huge for both teams, but Senegal seemed unfazed, bursting into a 3-0 lead by half-time. The second half saw Uruguay throw everything at the Senegalese to turn the game around – and they did in fact get it back to 3-3 with just a couple of minutes remaining, but it was too late; Senegal got their draw and moved on to the knockouts while Uruguay headed back to Montevideo. The match had been extremely bad-tempered with a busy referee handing out 12 yellow cards – not one for the faint-hearted.

Senegal's reward for coming second in the group was a round of 16 tie against Sweden. After falling behind early, Henri Camara equalised in the first half. That remained the score entering extra time, with the golden goal rule in place. Fourteen minutes in, Camara jinked into the Swedish area before his shot dribbled past keeper Magnus Hedman, going in off the post. Senegal followed in Cameroon's footsteps to become only the second African team to reach the quarter-final stage, where they faced another surprise package in Turkey. Again, the tie went into extra time, this time goalless, until İlhan Mansik, the Turkish substitute, ended the Lions of Teranga's dream. But there was no shame in the Senegalese camp – they had enjoyed a terrific tournament and made their country proud.

France, meanwhile, were looking to bounce back – after all, Argentina had followed their 1990 opening defeat by getting to the final. But the group opener had shown how much they missed Zidane. Their play was too predictable, lacking that spark of genius that could open a tightly organised defence. Hoping for a better performance against Uruguay, they went down to ten men after just 25 minutes after Henry received a straight red for a studs-up challenge, leaving them with a mountain to climb. Try as they might, the French could not find a way through and once again failed to score, this time suffering a goalless draw. Their humiliating World Cup defence then finally ended in a 2-0 loss to Denmark; 270 minutes played, no goals scored and a solitary point. *Les Bleus* slunk home, their tails between their legs – coach Roger Lemerre being replaced by Jacques Santini.

Teams

Senegal: Sylva, Coly, Diatta, Malick Diop, Daf, Cissé (c), N'Diaye, Bouba Diop, Diao, Fadiga, El Hadji Diouf
Manager: Metsu
France: Barthez, Thuram, Leboeuf, Desailly (c), Lizarazu, Vieira, Petit, Wiltord (Cissé 81), Djorkaeff (Dugarry), Henry, Trezeguet
Manager: Lemerre

Iconic moment

The joyous dancing of the Senegalese after scoring against France. Roger Milla had set a high bar in 1990 with his corner-flag wiggle but Papa Bouba Diop accepted the challenge with aplomb. The way he removes his shirt and so carefully places it on the pitch before calling his team-mates to the dance off. Seven of them without a care in the world – and luckily no yellow cards then for shirt removal as at least two were in that state. Pure box office gold.

Trivia fact

After the World Cup, El Hadji Diouf made a career for himself playing in England and Scotland, starting at Liverpool before then also representing Bolton Wanderers, Sunderland, Blackburn Rovers, Rangers, Doncaster Rovers and Leeds United over a 12-year spell. Wherever he went, controversy seemed to follow. He was accused of spitting incidents four times during that period, resulting in Bolton manager Sam Allardyce considering sending him to a sports psychologist. That still didn't prevent him from receiving cult hero status among Bolton fans, who loved his directness and flair.

Game 28

2002 World Cup

Italy v South Korea

18 June 2002
Daejeon World Cup Stadium, Daejeon
Attendance: 38,588
Stage: Round of 16

WORLD CUP CLASSIC

Why you should watch it

With South Korea acting as joint hosts of the 2002 tournament, there was huge excitement throughout the nation. Despite having qualified for the previous four World Cups, they were yet to win a game or get beyond the group stage. National pride dictated this time that preparation be meticulous – famed manager Guus Hiddink was brought in to manage the team in January 2001, having led PSV Eindhoven to three successive league titles and a European Cup triumph in the late 1980s before managing the Dutch national team at the 1998 World Cup. The early response to his leadership was tepid – it was felt that he was not taking the responsibility seriously enough, especially after a 2-1 defeat to the USA in the six months before the tournament. But he led the Korean squad into a concentrated preparation period, knowing that the nation was hoping to get their first World Cup win and knockout phase participation.

Their opening game in Busan saw them face Poland in front of almost 50,000 fans. To their delight, in their 15th World Cup match, South Korea finally tasted victory, overcoming the Poles 2-0. Next up were the USA, who had surprisingly beaten Portugal in their opening match. A crowd of 60,000 packed into the Daegu World Cup Stadium where a first-half goal seemed to be giving the Americans another victory until Ahn Jung-hwan equalised with 12 minutes remaining. That meant that a draw against Portugal would yield a place in the round of 16 – but the Koreans went one step better, beating them 1-0 thanks to a Park Ji-sung goal with 20 minutes remaining. Therefore South Korea topped Group D, lining up to face the runner-up of Group G, containing Italy, Mexico, Croatia, and Ecuador.

Pre-tournament expectations were for Italy to top Group G, and so the Koreans should have been delighted with avoiding them by winning their own group. After all, Italy had been losing finalists in 1994 and quarter-finalists in 1998 as well as qualifying with an unbeaten record – six wins and two draws. Their team was full of talent – Gianluigi Buffon, Fabio Cannavaro, Paolo Maldini, Francesco Totti, Christian Vieri and Alessandro Del Piero, just to name a few. They were managed by the legendary Giovanni Trapattoni, who had led Juventus to six Serie A titles and all three major European trophies, before also winning league titles managing Inter Milan and Bayern Munich. Much preferable to face Mexico, Croatia, or Ecuador.

But things had not turned out how South Korea would have hoped. While Italy won their opener, defeating Ecuador 2-0, they then suffered defeat at the hands of the Croatians, despite having been ahead with 17 minutes remaining. With Mexico winning both their games, Italy needed to win against them to top the group. Instead, they almost lost – Mexico leading 1-0 until Del Piero saved the *Azzurri* with a late equaliser. Mexico finished first, setting up a meeting against the USA, while Italy drew joint hosts South Korea. Trapattoni and the Italian media came out of the group stage convinced that a conspiracy existed to eliminate them – their paranoia based upon several goals being ruled out for offside.

The good news for South Korea was that Italy would be without their usual defensive pairing of Fabio Cannavaro and Alessandro Nesta due to suspension and injury respectively. But they would still have to face an attack containing Totti,

Vieri and Del Piero – all outstanding players. While the Italian team was full of top European league experience, the Koreans only boasted a couple of players who plied their trade on that continent. The most well known was Ahn Jung-hwan, who was on loan with Italian side Perugia.

It was sure to be an incredible atmosphere within the Daejeon World Cup Stadium as the Red Devils' fanbase congregated to see if they could eliminate a European superpower.

What happened?

The players were greeted by a sea of red and white as the Korean fans flew flags and held up cards to provide a breathtaking backdrop. Of note in their choreography was the spelling out of '1966 Again' – a reminder to the *Azzurri* of their infamous World Cup defeat at the hands of neighbours North Korea. Given the frenzied atmosphere, Ecuadorian referee Byron Moreno would need to keep a tight grip on the game. With his slicked-back hair, Moreno's whistle got the round of 16 tie started.

The game was just five minutes old when Moreno's first big decision arose. A Korean free kick into the penalty area saw Seol Ki-hyeon go down after seeming to tangle with Christian Panucci. Moreno had absolutely no hesitation in pointing to the spot, immediately surrounded by protesting Italians, although the replay showed that Panucci had grabbed Seol's shirt, vindicating the decision. Penalty duty fell to striker Ahn – he drove it low towards the corner but watched as Gianluigi Buffon made a great save. Korean fans wondered whether the miss would come back to haunt them.

A couple of minutes later, a Korean defender required treatment as a flailing arm from Vieri left him pole-axed. The Italians started to exert pressure but found space difficult against a fast, pressing Korean side. Then a corner to Italy saw Vieri muscle in to head at the near post, putting Italy ahead – Vieri celebrating by putting his finger to his lips to indicate that the Korean crowd should now quieten down. It was his fourth goal in four games, and suddenly the penalty miss was looking more fatal.

Following on from Vieri's flailing arm, Totti was involved in a similar incident just minutes later. Jumping for a ball against Kim Nam-il, his arm caught the midfielder in the face, leaving him rolling on the ground. The Korean players surrounded Moreno who, to their displeasure, produced only a yellow card for the Roma legend. It seemed fair – there was no obvious malicious intent on Totti's behalf – but the game was becoming spicy.

Ten minutes before half-time, Ahn sold Iuliano a superb dummy, sending him totally the wrong way before shooting just wide. Aside from the penalty, it was the best chance the Koreans had produced to date. Italy immediately attacked back and a lovely interchange between Damiano Tommasi and Totti produced a good save from Korean keeper Lee Woon-jae.

As the half-time whistle approached, Korea won a corner. As the ball came in, Francesco Coco moved towards it before clutching his face and waving for attention. The camera zoomed in to show blood pouring out of a gash above the eye, which came from a collision with his own team-mate Tommasi's elbow. Stitches would be needed but Coco bravely played on, head swathed in bandages.

Elbows continued to be the theme as the second half got underway, when Del Piero was adjudged to have fouled defender Kim Tae-young, who reacted by throwing an elbow. With Kim already on a yellow and inside his own penalty area, it was a risky response, but Moreno surprisingly let it go unpunished. The game continued to flow back and forth, with Vieri guilty of missing a great chance when put clean through by Totti, horribly mis-hitting wide.

With time running out, the Koreans pressed forward but the famed Italian defence held resolute. Just two minutes remained when a chip into the Italian box fell to Panucci. Off balance, he could only block the ball while falling backwards, gifting Anderlecht striker Seol the chance to hammer it past Buffon. A mass of red and white exploded into ecstatic celebration as extra time loomed. But then hearts moved to mouths as Tommasi whipped in a low cross right to Vieri on the edge of the six-yard box. With the goal right there, Vieri sliced his finish off his weaker right foot, an incredible miss from the Inter marksman. As the final whistle blew, the question now was how costly that Vieri miss would prove to be.

With the golden goal rule in place, the game now moved into its most dramatic, and famous, period. South Korea had done fantastically to not only hold Italy so far but to look the better team for significant periods. They had shown no fear in attacking the *Azzurri* rather than playing conservatively – but did they still have enough in the tank to maintain the pressure?

An early free kick to South Korea saw substitute Hwang Sun-hong attempt a cheeky shot under the jumping Italian wall, almost fooling Buffon. This was years before this kind of shot became more commonplace, combatted by the 'draught excluder' player tactic. Then, 13 minutes in, the game exploded into controversy. Totti received the ball on the edge of the Korean area, spinning his marker before going down under a challenge as he was preparing to shoot. Italian arms everywhere rose in unison, eyes turning to referee Moreno in expectation of a penalty award. Instead, to their horror, he produced a yellow card, booking Totti for simulation. After a few seconds, he seemed to recall that Totti had already been booked and so out came the red. Surrounded by furious Italians, Moreno calmly waved them all away, his face stony and emotionless. Italy were down to ten men and a frustrated Trapattoni could only punch the perspex dugout in anger.

As the first half of extra time finished, the Italians needed to clear their heads and regroup. Four minutes into the second half, Vieri received the ball in midfield and slipped a ball through to Tomasso. Rounding the keeper, it looked like the golden goal – until the linesman's flag was raised. The replay showed it to be extremely tight but Korea were still alive. But then just three minutes later, Seol was caught chasing a ball back towards his own goal. For some inexplicable reason, with Guttuso right behind him, the Korean decided to attempt a cute back-heel. It fell right into Gattuso's path, and a winner seemed inevitable until a fantastic save from Lee left Guttuso on his knees, staring up at the heavens in disbelief. It was a perfect demonstration of why defenders are defenders and not strikers.

With penalties just three minutes away, a long crossfield pass found substitute Lee Chun-soo in space on the left. He knocked the ball back to Lee Young-pyo, who swung it into the area, where Ahn rose above the taller Maldini to place a header into the bottom corner. The player who had missed the penalty ran off in celebration to be swamped by team-mates and coaching staff. Hiddink punched the air in delight as the Italians stood stunned. The 38,000 Koreans in the stands danced, while on commentary Barry Davies was beside himself, 'But what a story here! Ahn Jung-hwan is the hero of Korea. Just listen to the noise! The golden goal … it doesn't do it justice. It's the red goal, that's what it is. Amazing.'

The South Korean who played his football in Italy for Perugia had just eliminated the *Azzurri* from the 2002 World Cup.

Final score
South Korea 2 (Seol Ki-hyeon 88; Ahn Jung-hwan 117) Italy 1 (Vieri 18)
After extra time; South Korea win on golden goal

What was the aftermath?

'Conspiracy – a secret plan by a group to do something harmful or unlawful.'

If the Italians had convinced themselves that they were the victims of a witch hunt in the group stage, this game put them over the edge. It was clear that Trapattoni was losing the plot as the tie progressed, kicking water bottles, and screaming at officials as well as attacking the dugout walls. Reports came in that the *Azzurri* had wrecked the changing rooms in frustration. The Italian media went into full conspiracy theory mode for weeks with accusations that FIFA had wanted South Korea to progress. Referee Byron Moreno became public enemy number one, his face shown online with devil horns among rumours that he had received a new Chevrolet post-tournament. Of course, it was allegedly red.

Naturally, there is delicious irony in Italians complaining about a footballing conspiracy. They are, after all, the nation that gave world football *Calciopoli* and *Scommessopoli,* among others. It does put one in mind of an expression involving pots and kettles.

However, some of the more reasoned Italian press did look introspectively. There was criticism of Trapattoni's defensive approach to the match – for example, bringing on Gattuso for Del Piero. *La Stampa* went as far as to say, 'Moreno, with his face that looked like a depressed cow, has allowed Italy to hide behind an umbrella made by cry babies.'

As for Ahn Jung-hwan, his only misfortune was to be on loan at Perugia. The bitter club president, Luciano Gaucci, swore that Ahn would never play for him again and proved true to his word. His contract cancelled, he moved on to Japan's J.League. But given his status in South Korea following his winning goal, the move from Italy was probably not too devastating for him.

The controversy did not end there for South Korea. Progress to the quarter-finals threw up a clash against Spain and in a game that ended 0-0 after extra time, South Korea won on penalties to bring further joy to the country. But again, the referee dominated the headlines. A second-half Spanish goal was disallowed for an alleged shirt pull after which Fernando Morientes scored a golden goal, only for the linesman to flag that the ball had gone out of play before being crossed – a decision that appeared incorrect on slower viewing. A furious Iván Helguera stated, 'What happened here was robbery. Everyone saw two perfectly good goals. If Spain didn't win, it's because they didn't want us to win. I feel terrible about this game.'

The South Korean Cinderella story finally ended in the semi-finals – a narrow 1-0 defeat to Germany through a late Michael Ballack goal. But no one could begrudge them their amazing run and the excitement it brought to the joint host nation – unless of an Italian or Spanish persuasion.

Teams

South Korea: Lee Woon-jae, Choi Jin-cheul, Hong Myung-bo (c) (Cha Du-ri 83), Kim Tae-young (Hwang Sun-hong 63), Song Chong-gug, Yoo Sang-chul, Kim Nam-il (Lee Chun-soo 68), Lee Young-pyo, Park Ji-sung, Ahn Jung-hwan, Seol Ki-hyeon

Manager: Hiddink

Italy: Buffon, Panucci, Iuliano, Maldini (c), Coco, Zambrotta (Di Livio 72), Tommasi, Zanetti, Totti, Vieri, Del Piero (Gattuso 61)

Manager: Trapattoni

Iconic moment

While the celebrations were huge within the stadium, it only held 38,000 people and so most Koreans had watched the game outdoors on huge screens erected within public venues. Fans were nearly all dressed in red and white, waving South Korean flags as they danced in joy. As fireworks exploded, it resembled a teenage pop concert more than a football match, supporters crying in ecstasy. Speakers blasted out songs celebrating Korea, lyrics echoed by the crowds, while some fans beat furiously on drums in time to the music. The country had never witnessed such a party.

Trivia fact

In recognition of his achievements as South Korea manager, Guus Hiddink became the first person to receive honorary South Korean citizenship. But that was not all – a private villa on Jeju-Do Island was also gifted to the Dutchman, as well as free flights for life on both Korean Air and Asiana Airlines. The Gwangju World Cup Stadium also got renamed – becoming the Guus Hiddink Stadium. One can only imagine what would have happened if South Korea had made it to the final.

Game 29
2002 World Cup

Brazil v England

21 June 2002
Stadium Ecopa, Shizuoka
Attendance: 47,436
Stage: Quarter-Finals

Why you should watch it

The astonishing story of the 2002 World Cup to date was the return of Ronaldo to the Brazilian team. After his health scare and subsequent loss in the 1998 final, he returned to Inter Milan for their 1998/99 season. It proved frustrating as he suffered injury problems, although he still scored 14 goals in his 19 games, enough to make him Inter's top scorer for the season. Worse was to come early in 1999/2000 when, during a game against Lecce, Ronaldo scored but then limped off ten minutes later. It transpired that he had ruptured a tendon in his knee that would require surgery, keeping him sidelined for almost six months.

Finally, on 12 April 2000, Ronaldo gingerly made his return, coming on as a substitute in a cup match against Lazio. Six minutes after entering, he received the ball in midfield and started running forward when, faced up by a defender, he jinked a couple of times before collapsing to the field, screaming in agony. Players and spectators reported hearing a sound like a gunshot as he crumpled down. Surrounded by shocked team-mates, a stretcher was immediately called, and Ronaldo taken off in tears, after which it transpired that his kneecap had exploded, leading to his physiotherapist calling it 'the worst football injury' he had ever seen. Most feared that it could be career-ending – and Ronaldo was still only 23 years old. One of the greatest young stars ever might have played his last match.

The next two years saw Ronaldo undergo two operations and extensive rehabilitation to rebuild the knee, an enormously frustrating and painful period for the player, who recalled many days of tears and agony. Unavailable for Brazil's qualification campaign in which the *Seleção* struggled, it was decided to risk including him for the 2002 tournament. Four years after the France final, and having spent most of the time injured, Ronaldo would start in their opening game against Turkey.

Turkey stunned the Brazilians by opening the scoring just before half-time – it looked as if Brazil's poor pre-tournament form would continue. But five minutes into the second half, Rivaldo swung in a cross from the left. As the ball dropped, Ronaldo stole between two defenders to stab the ball home – *O Fenômeno* was back. It was a beautiful moment in world football – a young star whose career looked done, scoring in his country's opening game of the World Cup.

Brazil went on to win with a late goal before then easily beating China 4-0, with Ronaldo on the scoresheet once again. Their final group match against Costa Rica saw Ronaldo score twice in the opening 13 minutes as Brazil finished with five. In three group games, *O Fenômeno* had bagged four goals and a round of 16 victory over Belgium saw him continue his trend of scoring in every game, resulting in a quarter-final with England.

Ronaldo was not the only redemption story of the 2002 tournament. Another player who had suffered a miserable 1998 World Cup was David Beckham following his red card against Argentina and the Three Lions' subsequent elimination. Having initially suffered abuse, he had gradually rebuilt his standing with England fans during their World Cup qualification campaign. Going into their final match at home against Greece, England needed a draw to gain automatic qualification, but a 66,000 crowd at Old Trafford looked in horror as Greece took a 2-1 lead into stoppage time. Then a free kick outside the area gave them one final chance to equalise. Beckham placed the ball down, stepped back – and bent it over the wall and into the top corner. In his home stadium, Beckham instantly became a national hero.

The group stage gave him the chance to exorcise the 1998 heartbreak. Drawn alongside Argentina, the two met again in Sapporo, and just before half-time, Michael Owen went down to draw a penalty – and up stepped Beckham. The captain scored; England won 1-0 while Argentina were eliminated. It was sweet payback for four years prior.

Two of the favourites for the 2002 tournament faced one another in Shizuoka – England against Brazil, Beckham against Ronaldo. The two teams hadn't met in a World Cup since the classic 1970 game and the famous hug between Pelé and Bobby Moore. A great match from the past – would they serve up another?

What happened?

The teams lined up with Brazil in their change strip of blue shirts while England wore their classic white. English nerves would have been heightened by the sight of the infamous Brazilian front three – the three Rs – Rivaldo, Ronaldinho, and Ronaldo. A talented attacking midfielder, Rivaldo had just completed a high-profile move from Barcelona to AC Milan, having scored 86 league goals over five seasons in Spain, including what has often been called the greatest hat-trick of all-time against Valencia, consisting of a curled free kick, a long-distance strike and bicycle kick. Ronaldinho, meanwhile, had recently joined Paris Saint-Germain – a player who always seemed to play with flair and a smile on his face, for whom life was a game on the beach full of flicks, turns and dribbles. Pairing those two with Ronaldo's finishing meant the Three Lions faced an uphill task.

The first 20 minutes were extremely cagey – both teams full of respect for each other as they sparred without creating any clear chances. But then an Emile Heskey pass aimed at Owen fell instead at the feet of defender Lúcio.

Running towards his own goal and trying to twist to control the ball, Lúcio only managed to deflect it to Owen, who needed no second invitation to bury the ball past Brazilian keeper Marcos. It was his second goal of the tournament, building on the reputation he had started in 1998. The Brazilians found themselves in an unfamiliar position of being behind.

England maintained control as the first half progressed, although they suffered a scare when Roberto Carlos launched one of his trademark savage left-foot drives that flew narrowly wide. It appeared that England were comfortably heading into the break ahead but then, in stoppage time, Ronaldinho went on one of his typical runs from midfield, step-over included, before slipping the ball out to Rivaldo who coolly side-footed it into the corner. Brazil had chosen the perfect time to equalise – allowing them to go into the break full of confidence while England would be kicking themselves for letting the *Seleção* back in. Would it prove the turning point of the game?

Just five minutes into the second half, Brazil won a free kick around 40 yards from goal and out wide. Brazilian and English players lined up on the edge of the penalty area, ready for the inswinger from Ronaldinho while England keeper David Seaman stood just off his line, ready to intercept any cross too near the goal. Ronaldinho surveyed the scene – and then hit the ball directly at the goal. Seaman scrambled back, throwing an arm up only to see the ball loop over him into the top corner.

English fans stood in astonishment. Had Ronaldinho really meant to score or was it just a poor cross that luckily ended up in the net? He had lobbed Seaman – but to be fair, Seaman was only narrowly off his line. Ronaldinho had placed the ball in the one place where it would result in a goal. Whatever the opinion about the deliberateness of the strike, Brazil had turned the tie around in just five minutes either side of the break.

An increasing pace saw the game swing from end to end, until a 50-50 ball fell between Ronaldinho and Danny Mills in midfield. Clashing for the ball, Mills spun around clutching his ankle. The replay showed Ronaldinho had caught the defender's instep, but it didn't look particularly malicious, although Mexican referee Felipe Ramos begged to differ – producing a straight red card. England now had 33 minutes to equalise against ten men.

With 20 minutes remaining, Brazilian manager Luiz Felipe Scolari brought on Edílson for Ronaldo to a chorus of boos from *Seleção* fans. Surely England would press home their advantage – but strangely enough, they didn't. Despite over half an hour with one man more, they failed to create any notable chances. Brazil saw out the match – England left to rue an inability to hurt a weakened opponent. Scolari's men moved on to their third semi-final in a row while England experienced yet another 'what if?' moment.

Final score
Brazil 2 (Rivaldo 45+2; Ronaldinho 50) England 1 (Owen 23)

What was the aftermath?

Poor Seaman was inconsolable as the final whistle sounded, slumping down in tears as his colleagues gathered round to console him. It was not totally his fault that England were out though – Ronaldinho's free kick landed in the perfect spot while a man advantage had been spurned. The feeling was that England had frozen, hesitant to believe that they could beat the Brazilians. Tales of an uninspired half-time talk from England manager Sven-Göran Eriksson emerged – the heat also blamed as an additional factor. It was probably a mix of reasons, but the result was that England once again bowed out in the knockout stages.

Brazil moved on to the semi-finals where they met Turkey for the second time. Having narrowly beaten them 2-1 with a late penalty in the group stage, they again won, this time by a solitary goal scored by Ronaldo. With the South Korean dream finally ended by Germany, the 2002 World Cup Final would be contested by the two countries, one of which had participated in each World Cup Final since World War Two except for 1978.

Teams

Brazil: Marcos, Lúcio, Edmílson, Roque Júnior, Cafu (c), Roberto Carlos, Kléberson, Silva, Ronaldinho, Rivaldo, Ronaldo (Edílson 70)
Manager: Scolari

England: Seaman, Mills, Ferdinand, Campbell, Cole (Sheringham 80), Beckham (c), Butt, Scholes, Sinclair (Dyer 56), Owen (Vassell 79), Heskey
Manager: Eriksson

Iconic moment

The game will always be remembered for Ronaldinho's goal – and the debate about whether he meant it or not. The man himself later told FIFA, 'When I hit the ball I wanted to shoot for goal, but maybe not exactly where the ball ended up. If I'm being totally honest, I was aiming for the other side of the net. What basically happened is that I hit my shot too hard and, as it travelled through the air, it swerved more and ended up looping over Seaman. There was nothing he could do about it and I suppose there was an element of luck involved … but a goal is a goal!'.

To this day, many English players remain unconvinced. Danny Mills's view: 'I will never accept that it was intentional. Rio [Ferdinand] asked Ronaldinho after the game if he meant to shoot and he just gave a shrug and grinned. His sheepishness suggests to me that it was a misguided cross.'

Only Ronaldinho will ever really know – but a player with his talent was more than capable of such cheek. And no one can ever begrudge such a joyful player his moment. After all, if anyone would try such a thing, it would be him. Playing beach football as ever.

Trivia fact

The scorer of five goals during the tournament, Rivaldo enjoyed an exceptional 2002 World Cup. However, it was marred by an infamous incident in Brazil's opening game against Turkey – which received more playback than any one of his goals. In stoppage time, as Rivaldo waited to take a corner, the Turkish defender Hakan Ünsal kicked the ball over to him. As the ball struck his thigh, Rivaldo went down clutching his face before rolling in 'agony' by the corner flag. Replay after replay just accentuated the ridiculousness of the acting. The poor Turkish player received a second yellow card and his marching orders – Rivaldo received a fine from FIFA, a blemished reputation, and a permanent meme.

Game 30

2002 World Cup

Brazil v Germany

30 June 2002

International Stadium, Yokohama

Attendance: 69,029

Stage: Final

Why you should watch it

Brazil's negotiation beyond England and then surprise package Turkey to reach the 2002 World Cup Final had seen Ronaldo's redemption story continue with him scoring six goals in six matches up to this point. Now it was just a matter of whether he could banish the 1998 demons and write his name into history on a high note. To become a world champion four years after his seizure in 1998 and near career-ending injury with Inter in 2000 would be the stuff of legend. Just one game now separated him from immortality.

Brazil's opponents in the final would be Germany – you had two teams with extremely strong World Cup pedigree but who had never met in a final before. The two teams represented a heavyweight contest, the Ali v Foreman of football. But this was not a German team that was as highly regarded as previous iterations. True, they had got to the final – but they had not set the tournament alight with their style of play.

The 1998 World Cup had seen Germany eliminated in the quarter-finals, which had resulted in the resignation of manager Berti Vogts, to be replaced by Erich Ribbeck. His first major tournament was Euro 2000, which saw Germany draw against Romania before then losing to England and Portugal and being eliminated in the group stage. The poor performance cost Ribbeck his job, to be replaced by legendary player Rudi Völler.

Drawn in a World Cup qualification group alongside England, Finland, Greece and Albania, the top team would automatically qualify for Japan and South Korea while second place would have to move on to a play-off. Beckham's last-minute free kick against Greece saw England top the group on goal difference – Germany coming second after having won five but also drawn against Finland twice and suffering one defeat. That one defeat was a humiliating 5-1 thrashing in Munich by England despite Germany having taken the lead after just six minutes – Michael Owen scoring a hat-trick for the Three Lions on a famous night for them.

Drawn against Ukraine in the playoff, Germany progressed to the finals with a 5-2 aggregate victory, but the qualification campaign had been underwhelming by their traditional standards. The group stage in the Far East did see them finish first, a draw against the Republic of Ireland bookmarked by victories against Saudi Arabia and Cameroon, helped by five goals from Miroslav Klose, but progress to the final thereafter was less than convincing. Three 1-0 victories against Paraguay, USA and South Korea suggested a relatively straightforward path had been trodden without much flare or panache. The wins against USA and South Korea both came through goals from emerging superstar Michael Ballack, who would join Bayern Munich that summer. A major setback for the Germans saw Ballack pick up a yellow card in the semi-final against South Korea, just four minutes before scoring the winner, which would see him suspended for the final. He would be a major loss for *Die Mannschaft*.

Germany's path to the final owed a lot to the fine performances of goalkeeper and captain Oliver Kahn. Up to this stage, Germany had only conceded one goal, a last-minute equaliser by Robbie Keane for the Republic of Ireland. Kahn had already become the first goalkeeper to keep five clean sheets in a tournament. Going into the final with torn ligaments in his right ring finger, the question was could Kahn produce a last heroic performance to keep Ronaldinho,

Rivaldo and, most importantly, Ronaldo at bay? The best keeper of the tournament against the best striker of the tournament: one of them was going to come out on top on the world's biggest stage – but who?

What happened?

The teams lined up, Germany for their seventh appearance in a World Cup Final and Brazil for their sixth, but surprisingly their first meeting in any finals game, in their traditional home kits. The early phase of the game saw the Germans on top, with a cross from Bernd Schneider almost reaching the dangerous Miroslav Klose just yards from goal. Then, 18 minutes in, the first real chance fell to Brazil, as Ronaldinho slipped a cute pass through to Ronaldo who, one-on-one against the imposing figure of Kahn, pushed the ball wide.

Ten minutes later, there was almost a carbon copy. Ronaldinho chipped a ball through to Ronaldo whose control failed him, allowing Kahn to gather at his feet. As half-time approached, Brazil continued to probe, with a curling shot from Kléberson hitting the bar. There was still time for another chance to fall to Ronaldo, whose sharp turn and shot was saved by the outstretched foot of Kahn. As the teams went into the break, Ronaldo must have been reflecting on his three chances – the first 45 minutes had seen Kahn win their duel and continue his impressive tournament record.

The first chance of the second half fell to Jens Jeremies, who found himself unmarked on a corner – however, his diving header was blocked by the boot of Edmílson. Germany's sharp start continued as Oliver Neuville struck an audacious free kick from around 40 yards out, which Marcos did well to push on to the post. Brazil reacted by creating a chance which fell to Gilberto Silva, who was denied by a sharp save from Kahn, before Germany again came close through a Dietmar Hamann shot. It looked like a goal must come soon – but for who?

With 23 minutes remaining, Hamann ran into trouble in his own half, allowing Ronaldo to steal the ball from him. A flick to Rivaldo set him up for a shot from outside the area, which Kahn saved but could only parry rather than holding. As the ball rolled agonisingly away from Kahn, Ronaldo swooped in to open the scoring. *O Fenômeno* had struck again – this time in a World Cup Final – and the grin on Ronaldo's face said it all as Brazil fans celebrated in a sea of yellow, while you could only feel for Kahn given his amazing performances thus far.

The momentum was now all with Brazil and, with the game about to enter the final ten minutes, Kléberson took the ball down the right. Looking up, he saw Rivaldo calling for a pass inside and duly obliged. Rivaldo stepped over the pass, fooling his marker, and allowing the ball to run on to Ronaldo at the edge of the area. One touch to control the ball and then a sweet shot into the corner saw Ronaldo grab his, and Brazil's, second. As John Motson in commentary noted, 'And Ronaldo is rampant now. Resplendent Ronaldo. Two for him, two for Brazil, and is that their fifth World Cup?'

Germany tried dragging themselves back – Marcos making a good save from substitute Oliver Bierhoff – but for a team that hadn't scored more than one goal during the knockout stages, it was too much to expect. The final whistle went, and cameras panned to a grinning Ronaldo, followed by a disconsolate Kahn standing alone within his goal, staring up at the heavens before throwing his water bottle into the net in frustration.

Final score
Brazil 2 (Ronaldo 67, 79) Germany 0

What was the aftermath?

Watching any great player triumph on the ultimate stage is always heartwarming, but to watch a player do so after going through trials and tribulations is even sweeter. And Ronaldo had certainly been through those. After the medical scare and listless performance at the 1998 final through the horrendous injury suffered at Inter, it was a miracle that he was even fit to play at the tournament. And while the Brazil team did include the likes of Rivaldo and Ronaldinho, all eyes would be on Ronaldo to provide the necessary finishing. Therefore, to end the tournament having scored eight goals in seven games – earning the Golden Boot – to be named in the tournament all-star team and to score both goals in the final, winning a fifth World Cup for your country, was an incredible achievement. In his own words, 'The goals crowned my work and the work of the whole team. I worked for two years trying to recover from that injury and today God reserved this for me and the Brazilian team. I am very happy.'

Despite his eight goals, Ronaldo did not pick up the Golden Ball for best individual performance at the tournament. That honour instead deservedly went to Oliver Kahn, who had almost single-handedly dragged a somewhat average German team by their standards to the final. The opening goal continued to haunt him, his feeling being, 'It was my only mistake in the finals. It was ten times worse than any mistake I've ever made. There's no way I can make myself feel any better or make my mistake go away.' But the rest of the world would appreciate what a fine performance he had put in that year.

At the end of 2002, Ronaldo received his third FIFA World Player of the Year award, which he sportingly dedicated to his medical team. It was a beautiful gesture that honoured those behind the scenes who had worked so tirelessly with him through such hard times. He had also invited the French surgeon who operated on his knee, Gerard Saillant, to the final, whose eloquent summary was, 'This gives hope to everyone who is injured, even those who aren't sportsmen, to see that by fighting you can make it. He's back to where he was – it's hugely satisfying, and I am very moved.'

If ever there was a story to inspire someone to fight through adversity, it is that of Ronaldo.

Teams
Brazil: Marcos, Lúcio, Edmílson, Roque Júnior, Cafu (c), Silva, Kléberson, Roberto Carlos, Ronaldinho (Juninho 85), Rivaldo, Ronaldo (Denílson 90)
Manager: Scolari
Germany: Kahn (c), Linke, Ramelow, Metzelder, Frings, Hamann, Jeremies (Asamoah 77), Bode (Ziege 84), Schneider, Klose (Bierhoff 74), Neuville
Manager: Völler

Iconic moment

The camera coverage of both Ronaldo and Oliver Kahn after the final whistle perfectly captured the conflicting emotions. With his iconic crescent-shaped tuft haircut, *O Fenômeno* was carried on the shoulders of team-mates, draped in a Brazilian flag, a grin as wide as the Copacabana. Pitching up in front of the Brazilian fans, he bathed in their joy. At the same time, German players took it in turns to console Kahn, who just stared off into the distance, oblivious to them. In a show of class, Brazilian captain Cafu also strode across from the celebrations to give Kahn some words of consolation.

Trivia fact

The referee on the day was Pierluigi Collina from Italy. A distinctive figure with his bald appearance, caused by alopecia, and intense stare, he is widely regarded as one of the greatest referees of modern times. He had also refereed Germany's 5-1 defeat to England, leading Kahn to comment ahead of the final, 'Collina is a world-class referee, there's no doubt about that, but he doesn't bring luck does he?' A referee who received great respect from players, he retired in 2005 after having officiated for 17 years.

Game 31

2006 World Cup

Australia v Japan

12 June 2006
Fritz-Walter-Stadion, Kaiserslautern
Attendance: 46,000
Stage: Group F, Round 1

Why you should watch it

Brazil, Italy, Argentina – everyone loves to watch the big guns compete at the biggest international competition every four years. But part of the beauty of each World Cup is the smaller teams – those nations who only rarely make the finals and to whom just being there is an event. The 2006 World Cup in Germany saw two such nations provide an entertaining group match early in the tournament.

Japan, affectionately known as the Samurai Blue due to their blue playing jerseys, had never reached a World Cup until 1998. Having finally made it after so many failed attempts, they left France with three defeats in the group stage, narrowly beaten by one goal by Argentina before also losing to Croatia and Jamaica. Being a joint host nation in 2002 meant automatic qualification where a passionate following drove them through the group stage to emerge with wins against Russia and Tunisia and a draw against Belgium, before losing out to surprise package Turkey in the round of 16. But it had proved that, finally, they could take their place on the world stage without embarrassment.

Qualification for 2006 had seen Japan win all their six matches in the second round of the Asian Football Confederation before topping the final group with five wins out of six to reach Germany. They came into the tournament with confidence, looking to recreate 2002 and reach the knockout stage once again.

Sport is a major part of Australian life – but football in 2006 was down the pecking order. Australian rules football, rugby and cricket all drew huge crowds, but football was still a niche sport. Reflecting this, Australia had only ever qualified for one tournament before 2006 – way back in 1974 when they travelled to West Germany to lose to both sides of the divide, East and West Germany, followed by a goalless draw with Chile. The process for Australia to qualify was always a strange one. Playing within the Oceania Football Confederation meant playing countries much smaller than themselves, creating trips to far-flung locations including Solomon Islands, Fiji, Tahiti, and Vanuatu. That gave the Socceroos a considerable advantage, which for example in 2006 saw them defeat Solomon Islands 9-1 on aggregate to win the OFC. That was the easy part.

The hard part was that the winners of the OFC then had to play against the fifth-placed team within CONMEBOL – the South American qualifying tournament – in a two-legged play-off. That meant teams like Australia or New Zealand would always need to overcome a South American side to reach the finals. In 2006, Australia faced two-time world champions Uruguay, a repeat of the play-off ahead of the 2002 tournament where the South Americans prevailed. The first leg in Montevideo saw 55,000 fans enjoy a 1-0 win to *La Celeste* before, four days later, the teams faced off again in Sydney, before almost 83,000 fans. This time Australia ran out 1-0 winners, meaning a tense penalty shoot-out. Two misses by Uruguay saw celebrations and a ticket to Germany.

Australia had players in their squad that had built reputations in the English Premier League. Managed by the experienced Guus Hiddink, who had been so successful leading South Korea four years before, the team included strikers Harry Kewell and Mark Viduka, both Leeds United regulars. They also had Everton midfielder Tim Cahill – a player with a fine scoring record for his position.

Placed in a group alongside world champions Brazil and a strong Croatian team, both Japan and Australia knew that their opening game was going to be crucial. Lose that and progression would be extremely unlikely. Both teams desperately needed a winning start – but which would prevail?

What happened?

The teams kicked off in their traditional kits – Japan in blue shirts, Australia in their gold shirts and green shorts, mirroring their national flag. The first chance fell to Leeds striker Mark Viduka, whose powerful shot was fumbled by Japanese keeper Yoshikatsu Kawaguchi, before Viduka hit it again, only for Kawaguchi to pull off a second save. Japan came back into the game – a shot from Naohiro Takahara pulled just wide of the post. Then, in the 26th minute, Shunsuke Nakamura picked up the ball out wide for Japan. Cutting inside, he swung a cross into the danger area, several players rushing to meet it including Australian keeper Mark Schwarzer who sped out of his goal to punch it clear. The ball floated over them all and into the net – leaving Schwarzer looking stunned on the floor as he appealed for a foul to no avail. The replay showed that Schwarzer had a valid claim – he appeared to get barged into by Takahara – but the goal stood, and Japan had an early lead.

As spectators still processed the opening goal, Harry Kewell saw a thunderbolt just tip the top of the crossbar – so nearly the perfect response. But try as they might, Australia couldn't produce a first-half equaliser – the Samurai Blue went into the half-time break maintaining their slender advantage.

The second half continued to prove frustrating for the Socceroos. To freshen things up, young Tim Cahill came on for Mark Bresciano in minute 53. With 20 minutes remaining, a free kick from just outside the area saw Viduka's powerful low shot saved one-handed by Kawaguchi. Japan continued to frustrate Australia and as the game edged towards the final minutes, it appeared that they were going to get the vital opening three points.

With just six minutes remaining, Australia won a throw-in. Piling on the pressure, defender Lucas Neill launched a long throw into the area, where Kawaguchi came out to punch but, in the melee, could only deflect it. The loose ball got stuck under a couple of players before Cahill pounced to sweep it into the corner. As the stadium exploded in yellow and gold, Cahill ran to the corner flag to unleash his trademark goal celebration – shadow-boxing the corner flag. Australia had just scored their first World Cup finals goal.

Suddenly Australia had the impetus and momentum to push on for a win. As the game entered the final minute of regulation, substitute John Aloisi received the ball with his back to goal on the edge of the area. A short pass set up Cahill just outside the box and his shot flew past Kawaguchi into the top corner as he wheeled away in delight. This time he could not even reach the corner flag before being submerged under a sea of yellow and gold bodies. Miraculously the substitute had scored twice in the space of just five minutes to set Australia up for their first World Cup victory.

A stunned Japan had no option but to throw men forward in a last-ditch effort to get something from the match. Leaving themselves open at the back, Aloisi picked up the ball in midfield and ran at the Japanese defence. Cutting between two tired players, he placed the ball past Kawaguchi for a stoppage-time third goal to kill off any hopes Japan had. In the space of eight minutes, Australian substitutes had scored three times to claim the much-needed win with Brazil and Croatia still to come. A thunder had emerged from down under.

Final score
Australia 3 (Cahill 84, 89; Aloisi 90+2) Japan 1 (Nakamura 26)

What was the aftermath?

Japan's defeat left them staring into the abyss, needing something positive against Croatia and Brazil. They did manage a goalless draw against the Croatians, but that then meant needing a result against the world champions. It seemed a possibility when they took a 34th-minute lead, but the dream evaporated as Ronaldo equalised just before half-time. Three second-half Brazilian goals saw the Japanese dream finally end.

Australia, meanwhile, met Brazil after their historic win and put in a spirited performance, going into the last minute still just 1-0 down before a Fred goal confirmed a 2-0 victory. That meant the Socceroos needed a draw or win against Croatia to move on to the knockout stages.

The fixture was especially meaningful for Australians – there exists a significant Croatian population in Australia following emigrant migrations in the 1960s and 1970s. The Socceroos got off to the worst possible start, conceding after just two minutes, but that seemed to wake them up as they then created several chances before earning a penalty seven minutes before half-time, which Craig Moore dispatched.

Guus Hiddink had dropped keeper Mark Schwarzer for this game and brought in Zeljko Kalac, who was of Croatian heritage. Sadly, for him, in the biggest match of his life, he fumbled a second-half shot from Niko Kovač and had to watch the ball roll agonisingly over the line, giving Croatia the advantage again. But then, with just 11 minutes remaining, up stepped Harry Kewell to equalise once more. The game then descended into chaos – Croatian defender Dario Šimić received a second yellow card and was off, Australian midfielder Brett Emerton received a yellow card and then shortly after a second yellow card and was off and then, most farcically, Croatian defender Josip Šimunić received a second yellow card, but not a resultant red. Referee Graham Poll, among all the confusion, forgot that Šimunić had already been booked, but three minutes later he gave Šimunić his third yellow card and therefore his marching orders. Australia held on and booked a famous place in the last 16.

The round of 16 game would prove to be a heartbreaking moment for all of Australia. A strong Italy side went down to ten men after 50 minutes with the dismissal of Marco Materazzi. Australia had been gifted a golden opportunity and pressurised the Italians, creating several chances. Heading into stoppage time, the game appeared to be heading for an extra half an hour, until Lucas Neill went to ground tackling Fabio Grosso and the referee pointed to the spot. Up stepped Francesco Totti and the Australian fairytale ended. But what a fairytale it had been.

Teams

Australia: Schwarzer, Moore (Kennedy 61), Neill, Chipperfield, Wilkshire (Aloisi 75), Emerton, Grella, Bresciano (Cahill 53), Culina, Kewell, Viduka (c)
Manager: Hiddink

Japan: Kawaguchi, Tsuboi (Moniwa 56), Miyamoto (c), Nakazawa, Komano, Nakata, Fukunishi, Alex, Nakamura, Takahara, Yanagisawa (Ono 79 [Oguro 90+1])
Manager: Zico

Iconic moment

Tim Cahill's iconic goal celebration would be seen many times throughout a successful career mainly in England, where he enjoyed eight seasons with Everton, scoring 56 times. It was later claimed by another Australian player, Archie Thompson, that the inspiration came from him. According to Thompson, he had first done the celebration in a 2005 friendly against Jamaica at a game played in London where Cahill was in the crowd.

After seeing the celebration, Thompson says that Cahill came down to see him and asked, 'Archie man, that was unbelievable! Do you mind if I take it to the Premier League and we can make it our own?' Cahill took it and ran with it as he scored 50 goals for the Socceroos, making him the nation's record goalscorer.

Trivia fact

The Oceania Football Federation is the only FIFA confederation that does not have a guaranteed spot in the World Cup finals. From 1986 onwards, the winners had to negotiate a play-off system for a spot – something that only Australia had managed to succeed in doing, and then only through a penalty shoot-out. It was for this reason, following the 2006 World Cup, that Australia decided to leave the federation and instead take its chance within the Asian zone qualification process. Since then, only one further OFC team has made it to the finals – New Zealand in 2010. But the 2026 World Cup, as part of its expansion to 48 teams, will finally see the winners of the OFC region automatically qualify. While New Zealand will be favourites, how refreshing it would it be to see someone like the Solomon Islands or Fiji grace the biggest stage of all.

Game 32
2006 World Cup

The Netherlands v Portugal

25 June 2006
Frankenstadion, Nuremberg
Attendance: 41,000
Stage: Round of 16

Why you should watch it

O Jogo Bonito. The Beautiful Game. Football fans all over the world have phrases for the game we love. We try to describe the joy of watching players at a level that most will never reach, doing things that us mortals can only dream about. Baggio, Ronaldo, Ronaldinho – so many skilled proponents who bring joy to our hearts – and those great, epic games when football becomes a true art form, which is what this book seeks to capture.

But for every light side there is also a dark one, as not every game can be a paragon of virtue. The irony is that, as true aficionados, we are supposed to decry those matches where sportsmanship goes out of the window and where anarchy reigns. But let's be honest here, there is a side to all of us, hidden deep down, that can't help admitting that occasionally a dirty game can be a guilty pleasure. It is like eating ice cream – we know we shouldn't really do it, but it releases endorphins that flood our brain.

If you get pleasure from such a car crash, then the crazier, the more enjoyable. And so we come to Portugal against the Netherlands on 25 June 2006.

Coming into this round of 16 match, Portugal had cruised through the group stage. This was a young, talented team containing such talent as Ricardo Carvalho, Luís Figo and Deco, managed by the great Brazilian coach Luiz Felipe Scolari, known affectionately as Big Phil. And then there was their young 21-year-old winger, Cristiano Ronaldo dos Santos Aveiro.

In 2006, Ronaldo was making a name for himself at Manchester United, terrorising Premier League defences. He had moved there for the 2003/04 season from Sporting CP, becoming the most expensive teenager in English football history, where his first three seasons had seen him play 137 games, in which he scored 27 goals. While he would later develop into a prodigious goalscorer, at this stage of his career he excelled more in beating defenders to set up others, using his pace and trickery to great effect. It was already obvious that the boy had a great career ahead of him.

The group stage had seen Portugal win all three of their matches, defeating Angola, Iran, and Mexico, all while just conceding one goal. That lined them up to play the runner-up of Group C, the so-called 'group of death', containing Argentina, Netherlands, Ivory Coast, and Serbia and Montenegro. Both Argentina and Netherlands won their games against the other two teams, before a goalless draw between the two of them saw the South Americans top the group on goal difference. That left the Netherlands to face Portugal in the round of 16.

The Dutch side included such gifted individuals as Mark van Bommel, Wesley Sneijder, Robin van Persie and Arjen Robben. Pitted against the young Portuguese talent, the world looked on, anticipating football of the highest skill. What it got instead was a horror show – but one where you couldn't resist peeping through your fingers. Be scared, be very scared.

What happened?

Right from the kick-off, the action commenced as Van Bommel saw his shot just skid wide of the post. Van Bommel was clearly pumped up for the match and that enthusiasm spilled in the other direction when, just two minutes into the game, he tripped Ronaldo who had neatly turned him, earning a yellow card. As Ronaldo went down, Dutch defender Khalid Boulahrouz tapped the ball into his head for good measure.

Boulahrouz then went one step further just five minutes later, a high foot raking his studs down Ronaldo's thigh, earning him a yellow card too. So, the game was seven minutes old and Russian referee Valentin Ivanov had flashed two yellow cards – he must have hoped that, by setting an early example, the players would cool down. It is the hope that kills you.

The game managed to reach the 20th minute in relative peace before Portuguese midfielder Maniche went through the back of Van Bommel. To his seeming disbelief, Ivanov pulled out his third yellow card of the game. But Maniche soon made up for his error as just three minutes later, Deco whipped in a ball from wide that was tapped back to Maniche, who took a couple of steps before firing past Dutch keeper Edwin van der Sar. It was early advantage Portugal.

The 31st minute saw a wild, sliding challenge by Portuguese midfielder Costinha completely wipe out Dutch midfielder Phillip Cocu – the tackle arriving well after the ball had been moved on. Yellow card number four was duly brandished. It was then Boulahrouz's turn to again pick on Ronaldo, this time again hitting the thigh he had earlier raked, leaving the young star to limp off the field unable to continue. A visibly distressed Ronaldo took his place upon the bench, the first player forced to leave the pitch during the game. He would not be the last.

The violence then abated for a moment to instead allow a display of skill from Van Persie, who sold two Portuguese defenders a beautiful dummy before shooting narrowly wide. But the moment was fleeting – shortly after, Dutch defender Andre Ooijer won the ball with a crunching tackle in midfield. As he offloaded it to a colleague, Costinha gave him a sharp kick on the ankle before hurriedly running off.

It could have been a second yellow but this time he escaped punishment, despite heated Dutch protests.

Next a loose ball fell to Robben in the penalty area. At thigh height, his high foot got there just before that of Portuguese defender Nuno Valente, who appeared to karate kick Robben in the ribs. Amazingly the referee once again kept his cards in his pocket.

The game moved into first-half stoppage time, and it appeared as if the players would have 15 minutes to cool down, four yellow cards having been issued and other wild challenges having gone unpunished. Then, ironically given the earlier fouls, Costinha decided to deliberately intercept a pass with his hand, despite no real danger. That left Ivanov with no choice but to issue a second yellow to the Portuguese defender, leaving the *Seleção das Quinas* with ten men at the interval.

The first 45 minutes had seen five yellow and one red card brandished. It seemed unlikely that the second half could get any worse. Oh, but it could.

The start of the second half saw Netherlands almost equalise – a shot cannoning back off the crossbar. Petit was brought on to replace Pauleta and within four minutes picked up the next yellow card for hauling down Van Bommel. Nine minutes later, Dutch defender Giovanni van Bronckhorst joined him in the book after halting a Deco run with a late lunge. As Van Bronckhorst lay apparently injured, Deco and team-mates made sure to tell the stricken defender exactly what they thought of the challenge. Figo especially seemed argumentative and, as the referee's back was turned, he planted a head-butt on Van Bommel, earning himself a flash of yellow too, which so easily could have been red. The game was fast spiralling out of control.

Revenge was quickly meted out as Figo took an elbow to the face from Boulahrouz. His reaction seemed somewhat overdone, setting off more disputes between the players, with Ooijer having to be dragged from the melee while heated substitutes joined in the action. Having escaped a possible red card earlier for repeatedly assaulting Ronaldo, this time it was one foul too many and Boulahrouz joined Costinha on the naughty step. The game was now ten against ten with nine yellow cards and two red as the count. And there were still 27 minutes to go.

With 12 minutes left, Deco experienced a rush of blood to the head, scything down substitute John Heitinga with no apparent attempt to play the ball. As the referee approached Deco, who somehow escaped a second yellow, Nuno Valente poked the prone Heitinga, only to be sent flying by an onrushing Wesley Sneijder, who, along with Rafael van der Vaart, picked up the Netherlands' fifth and sixth yellow cards.

Three minutes later Valente and Ricardo picked up seventh and eighth yellow cards for the Portuguese. Almost straight afterwards, a free kick was given against Deco for handball. As the Dutch rushed to take it, Deco refused to hand the ball over, and having just had one narrow escape, this time he would not be so lucky. A ninth Portuguese yellow card was produced, Deco was off the field, Portugal were down to nine and the game was descending into anarchy.

There was still time for a final flourish as, in stoppage time, Van Bronckhorst took out Tiago and became the fourth player sent off. Finally, the final whistle sounded to end the madness. As the dust settled, the final tally was counted – nine yellow and two red cards for Portugal and seven yellow and two red cards for the Netherlands. As commentator Gary Bloom put it near the end of the game, 'This is just getting silly.'

Final score
Portugal 1 (Maniche 23) Netherlands 0

What was the aftermath?

It did not take long for this game to earn its own nickname – 'The Battle of Nuremberg'. The referee, Valentin Ivanov, received criticism for the number of cards brandished, although on review he could have issued more at some points. There were at least a couple of nasty challenges that avoided punishment. FIFA president Sepp Blatter reacted by saying that Ivanov should have issued a yellow card to himself for his performance – a crass statement that was soon retracted. It reached the point where Ivanov's father, Valentin Ivanov Snr, a former Russian footballer, came out and publicly defended his son.

Controversy followed Portugal into their quarter-final against England when Wayne Rooney got tangled up with Carvalho with about 30 minutes remaining, stamping on the defender in frustration. The Argentine referee was immediately surrounded by Portuguese players pleading with him to send Rooney off, including his Manchester United team-mate Ronaldo. The red card was produced, and Ronaldo was then caught on camera winking at the bench. Naturally, the English press and punditry went into overdrive, predicting that the relationship between the two would be permanently damaged. Ex-England striker Alan Shearer going so far as to predict that Rooney would 'stick one on him [Ronaldo]'.

Of course, Manchester United boss Sir Alex Ferguson had no intention of letting an incident such as this derail his team. He made sure that the air was cleared in pre-season, ensuring the two stars would continue to gel. They did – Manchester United went on to win the next three Premier League titles with both in their side.

After Rooney's red card, England managed to hold out for penalties before Portugal finally overcame them. That took them to a semi-final against France, the first time they had reached that stage since 1966, which they narrowly lost 1-0 before then also losing the third-place play-off to Germany.

Teams

Portugal: Ricardo, Miguel, Meira, Carvalho, Valente, Costinha, Maniche, Figo (c) (Tiago 84), Deco, Ronaldo (Simão 34), Pauleta (Petit HT)

Manager: Scolari
Netherlands: Van der Sar (c), Boulahrouz, Ooijer, Mathijsen (van der Vaart 56), Van Bronckhorst, Van Bommel (Heitinga 67), Sneijder, Cocu (Vennegoor of Hesselink 84), Van Persie, Kuyt, Robben
Manager: Van Basten

Iconic moment

As the final whistle sounded on the madness, the camera panned to the sidelines, where Barcelona team-mates Van Bronckhorst and Deco were sitting side by side, both having been dismissed, still in their respective team kits. They seemed to be calmly discussing the events, like two friends in the crowd, with Boulahrouz next to them. The image of the 'bad boys' corner' came to mind.

Trivia fact

Sixteen yellow cards feel like an unbeatable sum in any future World Cup game. But it has been surpassed. The 2022 finals saw 18 yellow cards issued in one match, beating Portugal vs the Netherlands by two. And one of the two participants in this record-breaker? The Netherlands again – as we will see later. A team famed for its beautiful football that can also mix it when needed.

Game 33

2006 World Cup

Germany v Italy

4 July 2006
Westfalenstadion, Dortmund
Attendance: 65,000
Stage: Semi-Final

Why you should watch it

A clash of the titans – a semi-final involving two of the most successful and strongest sporting nations in the world. In the white corner we have Germany – three times world champions, four times losing finalists – while in the blue corner we have Italy, also three times world champions, two times losing finalists. A combined 12 appearances in World Cup Finals between them, and one of them would go on to a 13th. These are the heavyweight match-ups that the World Cup is made for. Winner to the final, loser going home.

Germany had the advantage of playing in front of their own fans as 65,000 packed out the Westfalenstadion. They had surprised everyone, including themselves, by reaching this stage. Not having to go through the qualification process, the last tournament that *Die Mannschaft* had participated in was Euro 2004, where they were eliminated in the group phase, drawing with the Netherlands and Latvia before losing to the Czech Republic, under the management of Rudi Völler. Because of that humiliation, Völler resigned, to be replaced by footballing legend Jürgen Klinsmann.

Klinsmann immediately set about trying to refresh an ageing squad but encountered issues in the transition. With automatic qualification, Germany were restricted to playing friendlies, producing some unconvincing displays, the most discouraging being a 4-1 defeat to Italy. The German media were highly critical, especially focusing on the fact that Klinsmann was still living in California and commuting, while heading into the tournament, Germany ranked 22nd in the world, hardly filling observers with confidence. Klinsmann stuck to his guns, selecting a youthful squad, with his most bold selection being Jens Lehmann as first-choice goalkeeper instead of Oliver Kahn. He was taking a gamble but, given their performance in Euro 2004, it was one worth taking.

The group stages saw Klinsmann silence his critics as his team won all three games, defeating Costa Rica, Poland and Ecuador while scoring eight goals, four of which came from Werder Bremen's Miroslav Klose. Sweden were easily dispatched in the round of 16, followed by an epic encounter against Argentina which saw the Germans win on penalties. Most importantly, the German people took the team to heart. With the concept of open-air viewing parties used, a festival atmosphere enveloped the country and the Germans were enjoying their rare status as plucky underdog.

If German football had concerns going into the tournament, it was nothing compared to what was happening in Italy. Following Euro 2004, the *Azzurri* had also changed manager, replacing Giovanni Trapattoni with another legendary club boss, Marcello Lippi. He oversaw a confident qualification process in which Italy won seven of their ten games, only losing once. But it was not results that would rock Italian football ahead of Germany 2006. It was *Calciopoli*.

In May 2006, a scandal broke in Italy centred around relationships between referees and certain club officials. An undercover investigation, including telephone tapping, revealed clubs trying to influence referee selections for games, as well as influencing referees themselves. Several clubs were implicated, the most significant of which was Serie A champions Juventus. With the investigation breaking just ahead of the World Cup, and several of the squad being

Juventus players, it was an unwelcome distraction as they awaited verdicts. The upside was that it produced a tight camaraderie within the squad – an 'us against them' victimised mentality.

The group stage was successfully negotiated with two wins and a draw against Ghana, USA, and Czech Republic. Italy then struggled against Australia as discussed earlier, only winning through a stoppage-time penalty, before easily seeing off Ukraine in the quarter-finals to set up the mouthwatering semi-final.

The feel-good surprise Germans against the scandal-threatened Italians – who would make it to yet another World Cup Final?

What happened?

The teams lined up in front of a passionate German crowd – the hosts in their traditional white and black and Italy in all blue. As the Germans got into the game, they came up against a strong, well-organised Italian defence, marshalled by captain Fabio Cannavaro who had been enjoying a tremendous tournament thus far. The first chance fell after 15 minutes to Italian midfielder Simone Perrotta, who broke the German offside trap only to be denied by Lehmann. As expected between two such fine sides, the game became cagey thereafter, with Italy probably enjoying the better possession, although after 34 minutes Germany produced their first chance which saw Bernd Schneider blaze over. As the half-time whistle sounded it remained goalless, both sides prodding and poking without producing many scoring opportunities.

Five minutes into the second half, Lukas Podolski went on a weaving run that required a brave dive at his feet from Gianluigi Buffon. Five minutes later, it was Italy's turn as Fabio Grosso broke through only for Lehmann also to throw himself at his feet. Another chance fell to Podolski but Buffon again held firm. As the clock ticked on,

Germany won a free kick just outside the area but Michael Ballack shot over, and shortly afterwards the referee blew to indicate extra time. Both sides were still sparring but with no breakthrough yet.

Extra time started in dramatic fashion as straight away substitute Alberto Gilardino went on a run down the right, cutting back from the byline to beat Lehmann at his near post, only to see the shot rebound off the post and across the goal. Two minutes later Italy struck the woodwork again – a corner ending up at the feet of Gianluca Zambrotta who smashed it against the top of the crossbar. The *Azzurri* were making a furious start to extra time, coming closer to scoring in the first three minutes than either team had in the previous 90. Shortly before the first break, exciting Juventus striker Alessandro Del Piero came on for Perrotta as Italy continued to dominate, although unable to find a goal.

Five minutes into the second period of extra time Italy again threatened – a ball into the area falling to Del Piero who tried unsuccessfully to turn before laying off to Vincenzo Iaquinta, whose shot was blocked. Germany immediately went up the other end, Podolski forcing a fine save from Buffon. The game was suddenly open as both sides looked to finish it before the dreaded penalties – end-to-end action as they swapped blows, like boxers trying to settle a fight in the final round. With three minutes left, Andrea Pirlo's shot needed all Lehmann's attention; both keepers were making fine saves and penalties now looked inevitable unless someone could produce last-minute heroics.

Lehmann's save from Pirlo resulted in a corner, which fell to the midfielder again on the edge of the area. Moving across the German defence, Pirlo's eyes scanning for an opening, he spotted defender Grosso in a yard of space. Pirlo slotted a no-look pass to him, which Grosso struck first time hard and low towards the far corner.

The camera panned in on Grosso as he wheeled away in delight, shaking his head from side to side, long hair flowing, yelling 'non ci credo' (I don't believe it) repeatedly as his team-mates raced to catch him. The joy on his face reminded one of Marco Tardelli back in 1982, also against then West Germany, after he scored in the final.

Germany had no choice but to throw everyone forward for the last minute, the crowd still stunned by the late drama. As they were still processing what they had witnessed, Gilardino broke away where, faced by a German defender, he held the ball just long enough to allow Del Piero to overlap, before playing a cute reverse pass. Del Piero squared himself up before side-footing past Lehmann into the corner. It was two goals in two minutes and the German team slumped to their knees, followed by inevitable shots of devastated fans in the stands.

Two great footballing nations had battled for 120 minutes, trading blows before Grosso landed the knockout punch. As the final whistle sounded, Klinsmann tried to console his devastated young team, while Cannavaro and Buffon embraced at the other end, knowing Italy were on their way to a sixth World Cup Final.

Final score
Italy 2 (Grosso 119; Del Piero 120+1) Germany 0
After extra time

What was the aftermath?

In past tournaments, elimination at the semi-final stage in their own country would have been viewed as a disappointment by the German media and public. But given the pre-tournament doom and gloom, the German team was feted for having brought joy over the summer. Their run had produced a feelgood factor throughout the nation – Klinsmann's young turks being lauded by all. The players were awarded the Silbernes Lorbeerblatt (Silver Leaf), the highest sports award in Germany, by the country's president, while Klinsmann himself received the Order of Merit. Exhausted, despite the media praise, Klinsmann stepped down as manager to spend more time with his family in California, to be replaced by his assistant Joachim Löw.

The *Azzurri* moved on to face France in the final – *Les Bleus* having eliminated Spain, Brazil, and Portugal in the knockout stages. In front of 69,000 fans in Berlin, France took an early lead through a Zinedine Zidane penalty, only for Marco Materazzi to equalise after 19 minutes. The game moved into extra time and, with ten minutes remaining, there occurred one of the most infamous moments in World Cup history.

Away from play, French captain and global superstar Zidane was being marked by Materazzi. As Zidane jogged past the defender in midfield, words appeared to be exchanged and suddenly Zidane turned on the Italian, head-butting him in the chest. Materazzi went to ground, and confusion reigned – the officials hadn't completely seen the off-the-ball incident.

The only one who had was the fourth official and so after consultation with him, referee Horacio Elizondo showed Zidane a straight red, who then tragically walked past the trophy in what was already known to be the final match of his professional career. It remains one of the saddest footballing images in recent years.

To this day, no one knows the total truth about what was said between them. Materazzi will just claim he was trash-talking while Zidane has only said it was an insult against his mother. Whatever happened, France were down to ten men. They held out for penalties where the *Azzurri* won, 5-3, to bring home their fourth World Cup trophy.

Teams

Italy: Buffon, Zambrotta, Cannavaro (c), Materazzi, Grosso, Camoranesi (Iaquinta 91), Pirlo, Gattuso, Perrotta (Del Piero 104), Totti, Toni (Gilardino 74)
Manager: Lippi

Germany: Lehmann, Friedrich, Mertesacker, Metzelder, Lahm, Schneider (Odonkor 83), Ballack (c), Kehl, Borowski (Schweinsteiger 73), Klose (Neuville 111), Podolski
Manager: Klinsmann

Iconic moment

Grosso's goal and celebration will be the best recalled image of the game. The best way to view it is on the Italian Sky Sports feed, which features commentator Fabio Caressa. Having already covered 119 minutes of action, his voice is already strained when Pirlo picks up the ball from the corner kick. But the next few seconds of action see Caressa's full emotional outpouring: 'The ball is cut out. It's Pirlo, Pirlo, Pirlo, still Pirlo, heel, shot … GOOOOAL! GOOOOAL! GOOOOAL! Grosso! Grosso! GOOOOAL! Goal from Grosso! Goal from Grosso! Goal from Grosso! One minute left! Incredible, incredible!'

It still makes the hairs on your neck stand when you hear it.

Trivia fact

It was at the 2006 World Cup that the concept of the Fan Fest officially took off. When South Korea co-hosted the 2002 tournament, reaching the semi-finals, it had electrified the nation, as the Red Devils' progress had been followed by thousands of fans who congregated in public to watch their team on huge screens. Estimates of seven million Korean viewers watching the semi-final on such screens were published, excited by the communal spirit as opposed to watching the game at home. The crowds were well behaved and garnered a lot of media attention.

In 2006 Germany decided to push the concept further. Twelve host cities were chosen and in each a site was designated for fans to gather and watch the games in the fine summer weather. Visiting supporters from around the world embraced the concept, and very soon some sites were having to be expanded to handle the huge crowds. Whereas in the past, ticketless fans had often created problems for the host nation, they were welcomed in 2006 and world media were beaming images of fans gathered in front of huge screens, emotions heightened by being part of a large crowd. Behaviour was good and a new precedent was set for future tournaments. The concept of the Fan Fest had been officially born.

Game 34

2010 World Cup

France v South Africa

22 June 2010
Free State Stadium, Bloemfontein
Attendance: 39,415
Stage: Group A, Round 1

Why you should watch it

After staging a first Asian tournament in 2002 within Korea and Japan, FIFA next turned to bringing the show to Africa, so the 2010 bidding process was therefore only open to African nations, attracting bids from South Africa, Egypt, and Morocco. In May 2004 it was announced that the finals would go to South Africa – a bid that had been backed by Nelson Mandela himself, who spoke of his love for the game and its importance to him and fellow inmates on Robben Island. As the tournament approached, rumours spread that South African infrastructure may not be ready in time and that FIFA were looking at backup plans, but as June 2010 rolled around South Africa was ready to welcome the world to the party.

Bafana Bafana were placed into a group stage alongside France, Uruguay, and Mexico – a tough assignment given that the hosts are automatically a top seed in the draw. Huge excitement swept the country for their first World Cup adventure, which kicked off in Johannesburg against Mexico, where an entertaining game saw South Africa take a second-half lead before Rafael Márquez equalised with 11 minutes remaining – a result that was viewed as a good start to the adventure. Next up were Uruguay who proved too strong with an attacking trio of Diego Forlán, Luis Suárez and Edinson Cavani – enough to give any opposition nightmares. Going into their final game, South Africa needed a win to give themselves any chance of moving on.

France had won the 1998 World Cup and were losing finalists in 2006 but had since suffered a poor Euro 2008 when they had been eliminated in the group stage, losing to Italy and the Netherlands with their only point being a goalless draw against Romania. That had placed pressure on coach Raymond Domenech, whose job it now was to lead France to South Africa despite restless public opinion. Qualification did little to squash concerns as France came second in their group and had to go through a two-legged play-off. Domenech then announced his squad, surprisingly omitting Patrick Vieira, Samir Nasri and Karim Benzema, meaning tension filled the air as they departed for South Africa.

Ahead of their first match, the first signs of discontent emerged. During a training session, Florent Malouda had to be restrained by captain Patrice Evra as he squared up to Domenech, leading to him being benched. A dull goalless draw against Uruguay led to further rumours, with legend Zinedane Zidane stating that Domenech had lost the dressing room. Next up for *Les Bleus* were Mexico, whose two second-half goals left France rooted to the bottom of the group. Half-time had seen André-Pierre Gignac emerge from the tunnel, replacing Nicolas Anelka, as it later transpired that Anelka had launched a tirade of abuse at Domenech during the break. Asked to apologise by the Fédération Française de Football (FFF), Anelka refused and was sent home in shame.

Events then exploded during the following day's training session, which also happened to be open to the public. Evra got into a row with the French fitness coach before storming off to the team bus, followed shortly by his team-mates where, curtains drawn, they drafted a short manifesto stating their opposition to Anelka's punishment. The whole episode was now being played out in front of a watching world – and the anarchy did not bode well for their last must-win game against the hosts. A French revolution was in full flight.

What happened?

A crowd of 39,000 packed out the Free State Stadium in Bloemfontein as the teams emerged to the sound of vuvuzelas. A plastic horn, around two feet long, the vuvuzela was a staple among South African fans – which when blown by such a crowd produced a magnified buzzing sound, which could be described as 'an acquired taste'. For those in the crowd, it could be a painful experience with a sound level of 120dB at short distance, the human pain threshold. Players complained that they interfered with their ability to hear team-mates while broadcasters cursed that it drowned out chants, trying to filter out the noise. But there was no doubt that, love or hate them, they added local spice to the proceedings. Combined with the colour and passion of the home fans, it made for a great atmosphere.

After 20 minutes, South Africa won their first corner. An inswinger from Siphiwe Tshabalala was met by defender Bongani Khumalo at the back post, who powered in a header to give *Bafana Bafana* a shock lead. The French nightmare was continuing as the stadium burst out in yellow and green dancing, accompanied by even louder vuvuzela buzzing.

Just five minutes later, things became even worse for *Les Bleus*. A loose bouncing ball in the South African penalty area saw French striker Yoann Gourcuff challenge MacBeth Sibaya, leaving Sibaya prone on the ground. To initial surprise, Colombian referee Óscar Ruiz produced a straight red card. Replays showed that Gourcuff had led with his elbow, before then focusing on Domenech, head in hands as the enormity of the last few days probably became overwhelming. He cut a tragic lonely figure on the sidelines.

South Africa now had a glorious chance to cement their advantage against the ten men of France and with eight minutes remaining of the first half, they did exactly that. A ball out to Tshabalala saw his cross deflected by Alou Diarra into the path of Tsepo Masilela who fired low and hard across the six-yard box where defender Gaël Clichy couldn't sort out his feet before Katlego Mphela rolled it into an empty net. It was all going horribly wrong for the French.

The start of the second half almost saw a third for South Africa as Mphela broke the offside trap, only to see his shot graze off the outside of the post. Mphela was now on a roll and another shot from him had to be well saved by Hugo Lloris as it headed into the corner.

Finally, with 20 minutes remaining, France got their act together. Bacary Sagna brought the ball through midfield before slipping a beautiful pass into Franck Ribéry who, one against one with the goalkeeper, coolly rolled the ball across to Malouda to put into an empty net. A glimmer of hope.

Still South Africa pushed forward – Tshabalala finding himself open in the area only to see his shot well saved before narrowly being beaten to the rebound. But in the end their two goals were enough – the final whistle blew and, apparently, Domenech didn't even have the grace to shake South African manager Carlos Parreira's hand. France were bottom of the group, going home, one point from three games against a backdrop of blame and recriminations.

Final score
South Africa 2 (Khumalo 20; Mphela 37) France 1 (Malouda 70)

What was the aftermath?

Sadly for South Africa, this win wasn't enough for them to progress. Uruguay had beaten Mexico at the same time, leaving Mexico and *Bafana Bafana* tied with four points apiece, but Mexico with the better goal difference. It would be the first time that a host nation would be eliminated in the group stages, but given who South Africa had faced, four points was no meaningless achievement. They could hold their heads high, having given their noisy supporters much to be proud of.

The same could most definitely not be said for France. Their whole campaign had been a disaster, both on and off the field, making them an international laughing stock. For some unknown reason, Domenech had decided to leave striker Thierry Henry on the bench until the 55th minute, despite being two goals down at that stage. The whole affair drove furious debate back home as discussion centred around the disgraceful behaviour of Anelka, the incompetence of Domenech and the plotting and scheming of the senior players within the squad. There was a feeling that none of the players had taken responsibility during the anarchy for grabbing everyone by the scruff of the neck and enforcing a team spirit. Instead, cowardice had reigned as senior players looked the other way.

Not surprisingly there was no way Domenech could survive such a debacle, being swiftly replaced by legendary player Laurent Blanc. The FFF banned the entire squad from the next France fixture and the five key players involved in the training ground mutiny were publicly named and shamed, as well as banned for short periods. Of course, French football moved on and regained its prestige, but the 2010 World Cup will forever remain a dark blot on their history – a prime example of what can happen when leadership goes missing.

Teams

South Africa: Josephs, Ngcongca (Gaxa 55), Mokoena (c), Khumalo, Masilela, Sibaya, Khuboni (Modise 78), Pienaar, Tshabalala, Mphela, Parker (Nomvethe 68)
Manager: Parreira

France: Lloris, Sagna, Gallas, Squillaci, Clichy, Diarra (c) (Govou 82), Diaby, Gignac (Malouda HT), Gourcuff, Ribéry, Cissé (Henry 55)
Manager: Domenech

Iconic moment

The television coverage of the French bench during the game told as much about their problems as the action on the field. Domenech holding his head in his hands as France were reduced to ten men. Henry sat passively on the bench, woollen blanket draped around his knees, looking like a sad bored tourist on a cold, grey English day at the beach. Body language said it all in those moments – disharmony reigned throughout.

Trivia fact

In our age of VAR, it is probable that France would not have been in Bloemfontein for this game. Having come second in their group behind Serbia, they had to negotiate a two-legged play-off against the Republic of Ireland to make the finals. The first leg in Dublin saw France take home a 1-0 advantage courtesy of a Nicolas Anelka goal. Four days later, the teams met once again in Paris, where the Irish struck first through Robbie Keane, then holding on to take the game into extra time.

Towards the end of the first period, France won a free kick just inside the Irish half. The ball was pumped deep into the penalty area, where Thierry Henry controlled it close to the byline before prodding it across the face of the goal for William Gallas to tap in. Immediately, every Irish player close to the action raised their hands and rushed towards the referee, indicating handball, in scenes very similar to when Maradona scored his first against England in 1986. Henry wheeled away in celebration before an ecstatic Parisian crowd as the referee indicated the award of a goal. It was then that TV viewers were privy to the slow-motion replay, which clearly showed Henry handled the ball to keep it in play before crossing. But it was to no avail – the goal stood, and France held on to book a place in South Africa.

Not surprisingly, the Irish players and media were incensed. There were calls to have the game replayed. There were calls to have the Republic of Ireland allowed to go to the finals as a 33rd team. Neither was to be – and to this day, it is still referred to in Ireland as 'Le Hand of Frog'. It would be one of several incidents that would eventually lead to the adoption of VAR.

Game 35

2010 World Cup

England v Germany

27 June 2010

Free State Stadium, Bloemfontein

Attendance: 40,510

Stage: Round of 16

Why you should watch it

Germany against England represents one of the great international rivalries. Back in 1990 the Germans had dominated proceedings ever since England defeated them in the 1966 World Cup Final and the semi-final in Italy saw that trend continue. The next instalment of the storied grudge match came along in 1996 when 'football came home' – England hosting the Euros for the first time. Within a summer when England became swept up with football fever, driven by a 4-1 thrashing of the Netherlands in a group match, they inevitably came up against the Germans once again at the semi-final stage, this time in front of a packed Wembley Stadium.

The lead-up to the game was soured by excess jingoism from the English press, most markedly with the *Daily Mirror* headline 'Achtung! Surrender! For You Fritz, ze Euro 96 Championship is over'. Once again, the game ended 1-1 in regular time and once again it went to a penalty shoot-out. And once again the Germans prevailed, leaving England to begin to believe that *Die Mannschaft* had a hoodoo over them.

But then some hope emerged. The group stage of Euro 2000 threw the two teams together once more and England finally got their first competitive victory over Germany since 1966. It was a narrow win, 1-0 thanks to an Alan Shearer goal, but a win, nevertheless. The 2002 World Cup qualifiers represented their next meeting with normal service resumed as Germany travelled to Wembley and left with a 1-0 win. But then came one of the most celebrated games in English history.

Saturday, 1 September 2001 saw England fly to the Olympiastadion in Munich for the return match. The Wembley game had seen Kevin Keegan in charge as manager, but the defeat prompted his resignation, leading to England's first foreign boss – Sven-Göran Erikkson. A Michael Owen hat-trick helped England to record an incredible 5-1 win – the image of the full-time scoreboard becoming iconic to fans of the Three Lions.

The rivalry then took a break, with just a couple of friendlies, until the 2010 World Cup. England went into the tournament with the usual ramping up of expectations by the media. The team had Frank Lampard and Steven Gerrard in midfield along with Wayne Rooney up front and were managed by serial winner Italian coach Fabio Capello – surely the trophy would be coming home this time? The pressure told as Capello's team squeaked out of their group following two draws against the USA and Algeria followed by a narrow 1-0 win over Slovenia – hardly convincing stuff. Germany, meanwhile, topped their group, beating both Australia and Ghana while suffering defeat against Serbia, meaning the two rivals were thrown together once again in the round of 16. Would the Germans continue their dominance or could England repeat their heroics of Munich 2001?

What happened?

The tension was palpable as the two teams emerged from the tunnel. This was their fifth World Cup meeting and all the previous encounters had ended level after 90 minutes (1966, 1970, 1982 and 1990). Germany lined up in their traditional white shirts while England were in red – the colour they had worn in that famous 1966 final.

The game almost got off to a storming start as Mesut Özil broke through after just four minutes, only to see his shot kicked over the bar by a falling David James in goal. Germany had come out the much sharper team and continued to make the running, putting pressure on the English defence. England could rarely get out of their own half and finally, after 20 minutes, the inevitable happened. A ball down the middle found Miroslav Klose in a foot race against Matthew Upson, the German striker muscling him off before poking it past James to give Germany the lead. It was route-one football that had caught the English centre-backs out of position and represented Klose's 50th international goal, placing him second behind the great Gerd Müller. No one could say that it hadn't been coming.

England were reeling and Germany continued to press home their dominance. Ten minutes after the goal, Thomas Müller played a cute reverse ball through to Klose, whose shot was well saved by James to deny him his second. Immediately England finally created a first chance as Jermaine Defoe headed against the crossbar, only to see the linesman raise his flag anyway. But it was only a momentary reprieve – some neat passing on the right saw Müller placed through. As English defenders were drawn towards him, Müller flicked the ball across to Lukas Podolski, who was unmarked in the penalty area. With all the time in the world, Podolski controlled the ball before hammering it low and hard through James's legs for Germany's second. The game was 32 minutes old, and England were being overrun.

England finally seemed to realise that they had been sleepwalking the first half an hour. For the first time, they threatened the German goal as Milner whipped in an excellent cross that saw Lampard prod past Manuel Neuer, only for Philipp Lahm to clear off the line. Germany reacted with a beautiful back-heel spin from Klose at the other end, fooling three defenders before the ball was smothered out for a corner. Back came England again – Steven Gerrard receiving a short corner before sending in a cross which Upson rose to head past Neuer.

Suddenly the whole momentum of the game swung. England had found a way back into a game that seemed to be running away from them, and almost immediately from the kick-off, the ball broke to Frank Lampard just outside the area. Without pause, his shot flew over the advanced Neuer, before hitting the underside of the bar and bouncing around the goal line. Neuer quickly grabbed the ball and ran forwards with it. The Guy Mowbray's commentary was immediate, 'It was in! No. That surely crossed the line! It's not been given! Surely that was in.'

Horrified England fans at home watched the replay, which showed that the ball had crossed the line by at least a foot – it wasn't even close – but the linesman had indicated nothing, and the referee let play continue. Refusing to let it faze them, the Germans immediately went back on the attack, Podolski just shooting narrowly wide.

The half-time whistle was serenaded with boos from the England supporters as the teams left the field. It would be important for the players to shake off the disappointment as quickly as possible – they should have been level but weren't and so they would just have to deal with that rather than stewing on it. But it had to hurt.

If Lampard was feeling aggrieved, he wasn't letting it affect his play. Six minutes into the second half, he struck a long-distance swerving free kick that rocketed against the crossbar. England were making the early running as they tried to equalise, Defoe almost through, only for Neuer to quickly come off his line and clear the danger. Both sides were trying shots from distance – Bastian Schweinsteiger next to narrowly miss.

Then, on 66 minutes, Lampard won another opportunity to fire in a free kick from just outside the area. This time his shot hit the wall and ended up being quickly cleared up to Müller. As he raced forward, it was suddenly three against two as Müller swiftly passed it on to Schweinsteiger, while continuing his burst forward. Schweinsteiger brought it into the middle before laying off again to Müller, who took one touch before firing past James. Just like that, Germany had gone from defence to scoring, England now facing a two-goal deficit.

German confidence soared and Müller almost added a fourth as the English defence looked in disarray. With England trying to get back into the game, Germany again broke from their own area just three minutes after the Müller goal. A long pass down the wing pitted Özil against Gareth Barry, resulting in Özil leaving him for dead down the line. As he headed towards the edge of the area, Özil looked up to see Müller again flying down the middle unmarked, allowing Özil to slip the ball across for Müller to tap in for his second and Germany's fourth. Three minutes, two breaks, two goals. As Mark Lawrenson on TV punditry duties put it, 'Sucker punch number two.'

It was always going to be nigh-on impossible for England to come back from such a deficit. Gerrard came close with ten minutes remaining, but England were despondent and never really threatened as the game finished. The referee ended proceedings and once again the Germans had prevailed over the Three Lions. The curse continued.

Final score
Germany 4 (Klose 20; Podolski 32; Müller 67, 70)
England 1 (Upson 37)

What was the aftermath?

While naturally the English media focused on the 'ghost goal', they also had to face the fact that England had just suffered their heaviest defeat at a World Cup. They had played poorly throughout the group stages and the Germans had exploited their simple 4-4-2 formation. The fact that they had only finished second in their group had led to the round of 16 clash with the Germans – something they should have avoided if they had played better.

While England flew home with their tails between their legs, Germany moved on to a quarter-final against Argentina, which happens to be an upcoming game for discussion.

One consequence of this tie was that FIFA president Sepp Blatter revisited tests by Adidas on designing a ball with an embedded microchip that could send a signal to the referee if the ball crossed the line. He had initially been against such technology, stating that early tests were only 95 per cent accurate and voting ahead of the 2010 tournament to ditch the technology. In June 2011, FIFA sanctioned testing that eventually led to the development of the goal-line technology that we are familiar with today, first adopted by the Premier League for the 2013/14 season and then the Champions League in 2016.

Teams

Germany: Neuer, Lahm (c), Friedrich, Mertesacker, Boateng, Schweinsteiger, Khedira, Müller (Trochowski 72), Özil (Kießling 83), Podolski, Klose (Gómez 72)
Manager: Löw
England: James, Johnson (Wright-Phillips 87), Upson, Terry, A. Cole, Lampard, Barry, Milner (J. Cole 64), Gerrard (c), Defoe (Heskey 71), Rooney
Manager: Capello

Iconic moment

While the 'ghost goal' is probably the most infamous moment, what also stands out are the third and fourth goals scored by Germany. Both were lightning-fast breaks that saw *Die Mannschaft* move from their own penalty area to eventually score, both times Müller adding the finishing touch. It was a sign of both the speed of the Germans and the naivety of the English, as well as the footballing gap between the two teams.

Trivia fact

The irony of England having a goal wrongly disallowed that crossed the line against the Germans was not lost on both nations. Thoughts immediately turned to the 1966 final, when England's third goal had been scored by Geoff Hurst – a turn and shot that hit the underside of the bar before bouncing down and out. In that case, England were awarded the goal, with replays proving inconclusive at the time. Naturally the Germans felt that it had been a 'home team' call and thus many there felt that the Lampard incident was karmic retribution.

Game 36

2010 World Cup

Ghana v Uruguay

2 July 2010

Soccer City, Johannesburg

Attendance: 84,017

Stage: Quarter-Finals

WORLD CUP CLASSIC

Why you should watch it

Going into the 2010 tournament, no African team had yet progressed beyond the quarter-finals, although two had successfully reached that stage: Cameroon in 1990 and Senegal in 2002. Cameroon had been desperately unlucky against England, being probably the better team on the night but losing 3-2 after extra time, while Senegal had also taken their match to extra time, losing out to Turkey through a golden goal scored just four minutes into the extra period. It felt like just a matter of time therefore before this glass ceiling would be broken.

Five African teams qualified, along with the host nation, to head to South Africa. These included Cameroon in their sixth World Cup appearance as well as two making only their second – Ghana and Ivory Coast. Ghana – known to their fans as the Black Stars – had a promising squad including several who played in Europe, such as Asamoah Gyan (Rennes), John Paintsil (Fulham), John Mensah (Sunderland), Sulley Muntari (Inter Milan) and Stephen Appiah (Bologna). Placed into a group alongside Germany, Serbia and Australia, Ghana beat Serbia with a Gyan penalty, and drew with Australia with another Gyan spot-kick, before narrowly losing 1-0 to Germany. It was enough for them to qualify for the knockout stages, where Gyan struck again, scoring an extra-time winner to defeat the USA. Therefore, Ghana found themselves in the quarter-finals, courtesy of three goals from Gyan, who was almost single-handedly firing the team along.

Their opponents in the quarter-finals would be Uruguay. They had impressed in the group stages, beating Mexico and South Africa while tying with France, before eliminating South Korea 2-1 with both goals scored by Luis Suárez.

The Uruguayans boasted a fearsome attack – the trio of Suárez, Diego Forlán and Edinson Cavani. Forlán was the most experienced, playing for Atlético Madrid having previously represented both Manchester United and Villarreal, and had just finished the season by scoring twice in the final for Atlético as they won the Europa League, taking the man of the match award. Cavani, meanwhile, was making a name for himself at Palermo, earning the nickname *El Matador* for his composure in front of goal. And then there was Suárez.

Suárez had moved to Ajax in 2007 where he was an immediate success. His first season saw him score 17 goals, while the next saw him net 22, second-highest for the season in the Eredivisie, earning him Ajax's player of the year award. The 2009/10 season saw his prowess grow even further as he netted 49 goals in all competitions, earning him the Dutch Footballer of the Year award. He was becoming a deadly marksman, worshipped in Amsterdam – but there was a dark side to him too. In his second season, coach Marco van Basten had expressed displeasure at the number of yellow cards Suárez earned as well as handing him a suspension for a half-time incident with his team-mate Albert Luque over the taking of a free kick. There was no doubting Suárez's skill, but he did have a temperament to match.

On 2 July the two teams lined up at Soccer City, Johannesburg. Would Gyan continue his hot form for Ghana and carry them to a first semi-final for Africa or would the Uruguayan attacking trio rule the day?

What happened?

Coming out into a stadium filled with blue, yellow, and red, while serenaded by the irrepressible vuvuzelas, the two teams lined up in their traditional kits, the first time they had faced one another in a senior game. It almost started terribly for Ghana as an early corner saw a Cavani header deflect off a defender, only for keeper Richard Kingson to make a reaction save. Suárez was next to threaten – a sharp shot from the edge of the area again requiring skilful intervention from Kingson. After those initial scares, the Black Stars began to gain composure, Gyan shooting narrowly wide from a swift counterattack.

As half-time approached, commentator John Helm observed, 'If they [Ghana] are going to get a goal, they are going to have to get it in the next 20 seconds,' at which point Sulley Muntari picked up the ball around 40 yards from goal and suddenly cracked a swerving ball into the corner, leading to the comment, 'What did I say!' Ghana had opened the scoring at the perfect moment, right before half-time, producing an explosion of colourful celebration around the stadium.

The lead would only last for ten minutes, however, as John Paintsil cluttered Jorge Fucile to the ground just outside the area. With a cross expected by most, Forlán instead whipped the free kick past Kingson to put Uruguay level. It was an audacious strike from the Atlético Madrid striker and meant that Forlán and Suárez now both had three goals apiece in the tournament to date – the vaunted attack was performing as advertised.

With their tails up, Uruguay maintained the pressure, Suárez continuing his personal battle with Kingson by drawing another sharp save. But neither side could produce a knockout punch before the referee's whistle indicated the need for extra time.

Extra time saw Kevin-Prince Boateng narrowly miss but as time progressed, penalties appeared inevitable. Then, with just 30 seconds left, Ghana earned a free kick, giving them one last opportunity to throw it into the mixer. The ball was whipped in, and a frantic scramble ensued before it fell to Stephen Appiah whose shot was cleared off the line by Suárez before being headed back at goal by Dominic Adiyiah. As the ball was about to go in, Suárez, still on the line, threw a hand instinctively up and pushed it out, thereby denying Ghana a certain winner.

The referee immediately pointed to the spot and Suárez was shown the red card. With what was likely to be the last kick of the match, up stepped Gyan, scorer of the two penalties in the group stage and hero against the USA. Keeper Fernando Muslera dived low to his right; Gyan hit it hard above him and then watched in horror as the ball struck the top of the bar and flew over. The referee immediately blew for full time as Gyan held his hands to his head and Muslera tapped the bar in thanks.

As Gyan's team-mates tried to console him, the game moved on to the penalty shoot-out. Forlán started proceedings by scoring and then came one of the most amazing acts of bravery ever seen in a World Cup. Just a couple of minutes after having missed the chance to put his team through, Gyan stepped forward to take Ghana's first penalty of the shoot-out. Few of us can imagine what emotions must have been flowing through him but all of us can appreciate the guts it took to step back into the spotlight. But he was coolness personified as he drilled the ball successfully into the top corner. Could redemption be on the way?

After five successful kicks, captain John Mensah saw his effort saved from a very short run-up, meaning advantage Uruguay with Ghana having taken one more, before Maxi Pereira duly blasted his over the bar and it was all square. As spectators' nerves were stretched to breaking point, Adiyiah, whose header had been blocked by Suárez, stepped up next and saw his penalty saved, meaning that if Uruguay's final penalty taker, Sebastián Abreu, scored, the South Americans were moving on. As his team-mates held their breath, Abreu stepped up and dinked a Panenka past Kingson. Uruguay were into the last four, Ghana were inconsolable and the world was treated to the sight of Suárez celebrating with his team on the field. As far as late dramatic endings to a game go, this was one of the craziest.

Final score
Uruguay 1 (Forlan 55) Ghana 1 (Muntari 45+2)
After extra time; Uruguay win 4-2 on penalties

What was the aftermath?

Not surprisingly, all the post-match talk was about Suárez's handball. It became a global discussion about morality and winning. Was Suárez a cheat? What if a player on your team had done the same, would you endorse it? Suárez had broken the rules with the handball, but the proper punishment had followed with a red card and penalty, Suárez himself commenting that he had 'made the save of the tournament' and that 'the Hand of God' now belonged to him, hardly endearing himself to all neutrals. To the Ghanaian coach, Milovan Rajevac, Suárez was a 'villain' and a 'cheat'. To the Uruguayan coach, Óscar Tabárez, these descriptions went too far, as he stated, 'Well, there was a handball in the penalty area, there was a red card and Suárez was thrown out. Saying that Ghana were cheated out of the game is too harsh. We have to go by the rules. It might have been a mistake by my player but I do not like that word "cheating".'

It was left to Gyan to add, 'I would say Suárez is a hero now in his own country, because the ball was going in and he held it with his hand. He is a hero now.'

While a devastated Ghanaian team headed home, knowing just how close they had come to writing African footballing history, Uruguay moved on to a semi-final against the Netherlands. By now it was fair to say that all footballing neutrals were rooting for the Dutch given the perceived injustice of the Ghana match. An early Netherlands goal was cancelled out before half-time by Forlán, before a second-half Dutch double placed the *Oranje* on their way. Uruguay did score a second in stoppage time, but it was too little, too late. The result most had been hoping for transpired – it would be the Netherlands that would go on to face Spain in the final.

Teams
Uruguay: Muslera, Pereira, Lugano (c) (Scotti 38), Victorino, Fucile, Fernández (Lodeiro HT), Pérez, Ríos, Cavani (Abreu 76), Suárez, Forlán
Manager: Tabárez

Ghana: Kingson, Paintsil, Vorsah, Mensah (c), Sarpei, Annan, Inkoom (Appiah 74), Asamoah, Boateng, Muntari (Adiyiah 88), Gyan
Manager: Rajevac

Iconic moment

The image that most recall, and which has become the one most associated with this match, is that of Suárez celebrating in the tunnel after Gyan's penalty miss. On receiving his red card, Suárez was shown leaving the pitch in tears, his shirt pulled up over the bottom of his face, being consoled by team-mates. He was the picture of distress. As Gyan's penalty rebounded up off the bar, the cameras focused again on the striker, who had turned to see what had happened, face still buried in his shirt. Suddenly he broke into a run of celebration, grinning as he pumped his arms in joy. From despair to elation in a matter of seconds – while you can understand his emotional response, it wasn't perhaps the best look to present in front of a global audience, many of whom were cheering for the underdog.

Trivia fact

This would not be Gyan's only major penalty incident of his international career. In the 2006 World Cup, Ghana had met the Czech Republic in the group stage. It took Gyan just two minutes to open the scoring and then, in the second half, Ghana earned a penalty. Gyan stepped up, only to see his shot rebound off the post, after which, adding to his frustration, he was shown a yellow card for taking the penalty before the referee had signalled that he was ready – a yellow card that forced Gyan to miss Ghana's next match against the USA.

Two years after the Uruguay game, Gyan again faced an important penalty as Ghana played Zambia in the semi-final of the 2012 Africa Cup of Nations. Just six minutes had elapsed when the penalty was awarded. Gyan took responsibility, only to see his effort saved, and eventually Zambia went on to win by a single goal.

However, despite these one-off penalty incidents, Gyan enjoyed a long and distinguished career with the Black Stars, playing over 100 times across 16 years and scoring 51 goals. He represented Ghana at three World Cups and seven Africa Cup of Nations tournaments, ending as Ghana's all-time leading goalscorer, and remains a legend in his home country to this day.

Game 37
2010 World Cup

Argentina v Germany

3 July 2010
Cape Town Stadium, Cape Town
Attendance: 64,100
Stage: Quarter-Finals

Why you should watch it

The 1986 World Cup Final – Argentina, led by the genius of Diego Armando Maradona, take a two-goal lead against West Germany, before being pegged back to 2-2 by two late second-half West German goals, only for Maradona to set through Jorge Burruchaga for an 85th-minute winner to seal one of the great tournament showpieces. The 1990 World Cup Final – West Germany, led by the power of Lothar Matthäus, gain revenge with an 85th-minute winner of their own, beating Argentina through an Andreas Brehme penalty to seal one of the worst World Cup Finals. The 2006 World Cup – the two sides meet again, this time in the quarter-finals, where yet another late goal from Miroslav Klose takes the game to penalties and a German victory in front of their home crowd. It was safe to say that Germany against Argentina had become a great World Cup rivalry over recent years, and so it was with great anticipation that the next chapter of this classic rolled around.

The Germans had reached this stage by comfortably beating England 4-1, meaning they had only lost one match in the tournament thus far. But Argentina had an even stronger record – they had won every one of their four games to date. The group stage had seen them overcome Nigeria, South Korea, and Greece, scoring seven goals in the process while only conceding one, including a Gonzalo Higuaín hat-trick against the Koreans. Higuaín was on the scoresheet once again in the round of 16, where Argentina again looked strong, comfortably overcoming Mexico 3-1, albeit including a clearly offside Carlos Tevez opener. This was a strong Argentinian team, including the likes of Ángel Di María, Tevez and Higuaín in attack, alongside a young number ten by the name of Lionel Messi.

Coming into the tournament, the Argentinian press had high hopes for the Barcelona wonderkid. He had played sporadically in Germany in 2006, when he had become the youngest player to represent *La Albiceleste* in a World Cup finals match, coming on as a substitute against Serbia and Montenegro. But when he really grabbed the public attention was during the 2007 Copa América where, despite Argentina losing to Brazil in the final, Messi was named Young Player of the Tournament. That performance, plus his scintillating form for Barcelona, meant much was expected from this youngster in South Africa.

But even Messi was not the focus of attention for the worldwide media within the Argentinian squad – that position could only fall to one person. The manager who had brought Argentina to the tournament was none other than the legend himself, Diego Armando Maradona. Maradona had taken the role in late 2008, despite having no previous experience in such a position, meaning that it was his job to ensure qualification for the 2010 World Cup finals. The process involved ten South American countries playing each other home and away, with the top four automatically qualifying. After a strong start, Argentina began to stumble, especially when suffering a humiliating 6-1 defeat in Bolivia, but eventually they scraped through in fourth. It had hardly been stirring stuff, but Maradona faced down his critics in a fiery post-qualification press conference when he basically told them what they could do regarding their views in no uncertain terms. I leave the reader to research that particular nugget.

What happened?

As the teams walked out into the Cape Town Stadium, the scene was magnificently framed by the iconic Table Mountain. Anticipation was high as the two top-scoring teams in the tournament, with so much World Cup pedigree, awaited kick-off – the question would be whether the goals would continue to flow or whether they would cancel each other out. The answer was not long in coming – Germany won a free kick inside three minutes which Bastian Schweinsteiger swung into the area as Thomas Müller ran in slightly ahead of his marker, glancing the ball past a stranded Sergio Romero in goal. It was just the start the neutrals were hoping for.

The cameras panned to a pensive-looking Maradona, resplendent in a grey suit, shirt and tie and sporting a salt and pepper beard, as he faced his first serious test of the tournament. Germany continued to press but slowly Argentina regained their composure, Messi showing his skill with a delicious pass that Tevez almost latched on to near goal. But when Germany did have the ball, their passing was beautiful. A great move down their right saw Müller burst into the area, where he cut the ball back to the waiting Klose. A second goal looked certain but Klose just got under the ball, his shot narrowly going over the bar.

Back came Argentina again, winning a free kick outside the German area, allowing Messi his first opportunity to test keeper Manuel Neuer. He tried a low shot that came back off the wall to Gabriel Heinze, who played a perfect pass into the area for Tevez. As Neuer rushed out, Tevez calmly squared it to Higuaín to poke into the empty net before both strikers turned to see the linesman's flag correctly raised for offside. Try as they might, *La Albiceleste* couldn't break through as the referee blew for half-time meaning Germany went into the break narrowly ahead – both sides playing some flowing football and the game still poised on a knife-edge.

With Maradona's words ringing in their ears, Argentina came out on the offensive – Di María hitting a long-range shot that only narrowly missed the post. Maradona could not contain himself, pacing around his technical area like a caged animal, his head in his hands. Messi was starting to take control, another pass from him setting up Higuaín whose shot was nervously handled by Neuer, as it looked likely that any next goal would come from Argentina.

But then it all fell apart for them. On 68 minutes, a ball was played to Müller with his back to goal. Falling under a challenge from behind, Müller still had the presence of mind to play a pass while on the ground, stabbing it through to Lukas Podolski to run into the area. Pausing for just a beat, Podolski assessed the situation before squaring a perfect pass beyond Romero to an open Miroslav Klose on the edge of the six-yard box. Klose would never score an easier goal as he tapped the ball into the empty net before knee-sliding in celebration. The Germans were two ahead.

Just six minutes later Argentina were again carved open, Schweinsteiger picking up a pass on the wing and turning to face two defenders moving towards him. Running forward, a drop of the shoulder saw him burst between them into the area. Facing another defender close to the six-yard box, Schweinsteiger glided past him too toward the byline, leaving him one-on-one against the onrushing Romero, who spread himself only to see Schweinsteiger cut a short pass back to defender Arne Friedrich who, like Klose, couldn't really miss from close range. It had been a sublime piece of magic from Schweinsteiger – worthy of the watching Maradona himself. Two tap-ins for the Germans in six minutes and a semi-final berth beckoning.

Argentina looked stunned and a wild shot from Tevez that flew miles over seemed to sum up their resigned mood. The two quick strikes had crushed their belief and it was now just a matter of whether they could hold the Germans to three. With a minute remaining, the Germans broke forward from their own half, Özil playing it to Podolski before making an overlapping run at speed. Podolski carried the ball forward before playing it back to Özil, who played a first-time wonderful, chipped cross over two Argentinian defenders to an unmarked Klose. The German marksman calmly side-foot volleyed the ball into the corner, sealing a magnificent performance by *Die Mannschaft*. Argentina had been well-schooled on the day by clinical German passing and finishing – it was left to Maradona to attempt to console his crushed players as they tried to comprehend what had befallen them.

Final score
Germany 4 (Müller 3; Klose 68, 89; Friedrich 74)
Argentina 0

What was the aftermath?

The four-goal defeat was the heaviest suffered by Argentina at a World Cup since 1974. While German coach Joachim Löw trumpeted his team's performance as 'absolute class', the post-mortem began within the Argentinian media. Naturally, given his stature, the managerial abilities of Maradona came under scrutiny. He immediately stated that he was considering his future, commenting, 'I may leave tomorrow,' but somewhat surprisingly, just 12 days after the defeat, the Argentinian Football Association announced that Maradona would be awarded a new four-year contract, leading up to the 2014 World Cup. But this decision was reversed another 12 days later, enraging the legendary ex-player. It would be Maradona's last game in charge of the national team – and quite a ride it had been.

Germany, meanwhile, moved on to face Spain in the semi-finals – a Spanish team that were redefining football under the leadership of Vicente del Bosque, bringing the term *tiki-taka* to a worldwide audience. With a midfield powered by the Barcelona pairing of Xavi and Andrés Iniesta and David Villa up front, who would also join the *Blaugrana* that summer, they were finally allowing Spain to live up to their potential at a World Cup, something they had always failed to do in the past. Spain dominated the game with a Carles Puyol header separating the two sides at the final whistle. For a second World Cup in succession, Germany had fallen at the semi-final stage.

Teams

Germany: Neuer, Lahm (c), Mertesacker, Friedrich, Boateng (Jansen 72), Khedira (Kroos 77), Schweinsteiger, Müller (Trochowski 84), Özil, Podolski, Klose
Manager: Löw

Argentina: Romero, Otamendi (Pastore 70), Demichelis, Burdisso, Heinze, Mascherano (c), Rodríguez, Di María (Agüero 75), Messi, Higuaín, Tevez
Manager: Maradona

Iconic moment

While it is tempting to again focus on Maradona on the touchline, Bastian Schweinsteiger's run to set up the fourth goal was breathtaking. To waltz past players of the quality of Ángel Di María, Javier Pastore and Gonzalo Higuaín before then having the composure to pull the ball back for Arne Friedrich to finish showed what a special player he was. It would be no surprise that he would go on to earn 121 caps for *Die Mannschaft* over 12 years, earning the nickname 'football god' from adoring Bayern Munich fans.

Trivia fact

Argentina's struggles to qualify saw them looking in real danger of missing out with two games remaining. They faced a critical home match against Peru in which a win was badly needed. As the heavens opened above Buenos Aires, a rain-soaked Argentina strained to break down the Peruvians. Then, early in the second half, they grabbed the all-important lead through Higuaín. It seemed Maradona was going to get his much-needed victory but, with just a minute remaining,

Hernán Rengifo snatched an equaliser. Maradona could only hold his head in dismay as the rain lashed down. Then came *El Milagro* (The Miracle). Two minutes into stoppage time, with the ball pinballing around the Peruvian penalty box, substitute Martín Palermo poked in a winner. As the stadium erupted, Palermo whipped off his shirt while the bench ran on to the field – including Maradona who dived into a full bellyflop on the drenched pitch. One could never argue that Maradona's life was uneventful.

Game 38

2014 World Cup

The Netherlands v Spain

13 June 2014

Itaipava Arena Fonte Nova, Salvador

Attendance: 48,173

Stage: Group B, Round 1

WORLD CUP CLASSIC

Why you should watch it

The 2010 World Cup had ended with a final between Spain and the Netherlands – a clash that would either see the Dutch finally quash the demons of being losing finalists in 1974 and 1978 or see the Spaniards, the perennial underachievers, finally reach the mountain top. The hope had been for an exciting battle between Spanish *tiki-taka* magic and Dutch attack – unfortunately what emerged was an ugly duel, mainly spoilt by Dutch fouling, although Spain were not completely guilt-free either. Goalless after 90 minutes, and with referee Howard Webb already having dished out nine yellow cards (one of which could/should have been red in the case of Mark van Bommel), the next 26 minutes produced two more yellow cards and finally a red for Dutch defender John Heitinga. It was then, with just four minutes remaining, that Andrés Iniesta put the watching world out of its misery, resulting in Spain's first World Cup. There was still time for three more yellow cards, to leave the final total at 14 yellows and one red. It had been an ugly affair that left no love between the two countries.

Spain going into the 2014 tournament had become the dominant force in world football, winning an unprecedented three major trophies in a row – the 2008 European Championship, the 2010 World Cup and the 2012 European

Championship. It was a golden generation that included names such as Iker Casillas, Sergio Ramos, and Xabi Alonso from Real Madrid along with Gerard Piqué, Jordi Alba, Xavi, Sergio Busquets and Andrés Iniesta from Barcelona. Barcelona had won the Champions League in 2009 and 2011 while Real Madrid had done the same in 2014 (the next four years would also see Barcelona or Real Madrid win each year). Spanish football was untouchable at both club and international level.

The team was led by Vicente del Bosque, who had overseen the 2010 World Cup and 2012 European Championship victories. He used the Barcelona midfield to embrace their style of play, which had become known as *tiki-taka*, at international level, a style that involved short passing to keep possession until spotting an opportunity, when a quick incisive move was made.

There was delicious anticipation when the draw for the group stages of the 2014 World Cup in Brazil paired Spain and the Netherlands together in Group B. Never had the two previous finalists met in a group stage. Even better, the game would be the opener. Immediately the tension began to rise, especially given the bad blood resulting from the previous violent clash.

While the 2014 Spain team was similar to that which had triumphed over the Netherlands in 2010, the *Oranje* had changed considerably. The 2010 team had been managed by Bert van Marwijk but, after a disappointing 2012 European Championship, he was replaced by Louis van Gaal, who became manager for a second spell. He made major changes to the squad, with the team that would start against Spain in 2014 only including four players from the 2010 final.

Would Spain once again be victorious or, this time, could the Netherlands avenge their 2010 loss?

What happened?

The 2010 finalists came out under the Brazilian sun to kick off their campaigns – both knowing the importance of getting that initial win under their belt. Both teams wore untraditional kits – Spain in all white against the Netherlands in all blue. Almost immediately, the Dutch produced the first opportunity, when Arjen Robben put Wesley Sneijder through on goal, only for Iker Casillas to throw out a strong arm to save Spain. It was an early warning that this rebuilt Dutch team meant business.

Spain began to get their famous passing game going, making neat triangles around the midfield, and after 27 minutes, one such move led to a lovely through ball to Diego Costa, who ran into the area before cutting back on defender Stefan de Vrij. As he did so, De Vrij's trailing leg appeared to trip the striker, who immediately went down, causing the referee to award a penalty.

The responsibility fell to Xabi Alonso, who lined up as Robben appeared to give keeper Jasper Cillessen advice on where he felt the kick would go. If Robben was trying to play mind games on Alonso, it failed as he fired it past Cillessen, who did however dive the correct way. Once again, Spain were 1-0 up against the Netherlands.

Spain were totally dominating play and almost grabbed a second when a beautiful pass from Iniesta took out both the Dutch midfield and defence to put David Silva through on goal. With Cillessen rushing out to meet him, Silva tried a cute chip that only narrowly missed. As half-time approached, it looked like the Netherlands would need something extraordinary to get back into the game, such was the Spanish dominance. And that is exactly what happened.

The ball was played out to Daley Blind just inside the Spain half, where he was hugging the touchline. Looking up, he launched a cross towards the area, where striker Robin van Persie was running along with a couple of defenders. Finding himself ahead, Van Persie watched the ball dropping towards him where, still around 18 yards out, he flew into a horizontal dive to lob a header past an astonished Casillas. It was an incredible piece of skill that saw the crowd erupt in appreciation as Van Persie ran to celebrate with the Dutch bench before being mobbed by team-mates. Despite being under the cosh for most of the half, the Dutch found themselves going into half-time on level terms thanks to a moment of pure magic.

Eight minutes into the second half, the Dutch conjured up another piece of trickery. A pass forward found Robben between two Spanish defenders. As the ball dropped, Robben controlled it with his first touch using his left foot, then immediately turned one defender with his right before his third touch was to rifle the ball past Casillas with his left. Three touches and the Netherlands were ahead – they had book-ended the half-time break with two memorable goals.

The holders suddenly looked shaken. They tried to get their short passing game going again, but the Dutch were flying. Breaking up Spanish play, Sneijder set up Robben at the halfway line who immediately flew at the panicked defence, before a short pass to Daryl Janmaat was flicked on to Van Persie, whose first-time drive rattled the crossbar. It had only taken a few seconds for the Dutch to move from defence to almost scoring again. Spain were now all at sea and next gave away an unnecessary free kick out wide. Sneijder's cross beat everyone, including Casillas, to drop at the far post, where it was headed in by de Vrij for his first international goal. The fact that Casillas, the world's best keeper, had completely missed the cross showed the state Spain were now in. The Netherlands were in heaven.

Still, Spain weren't world champions without reason. A shot was charged down, falling to César Azpilicueta out wide. His cross was met by substitute Pedro whose header was incredibly parried off the line by Cillessen before Silva bundled it home. But, to Dutch relief, Silva was correctly flagged for offside, and the Netherlands' two-goal lead remained intact.

The madness continued when, with 18 minutes remaining, Sergio Ramos played an easy back-pass to Casillas. There appeared little danger until Casillas's first touch to control the pass was too heavy. He immediately realised his error as he an Van Persie raced for the loose ball where, to Casillas's horror, the forward emerged with it before poking it into an empty net. As Van Persie wheeled away, tongue out in celebration, Casillas could only look at the ground, hands on hips in dismay. The game was turning into a rout.

A conga line of Dutch supporters all clad in orange began to snake around the ground as Spain tried to pick themselves up. They seemed to have no answer to the speed of the Netherlands and, with still ten minutes remaining, things went from bad to worse. A fast ball from defence found Robben in his own half and he once again turned on the jets. Outpacing Ramos, Robben initially tried to go around Casillas, before turning back into the centre of the area. As Casillas scrambled after him, and two Spanish defenders stood to block the line, Robben calmly centred himself before lashing the ball into the top corner. It was another remarkable show of speed and clinical finishing, placing the Dutch in fifth heaven and the reigning champions in shambles. Even the normally taciturn Van Gaal could not suppress a huge smile of joy. Everything that could go right for the Dutch most definitely did, while for Spain, it was the first time that they had conceded five goals in an international since 1963.

The Netherlands were now enjoying themselves and another move saw them oozing confidence as they passed through the Spanish defence to create yet another opportunity, this time for substitute Georginio Wijnaldum, although Casillas was up to the task. The ball then found Robben whose vicious volley was again saved. If it had been a boxing contest, the referee would have stopped the fight at this point, and thankfully for Spain, the end did come shortly thereafter. They had been humiliated by a Dutch masterpiece that Rembrandt would have been proud of.

Final score
Netherlands 5 (van Persie 44, 72; Robben 53, 80; de Vrij 64) Spain 1 (Alonso 27 pen)

What was the aftermath?

The 5-1 defeat was the highest ever suffered by a defending champion at a World Cup. Spain had only suffered one worse defeat in any previous World Cup – losing 6-1 to Brazil back in 1950. This loss stunned the footballing world given Spain's recent dominance of the game, including qualifying for the 2014 tournament without a defeat, so they would now head into their second match against Chile needing at least a point to still have a chance of moving on to the knockout stages.

Unfortunately for Spain, they again failed to live up to their potential. Two first-half goals from Chile saw the defending world champions eliminated in the group stage after just two games – a shocking performance from one of the pre-tournament favourites. They did win their final group match – a meaningless encounter against Australia – 3-0, but that was little consolation. After three major championship victories in a row, Spain were on an early flight home.

The Netherlands, meanwhile, went on to defeat both Australia and Chile and topped the group with maximum points. This earned them a round of 16 match against Mexico and, with two minutes remaining, it looked like they were joining Spain as they sat a goal down. But then two goals in the next six minutes saw them make a miraculous recovery, winning with a hotly disputed penalty that broke Mexican hearts. Their quarter-final was a dull affair as the Netherlands and Costa Rica played out a goalless draw over 120 minutes, before the Dutch triumphed on penalties, while their semi-final was also goalless, this time against Argentina, before penalty misses by Ron Vlaar and Wesley Sneijder put an end to the Dutch dream.

As so often, the Netherlands had come close but been unable to cross the final hurdle. But they had successfully humiliated the greatest team in the world, thus ending Spain's era of dominance.

Teams

Netherlands: Cillessen, Vlaar, de Vrij (Veltman 77), Martins Indi, Janmaat, Blind, de Guzmán (Wijnaldum 62), de Jong, Sneijder, Van Persie (c) (Lens 79), Robben
Manager: Van Gaal
Spain: Casillas (c), Azpilicueta, Piqué, Ramos, Alba, Xavi, Busquets, Alonso (Pedro 62), Silva (Fàbregas 78), Iniesta, Costa (Torres 62)
Manager: del Bosque

Iconic moment

Van Persie's header to tie up the game just before half-time became a viral image – commonly referred to as the Flying Dutchman. It was such a strange header – it resembled a diving header but then instead of the usual power, he somehow contrived to lob the ball with his head over Casillas. However many times one views it, it remains difficult to understand quite how he did it, and how his brain processed the action so quickly. Seeing him in mid-air, he bends his back like a salmon leaping up a rapid.

The goal was rightly a finalist for the 2014 FIFA Puskás Award – only beaten by James Rodríguez's shot for Colombia against Uruguay.

Trivia fact

Since their 2010 triumph, Spain had one particularly new addition in their starting 11 – Diego Costa. A striker for Atlético Madrid, he was coming off a season where Atlético had reached the Champions League Final, during which he had contributed eight goals in their campaign. Atlético had also secured their first La Liga title for 18 years, with Costa netting 27 times, so including him in the Spanish team was a no-brainer – except that Costa was Brazilian.

Born in Lagarto, Brazil, Costa had moved over to play in Portugal at the age of 17 before being signed one year later by Atlético. In March 2013, he made his debut for the *Seleção* in a friendly against Italy. But then, seven months later, Costa declared that he wished to play football for Spain which, having been granted Spanish nationality and only having played in friendlies, is allowable under FIFA rules. He became a Spanish player – a decision that was not well received by Brazilian football authorities and supporters, leading manager Luiz Filipe Scolari to comment, 'A Brazilian player who refuses to wear the shirt of the Brazilian national team and compete in a World Cup in your country is automatically withdrawn. He is turning his back on a dream of millions, to represent our national team, the five-time champions in a World Cup in Brazil.'

Game 39

2014 World Cup

Brazil v Germany

8 July 2014

Estádio Mineirão, Belo Horizonte

Attendance: 58,141

Stage: Semi-Final

WORLD CUP CLASSIC

Why you should watch it

There can be no greater pressure felt by any team in world football comparable to Brazil hosting a World Cup. For a nation that always expects its team to win ahead of every tournament, playing in front of their own supporters ratchets the pressure to unbelievable levels.

Before 2014, Brazil had only hosted one World Cup, back in 1950, although for that tournament there was no World Cup Final – instead, a final group of four played each other, with whoever ended top of the table becoming world champions. Brazil were pitted against Sweden, Spain and long-time rival neighbours Uruguay. The *Seleção* were in imperious form, thrashing Sweden 7-1 and then Spain 6-1, with striker Ademir scoring six of those goals while Uruguay won one and drew one, meaning that in the final game, Brazil would only require a draw against Uruguay to lift the Jules Rimet Trophy.

Based on their form, it was widely predicted that Brazil would go one better and get the victory. National newspapers were declaring Brazil as world champions for days while the mayor of Rio proudly declared ahead of the match that Brazil would be hailed as winners. A rumoured crowd of over 200,000 packed the Maracanã to witness Brazil's coronation – at this time in history, they had never won the World Cup.

And two minutes into the second half, Brazil took the lead. The trophy was coming home.

And then, with 24 minutes remaining, Uruguay equalised through Juan Schiaffino and suddenly Brazilian nerves were jangling. With just 11 minutes left on the clock, the unthinkable happened – Alcides Ghiggia shot Uruguay into the lead. A stunned, silent stadium watched the minutes ebb by until the final whistle sounded. Brazil had lost the World Cup in their own backyard.

The loss became an event of national mourning – known forever as the *Maracanazo.* Suicides were reported around the country until the mourning turned to anger and recriminations against those players the crowd felt were most to blame. The Brazilian team had played in their national colours of white shirts with blue collars – these were ditched and replaced by the now famous yellow and green. Of course, Brazil went on to win five World Cups after this tournament, but the *Maracanazo* had always remained in the consciousness of fans. Naturally, with Brazil hosting for the first time since then, the story was retold as part of the narrative, but it was 64 years ago – an ancient tale that surely had no relevance in modern football.

Responsibility for winning the trophy on home soil had fallen to Luiz Felipe Scolari. While Brazil had a competent team, the poster boy was young superstar Neymar, a striker who had attracted all of Europe with his scoring record at Santos, before moving to Barcelona in 2013 for an undisclosed fee (later shown to be around €86m) to join up with Lionel Messi and later Luis Suárez to form the celebrated MSN attack. Although only 22 years old, he was seen by the Brazilian public as the talisman that would bring them a sixth World Cup. The pressure on his young shoulders was enormous.

Brazil came through the group stage with two wins and a draw, topping the table with Neymar scoring four of their seven goals. That led to a nervy round of 16 tie, which saw them need penalties to overcome fellow South Americans Chile before dispatching another local rival, Colombia, 2-1 in the quarter-finals. Their progress to the semi-finals had been a little shaky, but that just reflected the pressure being felt by the *Seleção* to deliver in front of their passionate fanbase.

The Colombia game had one moment of horror for Brazilian fans. Just two minutes from the end, Neymar received a knee in the back which saw him substituted off in agony. He had suffered a fractured vertebra, so ending his tournament, meaning Brazil would have to face their semi-final without him.

Their opponents would be Germany who, like Brazil, were also unbeaten throughout the tournament. They had topped their group before narrowly beating Algeria after extra time and then eliminating France with a 1-0 victory. The German attack was led by Miroslav Klose, playing in his final tournament for *Die Mannschaft* at the end of a long and successful international career. In the group stages, he scored his 15th World Cup goal, tying the record held by Ronaldo and becoming only the third player to score in four different World Cups. The Brazilian crowd did not want to see Ronaldo's record fall in this of all games.

The teams ranked second and third in the world met for only the second time in a World Cup match. Five-times winners Brazil against three-times champions Germany. It promised to be a hard-fought close titanic battle, with maybe one vital goal separating the two sides.

What happened?

A sea of yellow welcomed the two teams out into the Estádio Mineirão in Belo Horizonte as over 58,000 packed in to greet their heroes. The question on many lips was how the *Seleção* would cope without Neymar, and the early indications were good as Marcelo fired a shot narrowly wide of the German goal. Brazil were pressurising but the Germans showed their speed on the break with a move that eventually ended in the first corner of the game after 11 minutes. Toni Kroos swung the ball into the area and, as six Brazilians moved towards the near post, the delivery sailed over them all to Thomas Müller, who found himself completely unmarked on the edge of the six-yard box. A simple side-footed volley gave the Germans just the start they would have been dreaming of, while throwing the Brazilian crowd into an early state of anxiety.

While Brazil attempted to work their way back into the game, Germany continued to look dangerous on breakaways, their speed causing the hosts' defence all sorts of problems. After 23 minutes another break down the right saw Brazil avert the danger, conceding a throw-in. A ball into Kroos saw Fernandinho commit to the interception, only to miss it and leave himself out of position. Kroos rolled it into the area where Müller was coming in from the right but, rather than shoot, the forward flicked it to Klose, whose first-time shot was well saved by Júlio César. But Brazil could do nothing about the rebound, which fell again to Klose, who gratefully accepted the second invitation. Klose had his 16th World Cup goal, Ronaldo's record had been broken and Brazil were in shock – this had not been the script.

Straight from the kick-off, Germany regained the ball and moved forward into the Brazilian half. Again, finding room down the right, full-back Philip Lahm was allowed to cross to an unmarked Müller. Thankfully for Brazil, Müller missed his shot, only for the ball to continue to an unmarked Kroos who made no such mistake, rifling it home with his left foot. The Brazilian defenders looked at one another in disbelief – it looked like it could already be game over after just 24 minutes. As the Germans celebrated, the TV cameras focused on stunned fans, resplendent in yellow and green face paint, trying to comprehend what they were witnessing. Brazil needed to regain their composure quickly.

Instead, they went into full panic mode. Just two minutes after Germany's third, Fernandinho lingered on the ball in midfield too long, allowing Kroos to sneak up behind him, steal the ball and play a short pass to Sami Khedira in the penalty area, who immediately played it back to Kroos to side-foot into an unguarded net. Three goals in three minutes had surely killed the game off. As the cameras again panned into the crowd, we got our first sight of tears as it all became too much to bear. Youngsters were on their way to being traumatised and possible years of therapy as the Brazilian defence went AWOL, allowing Germany to ruthlessly punish them.

Trailing 4-0 after just 26 minutes, all Brazil could really do was to try and stem the tide until half-time where maybe they could reorganise. But the Germans were having none of it. The clock had reached 29 minutes when Mats Hummels broke up an attack, before being allowed to run unchallenged deep into the Brazilian half. When finally a tackle came, Hummels won the clash, poking the ball to Khedira, who, as with the fourth goal, again elected not to shoot but instead to pass it on to Mesut Özil. Three Brazilian defenders converged on him, but he simply passed the ball back to an unmarked Khedira. The commentary says it all, 'They're queuing up, they're all going to score at this rate … and the Brazilians look as if they want to go to the dressing room already.'

Just under a third of the game gone and it was 5-0 to Germany.

Thankfully for Brazil, they did manage to hold out for the remainder of the first half. One can only imagine what Scolari could have said to them – what do you say to a team that is five goals down in a World Cup semi-final at home? An early second-half chance fell to Oscar, whose shot was saved, but it did at least provide some evidence of life. Perhaps the Germans were going to slow down for the second period, seeing out the game while avoiding any injuries. If they were, then taking it easy would not apply to keeper Manuel Neuer, who pulled off a remarkable double save to prevent Paulinho from scoring. He seemed set on ensuring a clean sheet.

Müller soon showed that Germany were still in the mood for more, hitting a curling shot that was well saved by César. Then, with 20 minutes remaining, Germany again moved the ball down the right where Khedira found himself completely unmarked on the wing and slotted into Lahm at the near post. With everyone expecting a shot, Lahm instead cut the ball into the middle, where substitute André Schürrle stroked it home. Once again it was just too easy – the right-hand side wide open for exploitation. Germany had now racked up six and their players seemed subdued in their celebrations, probably realising that the game had entered full humiliation stage. Brazil's worst defeat in history – 6-0 against Uruguay back in 1920 – had been equalled.

The clock slowly moved towards the last ten minutes, every minute probably feeling like an hour to the shocked Brazilian fans who just wanted this to end. But it was not over yet. A ball down the left wing found Müller who instantly flicked it into the area where Schürrle was running in completely unmarked yet again. One touch to bring the ball under control and then a left-foot shot into the roof of the net. Seventh heaven.

Finally, finally the 90th minute came around and Özil almost added an eighth before a through ball to Oscar allowed him to cut across the area before sliding it past Neuer. Never, in the history of Brazilian football, had a goal scored in front of a home crowd been so quietly received. Neuer wasn't to get his clean sheet after all, although I am sure he got over that quickly.

The referee finally called a halt to the agony and the few remaining Brazilian fans responded with a chorus of boos as their team sank to its knees.

Final score
Germany 7 (Müller 11; Klose 23; Kroos 24, 26; Khedira 29; Schürrle 69, 79) Brazil 1 (Oscar 90)

What was the aftermath?

Brazil had lost 7-1 – what could be said about such a defeat? Scolari stated that it was the 'worst loss by a Brazilian national team ever', before adding that it was 'the worst day of my life' and resigning. Some players issued public apologies to the Brazilian people. Striker Fred was so traumatised that he announced his retirement from international football. The Brazilian media competed in seeing who could print the most dramatic headline – examples including 'The Biggest Shame in History', 'Brazil is Slain' and 'Historical Humiliation'. In memory of the 1950 *Maracanazo*, this game quickly became dubbed the *Mineirazo*, meaning 'the Mineirão blow'.

Most agreed that Germany had been reasonably classy about the whole thing. Mats Hummels talked after the game about how, at half-time, they realised that they should not humiliate the Brazilians, but that did not mean taking their foot off the gas, just instead subduing any celebrations. The sixth and seventh goals were examples of that and at no stage did the Germans take to showboating. It was their job to win, and they exploited Brazil's open defence to the full. They did however express surprise at how easy it had been, commenting on the lack of Brazilian defending and how the *Seleção* had rapidly fallen apart. The Brazilian press appreciated the German approach, calling them the 'world champions of sympathy'.

In a cruel last blow, Brazil were dragged on to the pitch once more to play a meaningless third-place play-off against the Netherlands. Still without Neymar, they were two goals down after just 17 minutes, ahead of an eventual 3-0 scoreline. Germany, meanwhile, went on to face Argentina in the final. Given the animosity between Argentina and Brazil, heightened by the Argentine media's gloating over the 7-1 result, Brazilian fans were firmly behind the Germans. They did not disappoint, scoring in extra time to secure victory and their fourth World Cup. A small consolation for home supporters at least.

Teams

Germany: Neuer, Lahm (c), Boateng, Hummels (Mertesacker HT), Höwedes, Khedira (Draxler 76), Schweinsteiger, Müller, Kroos, Özil, Klose (Schürrle 58)
Manager: Löw

Brazil: César, Maicon, Luiz (c), Dante, Marcelo, Gustavo, Fernandinho (Paulinho HT), Hulk (Ramires HT), Oscar, Bernard, Fred (Willian 70)
Manager: Scolari

Iconic moment

During every World Cup, some of the most iconic moments are often scenes of fans either celebrating or in mourning. Given that this was Brazil, whose fans are among the most passionate in the world, and that they had just been thrashed 7-1 in their homeland, the camera shots of fan reactions were priceless. There was the old moustachioed fan, clutching a replica World Cup trophy while being consoled. There were the women all in yellow with flowered wreaths in their hair, sobbing. But most famous of all, there was the man in a Brazil shirt tearing at a small Brazilian flag with his teeth. Being a football fan can be a brutal pastime.

Trivia fact

In Brazil, '7-1' (in Portuguese: *sete a um*), has become a metaphor for a crushing defeat, while 'goal for Germany' (in Portuguese: *gol da Alemanha*) is used as an exclamation after a mishap.

Game 40

2018 World Cup

Portugal v Spain

15 June 2018

Fisht Olympic Stadium, Sochi

Attendance: 43,866

Stage: Group B, Round 1

WORLD CUP CLASSIC

Why you should watch it

The 2014 World Cup saw Spain's dominance from 2008 to 2012 finally brought to a halt in Brazil, marked by elimination in the group stage. The 2016 European Championship held in France saw Spain finish second in their group, behind Croatia, and therefore have to face Italy in the round of 16, where a two-goal defeat saw them eliminated, continuing their downfall from their previous giddy heights.

The tournament did, however, see the emergence of a surprise winner. Portugal were lucky to qualify for the knockout rounds, drawing all three of their group games against Iceland, Austria and Hungary. It was hardly inspirational stuff and was followed by a round of 16 1-0 victory over Croatia, a quarter-final penalty shoot-out win over Poland and a 2-0 semi-final victory over surprise package Wales. But scruffy as it was, Portugal found themselves in the final against France, in front of 75,000 French fans at Saint-Denis. A goalless match went into extra time before substitute Eder scored in the second period to give Portugal their first major trophy.

While the team had a breadth of talent, its leader was undoubtedly the superstar forward Cristiano Ronaldo. Along with Lionel Messi, the two of them dominated football during the 2010s, winning every Ballon d'Or from 2008 to 2017, Ronaldo claiming five of those. He had earned his first cap for Portugal back in 2003 and had since represented his country at the 2004, 2008, 2012 and 2016 European Championships as well as the 2006, 2010 and 2014 World Cups. While playing in the 2016 European Championship, he had passed Luís Figo to become Portugal's most capped player, his 128th appearance at the time, as well as equalling Michel Platini's all-time scoring record across the competition of nine goals. In the final, he had to leave the field injured after 25 minutes following a challenge with Dimitri Payet, but cheered his team on from the sidelines before proudly getting to lift the trophy as team captain.

Post Euro 2016 he had led Portugal to Russia through a qualification group where they won nine of their ten matches, only losing to Switzerland away. Those ten games saw Portugal score 32 goals, of which 15 came from the boot or head of Ronaldo. As usual he was proving the inspiration for the *Seleção das Quinas* and so entered the 2018 World Cup as a fully fledged Portuguese legend with just over 150 caps and almost 80 goals.

Spain, meanwhile, had gotten some of their old magic back during the qualification process. Drawn in a tough group alongside Italy, they won nine of their matches and drew the other away in Italy, who they defeated 3-0 in the return match. Thirty-six goals had been scored with Diego Costa, Isco, Álvaro Morata and David Silva grabbing four apiece. But then, just two days before the World Cup would commence, their preparation was rocked.

Spain's manager was Julen Lopetegui, who had been appointed in July 2016 following the legendary Vicente del Bosque's retirement. He had led them through their strong qualification campaign and had an unbeaten track record to date. But on 12 June the news broke that Lopetegui had agreed to take over at Real Madrid at the end of the tournament. The news caught the Spanish Football Federation by surprise as they claimed no knowledge of this and, angered, they reacted by sacking Lopetegui with immediate effect. Three hours after this announcement, they followed it up by saying that the director of football, Fernando Hierro, would take control of the team for the World Cup. It was not an ideal way to head into their opening game.

Drawn together in Group B, the clash of the two Iberian superpowers was the opening game for both teams, both desperate to get off to a winning start, or at least avoid an initial loss. Their most recent World Cup meeting had been in 2010 when Spain had won by a single goal in the round of 16. Would Portugal continue their fine recent form, or would Spain remain leaders of Iberia? Could Ronaldo continue his incredible scoring record?

What happened?

I haven't talked about where I watched games in this book – but this one does have a particularly good memory for me. My family and I were in Lisbon on holiday, and we walked up to a picturesque street bar, with a view over the city, where they had a big screen set up for the match. My older son, being 19, was still very excited that he could drink a beer in Europe as opposed to being unable to do so back in the US. So we grabbed some drinks and food and settled in with the locals as they cheered on their beloved Portuguese heroes.

As the teams came out, Portugal were in the rare position of being one of the pre-tournament favourites, even ahead of traditional rivals Spain. And the game got off to a quick start. After just four minutes, Ronaldo ran at Nacho on the edge of the Spanish penalty area. Throwing one of his trademark step-overs, he drew the defender into a challenge, before flinging himself to the ground in response. On replay there did appear to be contact, and it would be Ronaldo himself who would pick himself up to take the resulting penalty. Placing it coolly past David de Gea, Ronaldo scored in his fourth successive World Cup, a Portuguese record, celebrating his 82nd international goal in usual style with a run to the corner flag and his trademark leap and pose. The game was only four minutes old and new coach Hierro must have been wondering what he had walked into.

Spain quickly began to regain their composure, with David Silva's snap-shot just clearing the Portuguese crossbar. Then, with 24 minutes gone, Spain played an uncharacteristic long ball, aiming for the combative Diego Costa who was isolated up front. Costa challenged Pepe for the high ball and the experienced centre-back went down, clutching his face, but play continued and Costa moved into the area, his path to goal shielded by a defender. A step inside, followed by another outside, managed to clear a tiny space for the Spanish forward as five Portuguese players converged on him, before firing the ball into the bottom corner. As the Spanish celebrated, the Portuguese surrounded the referee to no avail. The replay looked inconclusive – Costa's arm seemed to have brushed Pepe, but the former Real Madrid man also did seem to overreact and it hadn't helped his case that, as soon as no whistle sounded, he bounced up to try and help the defence, seemingly OK.

Spain now had the momentum, and their passing game began to tick again. Iniesta stroked one of his typical slide-rule passes through to Jordi Alba but it was narrowly cut out. The ball fell on the edge of the area to Isco who blasted it against the underside of the crossbar. It looked like Alba would bundle the ball in as it bounced down, but Portuguese keeper Rui Patrício made a great stop. Isco appealed but the referee indicated that goal-line technology showed that the ball had not crossed the line. It had been a narrow escape for Portugal.

Spain were purring and a lovely move made up of their characteristic short passes saw Andrés Iniesta come close to giving them a first-half lead. It seemed like the two teams would be tied at the break until a ball forward was well controlled by Portuguese forward Gonçalo Guedes. As he turned, the ball was poked away from him, falling to Ronaldo on the edge of the area whose shot was low and hard, but straight at de Gea. Horrified Spanish fans looked on as de Gea bent to stop the shot, only to find the ball squirming through his grasp and rolling on into the net. Against the run of play, Portugal were ahead again and Ronaldo had his second, knee-sliding in celebration as a stunned de Gea stared up at the heavens.

Looking to get level once again, Iniesta earned Spain a free kick just outside the penalty area ten minutes into the second half. Silva floated the ball towards the far post where Sergio Busquets outjumped his marker to head the ball right across the area for Costa to poke in his second. Spain were back on level terms and the game was turning into a personal duel between Costa and Ronaldo.

Once again the momentum was with Spain, and this time, they took full advantage. Some more beautiful short passing around the Portuguese penalty area saw the ball break to full-back Nacho running in on the right. Without breaking stride, Nacho slammed the ball across the goal and in off the post. It was a venomous strike that Rui Patrício could do nothing about, redeeming Nacho after giving away the penalty earlier. In the space of just three minutes, Spain had completely turned the game on its head.

As the game moved towards the end, Spain seemed to have everything under control. Pulling players back deeper, they set up to see it out, and with a couple of minutes left the plan was working, with little threat to the Spanish goal. But then a long ball to Ronaldo saw him brought down from behind right on the edge of the penalty area. It was the one thing Spanish fans must have been dreading – a late chance for Ronaldo to have a clear strike at goal, free kicks being one of his several specialties. Could the captain save his side and secure a World Cup hat-trick?

With the wall set, Ronaldo strode back and took a deep breath, staring intently at the target, his face a picture of intense concentration. Stepping forward, his shot dipped over the wall and into the top corner, de Gea rooted to the spot. It was absolute perfection. When the moment came, Portugal's leader had once again delivered.

There was still time for late scares as first Portuguese substitute Ricardo Quaresma weaved into the area before his shot was blocked, and then a Ronaldo header sailed narrowly wide. But in the end the two Iberian rivals shared the points in a thoroughly entertaining game. My family and I finished our beers and wandered off into the night, happy to have witnessed such a match under a cool Lisbon sky.

Final score
Portugal 3 (Ronaldo 4 pen, 44, 88) Spain 3 (Costa 24, 55; Nacho 58)

What was the aftermath?

With Morocco and Iran the other two teams in the group, Spain and Portugal went on to qualify for the knockout stages, Spain taking the top spot by virtue of goals scored as both teams remained unbeaten. Surprisingly, neither side would get through the round of 16. Portugal were eliminated by an Edinson Cavani double against Uruguay while Spain were taken to penalties by hosts Russia in a packed Luzhniki Stadium in Moscow, where misses by Koke and Iago Aspas saw them join Portugal on an early flight home.

Teams

Portugal: Rui Patrício, Cédric, Pepe, Fonte, Guerreiro, Carvalho, Moutinho, B. Silva (Quaresma 69), Guedes (A. Silva 80), Fernandes (João Mário 68), Ronaldo (c)
Manager: Santos

Spain: de Gea, Nacho, Piqué, Ramos (c), Alba, Busquets, Koke, Silva (Vázquez 86), Isco, Iniesta (Thiago 70), Costa (Aspas 77)
Manager: Hierro

Iconic moment

It could only be the 88th-minute free kick by Ronaldo. As soon as it was awarded, you just knew that he would deliver, as he so often has for both club and country. A player born for the big moment and the spotlight, he was a study in focus as he prepared to take the kick, before his perfect technique did the rest. It was a just reward for the endless hours spent on the training ground – something that Ronaldo has a deserved reputation for. Often quoted as first to arrive and last to leave training sessions, Ronaldo showed that hard work mixed with genius is a powerful combination.

Trivia fact

Playing in the 2022 finals in Qatar, Ronaldo became the first player to score in five World Cup tournaments when he found the net against Ghana. His overall tally is not overly impressive, eight goals over 18 appearances, but his longevity is. At the time of writing, Ronaldo has scored 128 goals for the Portugal first team over 205 appearances – making him both the top scorer for any international team in history as well as the only player to earn 200 caps for their national side. A remarkable player indeed.

Black, Blanc, Beur – French fans celebrate by the Arc de Triomphe after Zidane's double against Brazil

How can a cockerel eat a lion? – Senegalese El Hadji Diouf torments the French in the 2002 World Cup opener

Just because we're paranoid doesn't mean they're not out to get us – referee Byron Moreno ignores Italian protests

But did you really mean it? – England's David Seaman scrambles back in vain as Ronaldinho's free kick nestles in the top corner

The ultimate redemption story – Ronaldo celebrates one of his two goals against Germany in the 2002 World Cup Final

The late, late show – Cahill is mobbed by Australian team-mates as his two late goals sink Japan

The Battle of Nuremberg – Portuguese midfielder Figo receives one of sixteen yellow cards

Non ci credo! – Azzurri ecstasy as Italy's Fabio Grosso sets off in celebration

It's a lonely job – French manager Raymond Domenech gets that sinking feeling in South Africa

Where's VAR when you need it? – German keeper Manuel Neuer looks back as Frank Lampard's ghost goal passes him

Morality vs winning at all costs – Uruguay's Luiz Suárez sets off a philosophical debate as he denies Ghana a last-minute winner

It was so much easier playing – Maradona can only watch on as Germany hammer his Argentina side in 2010

Defying physics – Robin van Persie's iconic header as the Netherlands crush World Champions Spain

A nation in shock – a Brazilian fan struggles to come to terms with their 7-1 defeat to Germany in the Maracanã

Yet another hat-trick – Portugal's Cristiano Ronaldo celebrates rescuing the Seleção das Quinas against neighbours Spain in 2018

Sweeper keeper failure – German keeper Manuel Neuer is robbed in the South Korean half as Germany exit the group stage

Off to the races – a teenage Kylian Mbappe shows his blistering pace against Argentina

A 10-second breakaway – Belgium's Nacer Chadli scores a stoppage-time winner as the Red Devils overcome the Blue Samurai

Good evening, Moscow! – French President Macron does his best 'Mick Jagger' as France win the 2018 World Cup

Football comes to the Arab world – Saudi Arabia players celebrate with their fans after shocking Argentina in their opening match

Do you think this is a little too much? – Japan's fans light up the 2022 World Cup ahead of their clash with Germany

Surely the ball is out?! – Spanish fans realise a ball is a sphere as Mitoma sets up Japan's winner

A bad case of déjà vu – German players contemplate a second successive group stage exit

What are you looking at, fool? – things get heated as Argentina and the Netherlands fight the Battle of Lusail

Precious, my precious – Argentinian legend Lionel Messi finally gets his hands on the World Cup trophy to cement his legacy

Game 41
2018 World Cup

Germany v South Korea

27 June 2018
Kazan Arena, Kazan
Attendance: 41,835
Stage: Group F, Round 1

Why you should watch it

Germany – opponents who strike fear around the world in international football. Looking at their World Cup track record since 1950, in 16 tournaments they had been involved in eight finals, winning four, and always got through the first group stage at a minimum. Their achievements are right up there, with only maybe Brazil as a comparable nation. Whenever a World Cup starts, Germany are always pencilled in as one of the favourites – and rightly so.

The prior tournament had seen Germany once again top the world, following on from their defeat of Argentina in the 2014 final. Euro 2016 witnessed a powerful German performance as they reached the semi-finals unbeaten before falling 2-0 to a strong France team in front of 64,000 mostly home fans packed into Marseille's Stade Vélodrome. And if that was not daunting enough for all future opponents, Germany qualified for the 2018 World Cup by winning all ten of their group matches, scoring 43 goals in the process and conceding just four. It was quite the statement and once again marked them as a team to be avoided if possible.

In Asia, meanwhile, South Korea had become one of the most consistently successful teams. They had qualified for every World Cup from 1986 onwards, with their standout performance being in front of their own fans in 2002 when they shocked the world to reach the semi-finals, eliminating Italy and Spain on the way, albeit tinged with controversy.

The 2014 tournament had seen them eliminated in the group stage without registering a win, but they were returning in 2018. Unfortunately, they found themselves in a tough group, thrown together with the defending champions, plus Mexico and Sweden. Given their lacklustre 2014 performance, South Korea were clearly the underdogs, with most experts making them favourites to finish bottom.

South Korea's opening match was against the Swedes – probably their best chance to get a result within the group. A second-half penalty for Sweden and a late spurned headed opportunity meant that the Koreans got off to a bad start, and they would need a result against Mexico to avoid being almost eliminated after just two matches. Once again, they found themselves down following a penalty before a second Mexican goal from Javier Hernández decided the affair. As the game approached its conclusion, South Korea were looking at 288 minutes since last scoring in a World Cup finals match, but that drought was ended when Son Heung-min grabbed a consolation goal in the 93rd minute. But it still ended with another defeat for the Koreans.

Mexico's win came on the back of a great opening game when they had shocked Germany by beating them 1-0 in Moscow, courtesy of a Hirving Lozano goal after 35 minutes and an outstanding defensive performance, especially goalkeeper Guillermo Ochoa. Germany registered 26 shots but could not get on the scoresheet. It appeared to be 'just one of those games' – there was no doubt Germany had dominated but luck was not on their side.

Normal service was expected as Germany faced Sweden next – but *Die Mannschaft* found themselves 1-0 down at half-time. Suddenly facing the possibility of two defeats, and an early exit, they managed to draw level early in the second half through Marco Reus, but then saw Jérôme Boateng sent off with eight minutes remaining. Sweden came close to snatching a win before Germany won a free kick in the 95th minute. Situated on the left-hand side of the area, expectations were of a cross swung into the centre, but instead Toni Kroos tapped it to Reus, who tapped it back for Kroos to whip into the top corner. Germany had looked World Cup elimination in the face and escaped with the latest winner ever scored in a finals game up to that point in time.

And so it was that South Korea and Germany met in the final group match. The Koreans still had a mathematical chance to progress – they would need to beat the Germans by two goals and hope Mexico beat Sweden – a chance that their manager Shin Tae-yong placed at 'one per cent'. For Germany, a two-goal win would take them through automatically. But they had shown themselves to be vulnerable in their first two matches. Would Germany get the win they needed, or could South Korea score a major upset?

What happened?

The two teams walked out into a packed Kazan Arena, bathed in afternoon sunshine – the South Koreans cheered on by their army of Red Devils supporters while the Germans sported their change kit of green jerseys. Conditions for the game were hot, something both teams would need to take into consideration when pacing themselves. The early running saw Germany dominating play but without really troubling the Korean goal, until then, against the run of play, a Korean free kick saw Jung Woo-young strike a nasty knuckleball that German keeper Manuel Neuer couldn't hold, instead managing to parry the ball to safety just ahead of an onrushing forward. The chance seemed to build Korean confidence and next a shot from Son Heung-min narrowly missed after 24 minutes. Back came Germany again but still they found it difficult to penetrate a well-organised Korean defence, and the first half ended goalless.

In the other match, Mexico and Sweden were also goalless after 45 minutes. That meant that, as the second half got underway, the live table had Mexico on seven points,

Germany on four, Sweden on three and South Korea on one. Both the Swedes and Koreans needed goals to try and open their paths.

Early in the second half, Germany had the perfect chance to open the scoring. A cross from Joshua Kimmich found Leon Goretzka completely unmarked in the middle of the penalty area; his powerful header was goal-bound before Korean keeper Jo Hyeon-woo threw a strong gloved hand out to deny him. It was the clearest chance so far. Germany were now on a roll, another chance quickly falling to striker Timo Werner who sliced wide.

It was at this point that news came through of a Swedish goal, meaning that the live table now had Sweden and Mexico on six points each in the top two spots, with Germany still on four and South Korea on one. Germany were facing elimination from a first-round group stage for the first time while South Korea were doomed whatever happened. German urgency picked up, but as they pushed forward, Sweden continued to press their advantage, scoring twice more so that, with 16 minutes remaining in both games, they were looking safely through, while Mexico now had to hope that the Koreans could continue to hold Germany at bay.

Germany continued to make chances – a header from substitute Mario Gómez was well saved before Gómez again came close to poking in at the near post. It was all one-way traffic now as Germany pushed for the vital goal, leaving themselves open to a counterattack. They continued to take shots from distance, not overly troubling the Korean goal, but this was Germany – it just felt like a matter of time before they would break through.

And then with four minutes remaining, an inswinging cross found Mats Hummels in the area. As the German fans leapt in anticipation, joy turned to horror as they watched the ball bounce off his shoulder and over the bar. Hummels held his head in disbelief – it had looked like a certain goal coming and with the game entering stoppage time, the world watched to see if Germany were really going out.

Four minutes into stoppage time, Korea won a corner. A low ball in bounced around before falling to defender Kim Young-gwon, unmarked on the edge of the six-yard box. Hardly able to believe his luck, he shot past Neuer and the Korean fans exploded into celebration until they spotted the linesman's flag raised. It went to a VAR check; they recommended the referee go to the monitor and after a moment he pointed back to the centre circle. Korea had snatched a possible late winner.

But with nine minutes of stoppage time, there was still time for Germany to create one more chance, again falling to Hummels whose header again cleared the crossbar. As German desperation increased, Neuer came forward. Losing the ball in the Korean half himself, he watched helplessly as a long ball was launched into the German half for Son to chase all alone. Getting to the ball just before it ran out of play, he side-footed it into the empty net and, unbelievably, it was all over for *Die Mannschaft*.

As the final whistle blew, the German players slumped to the ground as the commentator declared, 'It has turned into a nightmarish road in Russia and Germany comes to an end.' The world champions had fallen at the first hurdle for the first time in their history.

Final score
South Korea 2 (Kim Young-gwon 90+4; Son Heung-Min 90+6)
Germany 0

What was the aftermath?

Sadly for South Korea, while they had defied the odds and achieved their two-goal victory over Germany, it was not enough to see them move on to the knockout phase following Sweden's victory over Mexico. But they could head home from the tournament with their heads held high and a historic victory under their belts.

The same could not be said for Germany, heading home after the group stage for the first time. German press were unforgiving in their reactions – *Bild* went with 'Speechless', the same headline it used when Germany thrashed Brazil 7-1 but now applied to losing to South Korea. *Die Welt* claimed 'Over and out', the *Rheinische Post* simply said 'Out', while *Frankfurter Allgemeine* highlighted 'Germany's downfall'. Former German players also lashed out, Michael Ballack posting on social media, 'You can always go out early with a bad team, but not with a team like this one!! Honest assessment must start!! Leadership? Personality? Mentality?'

A lot of praise was lavished on to South Korea's goalkeeper, Jo Hyeon-woo, who had not been beaten despite 28 German shots. Given that Mexico qualified thanks to the Koreans' victory, someone on Wikipedia updated his home page to read, 'He is also known as the Mexican Saviour or the one true god.' Surprisingly, coach Joachim Löw stayed on after the tournament. Germany's woes continued over the next three years, including a 6-0 loss to Spain in the 2020/21 UEFA Nations League and defeat to England in Euro 2020, which would prove to be his undoing, causing his 15 years in the job to finally end.

Teams

South Korea: Jo Hyeon-woo, Lee Yong, Yun Young-sun, Kim Young-gwon, Hong Chul, Lee Jae-sung, Jung Woo-young, Jang Hyun-soo, Moon Seon-min (Ju Se-jong 69), Koo Ja-cheol (Hwang Hee-chan 56 [Go Yo-han 79]), Son Heung-min (c)

Manager: Tae-yong

Germany: Neuer (c), Kimmich, Hummels, Süle, Hector (Brandt 78), Khedira (Gómez 58), Kroos, Goretzka (Müller 63), Özil, Reus, Werner

Manager: Löw

Iconic moment

The sight of Manuel Neuer playing as a midfielder as Germany went all out to try and find an equaliser in the dying minutes. While Neuer is famous for his ability with his feet for a goalkeeper, it is not his full-time profession and it showed as he lost possession and allowed South Korea to launch the ball forward for Son Heung-min to tap into an empty net. It summed up Germany's desperation at that moment.

Trivia fact

Given the inferiority complex that England has felt in relation to Germany for decades in footballing terms, there was a certain amount of gloating in the English press. *The Sun* went with a full front-page headline that read 'Schadenfreude – noun (from the German): Pleasure derived from another person's misfortune', while *The Times* said 'Day the Germans just disappeared'. Given the events of 2014, Brazilians also derived some pleasure from Germany's downfall, with Fox Sports Brazil simply posting 'AHAHAHAHAHAHAHAHAHAH' on social media. Neither England nor Brazil would go on to win the tournament, so it was a case of gloating while they could.

Game 42

2018 World Cup

Argentina v France

30 June 2018

Kazan Arena, Kazan

Attendance: 42,873

Stage: Round of 16

WORLD CUP CLASSIC

Why you should watch it

As the 2018 World Cup rolled around, there were two players vying for the title of best player in the world. Cristiano Ronaldo had won five Ballon d'Or awards out of the last ten, including the most recent two, while the other five had gone to Argentinian superstar Lionel Messi. They were clearly in a league of their own.

While both were recognised for their outstanding contributions to their respective clubs – Ronaldo for Real Madrid and Messi for Barcelona – Ronaldo had achieved more at an international level. He could point to leading Portugal to the 2016 European Championship, while Messi could not point to any international titles while representing Argentina. Argentina had reached the 2014 World Cup Final, but Messi had been quiet during that match, and they had also reached the finals of the last two Copa América tournaments but again had lost both, to Chile in 2015 and 2016. There was a feeling that, to really enter the pantheon of greats, Messi needed to lead Argentina to a tournament victory and until that time, talk would always be of how Maradona had won the 1986 World Cup and so Messi could not be compared without a similar achievement.

So it was that Messi and Argentina entered the 2018 World Cup with that pressure upon them. They had come close in 2014, losing the final to an extra-time goal from Mario Götze for Germany, and hence they desperately wanted to go one step further. They had been less than convincing during the CONMEBOL qualification process, requiring a Messi hat-trick in their final game against Ecuador to assure themselves of a place in Russia, and that shaky form had continued into the group stage where, drawn alongside Croatia, Nigeria, and Iceland, they opened by only drawing against the Icelandic minnows. That was followed by a 3-0 beating by Croatia, leaving Argentina needing to defeat Nigeria in the final match to move on to the round of 16. With four minutes left the teams were tied, and Argentina were facing a group-stage exit. It was then that Marcos Rojo saved *La Albiceleste* with a late winner meaning Argentina were through by the skin of their teeth.

Coming second in their group, they would face the winners of Group C, the strong France team including the likes of Paul Pogba, Antoine Griezmann and Raphaël Varane. But there was also a young striker within their team who was starting to garner international attention.

In December 2015, Kylian Mbappé broke into the first team at Monaco and made his debut at the tender age of 16 years and 347 days. The next season, 2016/17, saw Mbappé establish himself as an extremely promising talent, becoming part of the Monaco team that won the Ligue 1 title and reached the Champions League semi-final, scoring 26 goals in 44 matches. That led to a loan move to Paris Saint-Germain where his form resulted in a call-up to the French squad for the 2018 World Cup, having represented them 15 times to date, scoring four goals. He was an exciting prospect, but it needed to be remembered that he was just 19 years old – a teenager on the ultimate stage.

The group stage saw France open with a 2-1 victory over Australia in which Mbappé did not score, but did become the youngest French player to start a World Cup match. Next up were Peru and, after 34 minutes, Mbappé became

France's youngest scorer at a World Cup, when at 19 years and 183 days he tapped the ball into an empty net following a deflected shot from Olivier Giroud. It was the deciding goal that, followed by a goalless draw with Denmark where Mbappé was rested on the bench, saw France ease into the round of 16.

All eyes turned to the upcoming clash between Argentina and France. Would Messi lead Argentina towards that first tournament win he so craved to make his mark on history or would *Les Bleus*, and their teenage sensation, succeed? The game did not disappoint.

What happened?

France got the game underway on a beautiful, sunny afternoon in Kazan. Early on, Mbappé showed his turn of pace, running at the Argentine defence and drawing a free kick as they panicked to stop him. Antoine Griezmann took responsibility and hit a beauty over the wall, curling and dipping right towards the top corner, where, with keeper Franco Armani rooted to the spot, it rattled off the crossbar back into play – just eight minutes gone and so nearly a French lead.

A couple of minutes later, a lack of control by Argentina in the France half let Mbappé break up the play. Immediately he sprinted forward, leaving three defenders floundering as he crossed the halfway line. His pace was terrifying as he just kept flying in a straight line until suddenly it was just Marcos Rojo between himself and the penalty box whereupon Mbappé accelerated again, burning past Rojo who tried to catch him but could only succeed in bringing him down in the penalty area. There was no hesitation from the referee – it was a clear foul. Mbappé had run two-thirds of the pitch at a searing pace – a terrifying sight for Argentinian players and fans.

Having come so close with the earlier free kick, Griezmann slotted the penalty calmly past Armani to give France a 13th-minute lead, before breaking into a somewhat bizarre goal celebration that resembled a drunk dwarf dancing.

Mbappé was proving hard to deal with, and just five minutes later Paul Pogba hit a long ball forward towards him as he sprinted through the defensive line. With one sublime touch he brought the ball under control at speed before being brought down by Nicolás Tagliafico. It looked right on the edge of the area – and nervous eyes turned to the referee, who signalled a free kick. This time Pogba tried his luck – his effort clearing the crossbar, but it was evident that Argentina just could not cope with the speed of Mbappé.

Slowly Argentina started to get back into the game, with a possible shout for a handball in the penalty area declined just before the half-hour. With four minutes remaining of the half, some neat passing found Ángel Di María unmarked around ten yards outside the penalty area. Allowed plenty of time, Di María cued up the shot, before unleashing a left-footed arrow into the corner. It was a beauty that Hugo Lloris could do nothing about; Argentina had drawn level at just the right time and a watching Diego Maradona, resplendent in sunglasses, punched the air in celebration.

Almost straight from the second half kicking off, Di María weaved between French defenders, drawing a foul to the left of the penalty area. The free kick was chipped in and found Messi at the far post where, trying a left-footed shot, he saw it deflect off team-mate Gabriel Mercado into the French goal to give Argentina the lead. It was lucky but the blue and white army of supporters weren't complaining – in the space of just seven minutes across both halves, they had turned the game around.

Immediately Mbappé tried one of his runs but Argentina were now doubling up on him – a foul by Di María was followed by Éver Benega following in to provide the first flashpoint of the match. France were then almost gifted an equaliser when a mix-up between Armani and substitute Federico Fazio allowed Griezmann to narrowly miss.

Then came another moment of magic. French midfielder Blaise Matuidi hit a beautiful ball up the line, inside the Argentinian defender, for left-back Lucas Hernandez to chase down and hit a first-time cross towards the edge of the penalty area. Suddenly right-back Benjamin Pavard appeared at full speed and, without breaking stride, smashed a first-time shot past Armani. The ball flew like a missile – he could not have hit it better however many times he repeated the attempt – his striking technique perfect. It was sublime and France were level again.

France had their tails up, and shortly afterwards Pogba sent a ball out to the right, where Hernandez again found space before whipping a cross in. The ball bobbled before settling at the feet of Mbappé. With lightning speed, he turned outside a defender to make space before firing it low and hard under Armani and, just as Argentina had scored twice in seven minutes, France had now done the same, meaning the lead changed for the third time. The teenager was announcing himself in front of a worldwide audience while Messi could only rub his eyes in disbelief as the game swung back and forth.

Argentina brought on Sergio Agüero – six years after that famous winner against QPR for Manchester City which catapulted him into legend – but it was all France. With Argentina still trying to regain their composure, Matuidi fed the ball forward to Olivier Giroud who flicked it into the path of the onrushing Mbappé. Without breaking stride, Mbappé slid the ball under Armani for a third French goal – and his second – in the space of just 11 minutes. It was fast, slick, one-touch football and Argentina were reeling.

One minute later, and Giroud almost added a fifth as France became rampant. Mbappé had a chance for a hat-trick but, for the first time all day, miscontrolled the ball and lost the opportunity. As the clock ticked down, Messi finally set off on one of his weaving runs, before weakly shooting straight at Lloris. It looked like it wasn't to be his day yet again.

The game moved into stoppage time before a cross from Messi found Agüero at the back post and his header beat Lloris to give Argentina a late glimmer of hope. There was still time for Nicolás Otamendi to pick up a yellow card for deliberately slamming the ball into a prone Pogba in frustration, leading to more shoving, but then it was all over; a fantastic game that had swung this way and that ended up with France winners. A sad Messi stared into space as French celebrations broke out around him – Mbappé, the centre of attention. A new superstar was forming.

Final score
France 4 (Griezmann 13 pen; Pavard 57; Mbappé 64, 68) Argentina 3 (Di María 41; Mercado 48; Agüero 90+3)

What was the aftermath?

This was the game that cemented Kylian Mbappé's reputation as the next big global star. While many were conscious of his potential before this tournament, his two goals and constant threat during this match made the whole world aware. His two goals were the first time that any teenager had scored twice in a tournament since Michael Owen in 1998 and the first time any teenager had scored twice in a World Cup finals match since the great Pelé in 1958.

And that reputation would only increase as the tournament progressed. France would eventually reach the World Cup Final – a game which will be highlighted later in this book, where I will discuss Mbappé's post-World Cup career some more.

As for Argentina and Messi, it was disappointment again. Immediately after the game, talk turned to internal issues within the camp, with rumours of discontent within the dressing room. There was talk that Messi was influencing team selection. There was discussion that manager Jorge Sampaoli was not getting the best out of

Messi. The elimination meant that Messi had now played 756 minutes of World Cup knockout round football and never scored a goal.

While he was enjoying a stellar club career at Barcelona, winning multiple La Liga and Champions League trophies in the greatest team of that era, he couldn't crack international success. He had been involved in four World Cups, coming close in 2014 when reaching the final, as well as four Copa Américas, where Argentina had suffered the agony of losing three finals. Messi had been so close to lifting a significant trophy for so long, but it still was not to be. The albatross would finally be removed in 2021, when Messi captained *La Albiceleste* to a single-goal victory over Brazil in the Maracanã, allowing him to finally proudly lift the Copa América aloft.

Teams

France: Lloris (c), Pavard, Varane, Umtiti, Hernandez, Kanté, Pogba, Mbappé (Thauvin 89), Griezmann (Fekir 83), Matuidi (Tolisso 75), Giroud
Manager: Deschamps
Argentina: Armani, Mercado, Otamendi, Rojo (Fazio HT), Tagliafico, Pérez (Agüero 66), Mascherano, Banega, Pavón (Meza 75), Messi (c), Di María
Manager: Sampaoli

Iconic moment

The run from Mbappé that resulted in the opening penalty. The speed with which he took off after collecting the ball in his own half was phenomenal and then to just use that speed to head almost in a straight line for the opponents' goal was incredible. He was indifferent to what was happening around him – his only aim was to just burn past everyone and he did exactly that, until the only way Argentina could stop him scoring was to bundle him over. It showed a confidence that only a teenager can have, combined with great ability.

Trivia fact

After the tournament ended, FIFA opened voting to the public for the goal of the tournament. Over three million votes were logged and once everything had been tallied there was a clear winner as Benjamin Pavard's screamer during this match deservedly took the award. As of the time of writing, Pavard has played for France 52 times and only scored on five occasions, with his first goal for *Les Bleus* being this one. Not a bad way to break your duck.

Game 43

2018 World Cup

Belgium v Japan

2 July 2018

Rostov Arena, Rostov-on-Don

Attendance: 41,466

Stage: Round of 16

WORLD CUP CLASSIC

Why you should watch it

Like their neighbours the Netherlands, Belgium often punch above their weight in major tournaments. The 1986 World Cup saw them reach the semi-finals before being eliminated by the skill of Maradona in his prime, then 1990 saw them reach the round of 16 before being undeservedly eliminated by England and David Platt's last-gasp winner. They also qualified for the 1994, 1998 and 2002 World Cups; 2002 had seen the Red Devils placed in the same group as co-hosts Japan, with whom they had drawn 2-2 in the opening group game, with all four goals scored in an eventful second half. They ended up finishing second behind the Japanese, resulting in a round of 16 match against Brazil which they lost 2-0.

Since 2002, however, Belgium had fallen on hard times. They had failed to qualify for the 2006 and 2010 World Cups, as well as the 2004, 2008 and 2012 European Championships – an unheard-of barren spell for them. But, as that era came to an end, a new generation of talent was starting to blossom. The 2014 World Cup saw Belgium win all their group games, before eliminating USA after extra time to set up a quarter-final against Argentina, which proved one step too far as they narrowly lost 1-0. It was a squad that contained the likes of Thibaut Courtois, Toby Alderweireld, Thomas Vermaelen, Vincent Kompany, Jan Vertonghen, Axel Witsel, Kevin De

Bruyne, Romelu Lukaku, Eden Hazard and Dries Mertens – who all played club football at the highest level. There was a feeling within world football that this Belgium squad would be competing for major honours over the next decade.

The 2016 Euros ended in disappointment as the Red Devils were shocked by a 3-1 defeat in the quarter-finals to Wales, and so they came into the 2018 World Cup with a squad that was yet to fulfil its undoubted potential. Responsibility lay with manager Roberto Martínez to lead the team deep into the tournament and Belgium looked fantastic in the group stage, winning all three games (including beating England 1-0), with striker Lukaku grabbing four goals. That gave them a round of 16 tie against the runners-up of Group H.

Japan had become the strongest team from Asia, appearing in every World Cup from 1998 to 2018 (including 2002 when they qualified automatically as co-hosts). In 2002 and 2010 they got out of the group stage, only to fall in the round of 16 to Turkey and Paraguay respectively, but both eliminations were close affairs – it felt like Japan were cursed to have the round of 16 as their ultimate ceiling.

The 2018 finals saw Japan placed into Group H, where they surprised again by beating a strong Colombia team 2-1 in their opening match, becoming the first Asian nation to beat South American opposition at a World Cup, helped by Colombia being reduced to ten men after just three minutes when a straight red card was issued to Carlos Sánchez, resulting in a penalty that Shinji Kagawa converted. Next, they twice came back from behind to draw 2-2 with Senegal before a 1-0 defeat to Poland condemned them to second place in the group. That would set them up for a meeting with Belgium and a rematch from 2002. Would this game be a similarly dramatic affair with a second half to remember?

What happened?

The game got underway with Belgium in all red and Japan in all blue on a beautiful evening in Rostov. Early on, the ball was played out wide to Mertens, who whipped in a quick cross right to the feet of Lukaku on the edge of the six-yard box. As a goal looked inevitable, the ball got caught under Lukaku's feet and Japan were able to scramble clear, but it was an early reminder of what this Belgian team was capable of. Japan started to settle into the game, creating a couple of chances through firstly a header from Takashi Inui and then a deflection from Yuya Osako that almost embarrassed Courtois. But to be honest, that was about all there was to the first half. As in 2002, the teams went into the break goalless with nothing to indicate that the game would be a memorable one.

As the second half commenced, there was a feeling that the contest needed a goal to spark it into life, and just three minutes in it got one.

Inui broke up a Belgian attack inside his own half and passed it forward to Gaku Shibasaki. Looking up, he played an inch-perfect pass behind Vertonghen into the path of the onrushing Genki Haraguchi. As Vertonghen tried to recover ground, Haraguchi settled himself before striking the ball past Courtois, and it nestled into the corner of the net. Haraguchi ran to the bench to be mobbed by team-mates and substitutes alike. Were Japan on their way to a major upset and a first quarter-final spot?

Suddenly it was a completely different game. Almost straight from the kick-off, Belgium launched an attack of their own that saw the ball break to an unmarked Eden Hazard on the edge of the penalty area, only for his first-time curling shot to come back off the post. Back came Japan whose subsequent attack broke down outside the Belgian area. Recycling play, the ball was played back to Inui, who stopped to consider his options before deciding to merely lash a shot into the bottom corner from distance. Seven minutes of the second half had elapsed and Japan had leapt into a two-goal lead. Inui again ran to the bench, his mouth wide open in apparent amazement at what he had just done, as it looked like Belgium's golden generation was going to miss another opportunity to achieve its potential.

Belgium had to lift their game now and the next chance again fell to Lukaku, who really should have scored with a close-range header that went wide. His facial expression summed up the frustration that the Red Devils must have been feeling at that moment, with nothing seeming to go his way. With 25 minutes remaining, manager Martínez gambled on a double substitution, bringing Marouane Fellaini and Nacer Chadli into the fray, knowing he had to try something to change the course of the game.

One of Fellaini's first touches of the ball was to win Belgium a corner. De Bruyne's cross pinballed around before being hit high into the air towards Vertonghen on the left side of the penalty area. As he watched the ball drop, his options seemed limited – most likely a header back into the middle – but instead, he powered a looping header over keeper Eiji Kawashima and into the top corner. It was a tremendous goal, a moment of magic, and dragged Belgium back into the game with 20 minutes remaining.

The match was now fast and furious as Belgium went after an equaliser. De Bruyne saw an effort blocked by defender Gen Shoji as he threw himself in front of the shot. From the corner, Belgium maintained the pressure, the ball eventually coming back out to Hazard on the left wing. Some neat trickery saw him create space to throw in a cross enabling the tall Fellaini to outjump the Japanese defence and head in an equaliser. Martínez's gamble had paid off and with 16 minutes remaining it looked like there could only be one winner – Belgium were flying.

Given the situation, it would have been completely understandable if shell-shocked Japan had withdrawn and tried to get into extra time, but instead they continued to attack and try to take the game to Belgium. Some sloppy defending allowed Kagawa to play in Inui whose shot was smothered by sliding Belgian defenders. It was edge-of-your-seat stuff as next Chadli saw his header well saved before chipping the rebound back in for Lukaku, whose close-range powerful header was again tipped over the bar by Kawashima – a spectacular double save from the 35-year-old. Back came Japan again and Courtois had to be alert to prevent a Witsel own goal. The tie was being played at a frantic pace as both teams seemed determined to win it in regular time.

The board went up to indicate four minutes of stoppage time. Still Japan pushed forward, earning a free kick that saw Courtois parry Honda's effort around the post. It was now deep into stoppage time and Japan's corner was confidently handled by Courtois, who immediately looked for a quick throw opportunity. Seeing Belgium players rushing out of his area, he rolled it into the path of De Bruyne who set off at speed through his own half, flanked by breaking colleagues. With Japan trying to get back and short in defence, De Bruyne advanced into their half before playing the ball wide to a sprinting Thomas Meunier, who played a first-time pass into Lukaku, who dummied and allowed it to run on for Chadli to slot in from close range. It had taken just seconds for Belgium to go from one end of the pitch to the other and both substitutes had now scored. As the Belgians broke into wild celebrations, the Japanese players were devastated, collapsing to the ground. They had gambled by pushing forward on the late corner, only to be punished, but it had been a valiant effort. Japan kicked off, but that would prove to be the last touch of the game – Belgium had come back from 2-0 down to win with almost the last kick. In the words of the great Sir Alex Ferguson, 'Football. Bloody hell.'

Final score
Belgium 3 (Vertonghen 69; Fellaini 74; Chadli 90+4)
Japan 2 (Haraguchi 48; Inui 52)

What was the aftermath?

As the dust settled on the drama, it was noted that Belgium had become the first team to come back from a two-goal deficit in a knockout-stage game and win inside 90 minutes since Portugal had recovered from 3-0 down against North Korea to win 5-3 in 1966 – a gap of 52 years which was testament to what the Belgians had achieved. They had been 2-0 down with 21 minutes remaining and still managed to turn it around; maybe the golden generation was finally going to prove itself on the highest stage.

Next up for the Red Devils was a quarter-final date with the mighty Brazilians, and if they could get past them, then they would indeed be serious contenders for the trophy. Two first-half goals set them on their way, and despite Brazil pulling one back in the second half, Belgium emerged victorious to reach the semi-finals for only the second time, the previous being back in 1986 against Maradona in his prime. There they would meet their neighbours – a strong France team with emerging superstar Kylian Mbappé. A tight game was settled by a Samuel Umtiti header, meaning that Belgium suffered their first defeat of any kind since losing to Spain in a friendly back in September 2016. They had come frustratingly close but had to settle for a respectable third place after defeating England 2-0 in the meaningless play-off.

Meanwhile, Japan went home to great praise from all. The game had been aired at 3am in Japan but thanks to #NebusokuJapan trending – which translated to 'lack of sleep Japan' – huge numbers watched on. Their fans had lit up the tournament and they had played with an attacking spirit. Their naivety may have cost them in the end but no one could fault them for having a go. They had, however, to face the heartbreak of yet again not being able to get past the round of 16.

Teams

Belgium: Courtois, Alderweireld, Kompany, Vertonghen, Meunier, De Bruyne, Witsel, Carrasco (Fellaini 65), Mertens (Chadli 65), Lukaku, Hazard (c)
Manager: Martínez

Japan: Kawashima, Sakai, Yoshida, Shoji, Nagatomo, Hasebe (c), Shibasaki (Yamaguchi 81), Haraguchi (Honda 81), Kagawa, Inui, Osaka
Manager: Nishino

Iconic moment

The break that led to the winning goal for Belgium. From the moment that Courtois rolled the ball out to De Bruyne to the moment that the ball crossed the line was just ten seconds but, in that time, the Belgian players managed to cover the whole length of the field, despite most of them having played 94 minutes at that stage. It was the very definition of a 'lightning-fast break' and the ultimate sucker punch.

Trivia fact

One of the saddest aspects of the last-minute defeat to Belgium was the loss of the Japanese fans. They had travelled to Russia in numbers and lit up the tournament with their enthusiasm and their painted faces. But what really impressed world audiences was their behaviour after every game. Not content to run off and party somewhere, instead they took the time first to clean up their area of the stadium. Footage went viral of supporters with bin bags picking up rubbish post-match with the explanation that Japanese society values cleanliness, and it is ingrained from an early age to clean surrounding areas. Whatever the explanation, it just made everyone love them even more and mourn their elimination.

Game 44
2018 World Cup

Croatia v France

15 July 2018
Luzhniki Stadium, Moscow
Attendance: 78,011
Stage: Final

Why you should watch it

The 12th World Cup that I have covered in this book so far, and only the fourth inclusion of a World Cup Final. Admittedly the 1986 final between Argentina and West Germany almost made the cut – if this had been 60 great games it would have been included – but so often finals are cagey affairs, unsurprising given the stakes, but sometimes to the detriment of the neutral viewer. In fact, it could be argued that the 1990 final was one of the worst games ever seen during any World Cup.

Luckily, the 2018 final ranks as a great game. France were appearing in their third final, having won the World Cup in 1998 before losing to Italy on penalties in 2006, powered by a strong squad. They had entered the tournament as the bookmakers' favourites and had gone through the group stage unbeaten, with only Denmark able to restrict them to a goalless draw. Then came that thriller against Argentina when teenage sensation Kylian Mbappé announced himself to the world with two goals and the winning of a penalty. The quarter-finals saw France comfortably deal with Uruguay 2-0 before they ended the dreams of Belgium's golden generation in the semi-final through a Samuel Umtiti header. *Les Bleus* had lived up to their pre-status as favourites, professionally making their way to the final unbeaten and only conceding four goals, three of which were scored by Argentina. Job well done so far.

The bigger story coming into the final was Croatia. A country with a population of only 3.9 million at the time of writing and covering less than 22,000 square miles that only gained independence in 1991 – they had a strong record to date. Their first venture into the World Cup saw them finish third in 1998, famously beating Germany 3-0 in the quarter-final before narrowly losing to France 2-1 in the semi-final, both goals unexpectedly scored by defender Lilian Thuram. Croatian striker Davor Šuker had been a revelation, receiving the Golden Boot for his six goals, ahead of the likes of Gabriel Batistuta, Christian Vieri and Ronaldo. They had then also qualified for the 2002, 2006 and 2014 tournaments, albeit they were eliminated in the group stage each time.

Qualification for the 2018 World Cup had seen Croatia come second behind a surprise Iceland team, who were achieving new heights for that country, including beating the Croats with a last-minute goal in Reykjavik. In fact, it was that defeat that partially accounted for the sacking of manager Ante Čačić, replaced by Zlatko Dalić in late 2017. Like Belgium at this time, Croatia were also witnessing the blossoming of a great team. The squad for 2018 included the likes of Dejan Lovren (Liverpool), Ivan Rakitić (Barcelona), Mateo Kovačić (Real Madrid), Marcelo Brozović (Inter Milan), Ivan Perišić (Inter Milan) and Mario Mandžukić (Juventus) – players at their peaks playing for top European clubs. And then there was their captain, Luka Modrić. Aged 32 going into the tournament, with over 100 caps, he was a world superstar in his sixth year with Real Madrid. Part of the team that won four Champions League titles in just five years, he would go on to win the Ballon d'Or in 2018. Small in stature, Modrić was the consummate midfielder, skilful in both a defensive and attacking role.

The group stages saw Croatia announce their potential, defeating Nigeria 2-0, Argentina 3-0 and gaining revenge on Iceland with a 2-1 win for a 100 per cent record. Their three knockout games were more tense affairs, with the round of

16 and quarter-finals both won on penalties against Denmark and hosts Russia respectively, before beating England 2-1 in the semi-final after extra time. They had shown their grit along the way, coming from behind in each of the three ties, gaining a reputation for doggedness and not knowing when they were beaten.

The final would see pre-tournament favourites France take on Croatia, a team that fought to the end of every game. A global audience of over one billion sat down to see if it would produce fireworks. They would not be disappointed.

What happened?

With the pre-match show ending on a hot evening, the two teams came out in front of a crowd exceeding 78,000 including dignitaries such as Russian president Vladimir Putin, French president Emmanuel Macron and Croatian president Kolinda Grabar-Kitarović. France lined up in all blue while Croatia wore their trademark red and white checked shirts. Straight away, Croatia applied pressure on *Les Bleus*, pinning them into their own half for much of the opening quarter of an hour. But then Antoine Griezmann drew a foul from Brozović close to the Croatian penalty area. With only Modrić as a wall, both sides filled the penalty area as Griezmann assessed his options. Deciding to float in a cross, the ball seemed to be flicked into the goal by French defender Raphaël Varane before replays showed that it was an unfortunate attempt to clear by Croatian striker Mandžukić that ended up beating his own keeper. The first own goal in a World Cup Final, it was a cruel blow for the player who had scored the winner against England in the semi-final just days earlier, but France had the lead after just 18 minutes.

The question now was whether Croatia could once again show their resilience and come from behind like the previous knockout rounds. Regaining their composure, a run from Perišić through midfield saw him fouled by N'Golo Kanté, earning the midfielder the first yellow card of the match.

Captain Modrić floated the free kick towards the far post where Šime Vrsaljko nodded the ball into the area. A brief spell of head tennis ensued before Perišić shimmied past a defender and fired a left-footed shot into the bottom corner, giving Hugo Lloris no chance. Croatia had been behind for just ten minutes.

Ten minutes later France earned a corner which Griezmann fired towards the near post, where Blaise Matuidi had stolen in front of his marker, Perišić. Narrowly missing Matuidi, the ball came off Perišić to go out for another corner – or so it seemed. But suddenly the French were appealing for handball. Six players turned to the referee simultaneously, all gesturing to their hands – a sign that something suspect had clearly happened. Referee Néstor Pitana of Argentina decided to check on the VAR monitor as TV replays indicated that the ball had struck Perišić's arm, although there was no clear intent. A huge call to make in a World Cup Final, Pitana viewed the replay several times before turning from the screen and pointing to the penalty spot.

Griezmann against Danijel Subašić from 12 yards. Griezmann calmly sent Subašić the wrong way, rolling the ball into the opposite corner, an ominous sign for Croatia as France had never lost a game in which Griezmann had scored.

The half-time whistle indicated the end of an opening 45 minutes in which France had registered just one shot on target and 34 per cent possession, yet were 2-1 ahead. Croatia were playing their part and could feel unlucky to be behind, but at least they could feel that the game was far from over given their dominance.

Croatia started the second half in a similar fashion to the first, attacking France from the off. A run from Rakitić allowed him to feed the ball through to Ante Rebić, whose powerful first-time shot with his left foot was tipped over by Lloris. Up to this stage, Croatia had done well in keeping Mbappé quiet, not allowing him to trouble them with his trademark speed, but a ball from Paul Pogba gave Mbappé his first real opportunity to run at them. His frightening speed saw him streak past defender Domagoj Vida but his shot was then saved by Subašić's feet. It was a warning that, while he may be quiet for periods, Mbappé could change the match in the blink of an eye.

Sensing that Mbappé had Vida concerned, Pogba sprayed another pass from midfield in behind the Croatian for Mbappé to chase down. Mbappé took him on again before sending a pass into the area that found Griezmann. With a little juggle, Griezmann set up Pogba on the edge of the area, whose first-time right-foot shot was blocked, rebounding back to his left foot from which he curled in France's third goal. It was a beautiful strike from the Manchester United midfielder, who, while struggling at club level still produced magic for *Les Bleus*. As Pogba was mobbed by his team and substitutes, French fans celebrated finally putting some daylight between themselves and the Croatians with 30 minutes remaining.

Mbappé was starting to show once again what an exciting talent he was. Just six minutes after Pogba's strike, Lucas Hernandez turned his marker on the wing before laying the ball off to Mbappé a few yards outside the penalty area. One touch to control, one touch to switch it on to his right foot – Mbappé drilled the ball into the bottom corner to send France into ecstasy.

In homage to the great Irish band the Undertones, commentator Peter Drury purred, 'Oh my word, teenage kicks, the ultimate teenage kick. The boy with the world at his feet.' He became only the second teenager to score in a World Cup Final, along with the legendary Pelé. Great company indeed.

France were coasting and needed to just keep things simple and calm while seeing out the game. Nothing stupid, nothing crazy, just play safe, but unfortunately Lloris did not get the memo. Just four minutes after Mbappé seemed to have sealed the trophy, Lloris received an easy back-pass from Umtiti. Slightly mis-controlling the ball, Lloris looked up to see Mandžukić bearing down on him. Instead of clearing to safety, Lloris decided to try and turn inside Mandžukić, who stretched out a leg to tackle Lloris, sending the ball into the empty net. France had gifted Croatia a sliver of hope – a moment of madness in front of a massive worldwide audience.

Realising the gift they had received, Croatia pushed forward looking for a third. An effort from Rakitić was deflected just inches past the far post. But France weren't in the mood to make any further mistakes and eventually the referee's whistle anointed them as world champions for a second time. *Allez Les Bleus.*

Final score
France 4 (Mandžukić 18 og; Griezmann 38 pen; Pogba 59; Mbappé 65) Croatia 2 (Perišić 28; Mandžukić 69)

What was the aftermath?

As the French players celebrated, the heavens opened, and rain poured down upon the stadium. France coach Didier Deschamps looked on proudly, in the knowledge that he had become only the third person to win a World Cup as both a player and manager, alongside Franz Beckenbauer and Mário Zagallo. Captain Lloris raised the trophy up to the sky, happy that his error would now be relegated to the dustbin of history, while Mbappé could only wonder how his life would change after such a performance, having received the FIFA Young Player Award for his performances and goals.

On returning to France, it was estimated that around one million people gathered on the Champs-Élysées to congratulate the conquering heroes.

Meanwhile, while they may have lost, the Croatian team could hold their heads high. Having finished third in 1998, they had now gone a step further – a fantastic achievement for such a small nation. Unlike Belgium, their golden generation had delivered on the biggest stage in reaching the final. Modrić was deservedly awarded the Golden Ball as the player of the tournament and the Croatians too returned home to great celebrations, with over half a million fans packing Zagreb.

Teams

France: Lloris (c), Pavard, Varane, Umtiti, Hernandez, Pogba, Kanté (Nzonzi 55), Mbappé, Griezmann, Matuidi (Tolisso 73), Giroud (Fekir 81)
Manager: Deschamps

Croatia: Subašić, Vrsaljko, Lovren, Vida, Strinić (Pjaca 81), Rakitić, Brozović, Rebić (Kramarić 71), Modrić (c), Perišić, Mandžukić
Manager: Dalić

Iconic moment

France's fourth goal – the combination of the fact that it effectively won the game for them along with it being scored by Kylian Mbappé. To see the teenager who had shown such talent throughout the tournament get his fourth goal before a global audience was a moment to enjoy. It was one of those moments when you instantly realised that his life would never be the same as he vaulted into superstar status.

Trivia fact

As the second half kicked off, a Croatian attack was suddenly interrupted by four pitch invaders. It later transpired that three of the four were members of the Russian punk band Pussy Riot, famous for protesting the Putin regime (the fourth invader being the husband of one of them). They had dressed as police officers and hailed their protest as 'Policeman Enters the Game'. One of the band, Veronika Nikulshina, even reached the centre circle, exchanging a high five with a bemused-looking Mbappé. The four were later sentenced to 15 days' imprisonment each for the act, having successfully brought to the world's attention their protest manifesto.

Game 45
2022 World Cup

Argentina v Saudi Arabia

22 November 2022
Lusail Stadium, Lusail
Attendance: 88,012
Stage: Group C, Round 1

Why you should watch it

Up to 1994, the venue for the World Cup was traditionally alternated between Europe and Latin America, before FIFA then decided to spread the game by situating tournaments in countries outside of these two continents, with 1994 occurring in USA, 2002 co-hosted by South Korea and Japan, 2010 taken to South Africa and 2018 awarded to Russia. But no World Cup had been hosted within the Arab world.

That all changed when the 2022 edition was granted to Qatar. However, given its location and summer temperatures, it also meant the first World Cup to be held in November and December, rather than the traditional June and July. It was an exciting moment for the Arabian region and would see the game brought in front of a football-loving people. There were of course criticisms of the award to Qatar, ranging from alleged bribery to migrant workers' conditions to treatment of LGBTQ+ people. But there was no doubt that Qatar was adequately prepared for the tournament, spending vast amounts on new stadiums and infrastructure, and the region had three teams in the finals – hosts and automatic qualifiers Qatar, along with Iran and Saudi Arabia.

Qatar had never qualified for a World Cup tournament before and, being brutally honest, would probably have struggled to reach this version if not for being the hosts. They did not disgrace themselves in the group stage but did exit having lost all three matches and scoring only one goal. Saudi

Arabia, on the other hand, did have considerable World Cup experience. This would be their sixth finals and, in the past, they had experienced some notable highlights, with their best performance in the USA in 1994 when they came second in their group. Kicking off against the Netherlands in 1994, they only lost to a winning goal scored four minutes from time, before then defeating Morocco 2-1 and beating a strong Belgium team by a single goal.

And what a goal it was. If you have never seen Saeed Al-Owairan's incredible run, stop reading now and go do so – you won't be sorry. One of the great World Cup goals of all time, it placed Saudi Arabia in the round of 16, where they fell to Sweden, who would eventually finish third overall. Since 1994, Saudi Arabia had only won one more game at a World Cup, against Egypt in 2018.

The 2022 draw saw Saudi Arabia placed in a tough group, alongside Argentina, Poland, and Mexico. They were ranked the highest outsiders for the tournament alongside Iran and Costa Rica. Argentina, meanwhile, were ranked third in the world by FIFA, with many selecting them as probable winners, having played 17 games within CONMEBOL qualification, drawing six and winning 11. They were on a 36-match unbeaten streak and had one of the greatest players of all time in their team – Lionel Messi. The squad was full of talent who plied their trade at the biggest clubs worldwide with everyone expecting them to cruise through the group – the key would therefore be who would get second place behind them.

Saudi Arabia were first to face *La Albiceleste*. Given that goal difference could be important, it was felt that limiting any damage would be their best hope. Get through this game maybe losing by a single goal and then focus on getting a result against Poland and/or Mexico. But Argentina had slipped up on seemingly straightforward opening matches before – famously being beaten by Cameroon in 1990 before still eventually reaching the final – so there was a precedent to give hope to the Saudis. Cameroon had defeated Maradona's Argentina, could Saudi Arabia possibly replicate such a shock against Messi's Argentina?

What happened?

Being in Qatar, the stadium was awash with Saudi Arabian fans, decked all in green, while Argentina brought along their usual huge following clad in blue and white – 88,000 overall creating a fantastic atmosphere as the teams lined up. Unsurprisingly much of the focus was on Messi, with the possibility that this could be his final opportunity to win a World Cup – a thought that had to be playing on the minds of the whole team as they prepared to kick off their campaign.

The game was only two minutes old when Messi almost opened the scoring after the ball fell to him within the penalty area, but his first-time shot was well saved by Mohammed Al-Owais. You felt that the Saudi keeper would be in for a busy afternoon. Soon afterwards, Argentina won a corner and as the ball was crossed in, midfielder Leandro Paredes went down in a tangle with a Saudi defender. The referee decided to check the incident on the VAR monitor before pointing to the spot, deciding that Saud Abdulhamid had fouled Paredes. Messi stepped up and rolled the ball into the corner. Ten minutes on the clock and Argentina were already ahead, ominous signs for Saudi Arabia, thoughts of damage limitation possibly already entering fans' minds.

Messi broke through again after 22 minutes to slot in a second, only for the assistant referee's flag to deny him. It was extremely close, but VAR did endorse the decision, albeit by inches. Five minutes later, it was the turn of Lautaro Martínez to break the offside trap and dink the ball past Al-Owais, but once again, after Martínez had celebrated with the crowd, the referee was pointed to the VAR monitor, and once again Argentina were denied a second. Saudi Arabia were playing a dangerous game and it felt like their luck would soon run out.

Ten minutes before half-time it was déjà vu as Messi put Martínez through again, for him to round Al-Owais and score, only for the goal to be chalked off for offside – to be fair, by quite a margin this time. Apart from the disallowed efforts though, chances were few and far between, with Saudi Arabia taking a physical approach towards which the referee was very lenient, keeping his cards in his pocket throughout the first half.

Saudi Arabia reached half-time just the one goal down – which after going behind after just ten minutes and with three offside goals was not a bad place to be. Saudi Arabia's French coach, Hervé Renard, must have then given an inspirational half-time team talk because the Saudis started the second half on the attack and scored after just three minutes. The ball broke to Saleh Al-Shehri who was one-on-one against Cristian Romero. Beating him to his left, Al-Shehri made enough space to strike the ball past Argentine keeper Emiliano Martínez and just inside the far corner to send the Saudi fans into ecstasy. Suddenly it was game on.

Argentina were rattled and it would get worse very quickly. Just five minutes after Al-Shehri's equaliser, Salem Al-Dawsari picked up the ball just inside the penalty box where, swerving past a challenge, he lashed a right-footed shot from the edge of the area that flew into the far corner beyond Martínez's outstretched hand. Argentine fans looked on in disbelief as the Saudi players wheeled away in celebration. Commentator Sam Matterface spoke for all when he asked, 'Who saw this coming?'

Argentina threw players forward in an effort to get back level. A ball across the area from Nicolás Otamendi fell at the feet of substitute Lisandro Martínez, whose deflected shot was well saved by Al-Owais. Another physical challenge from the Saudis finally saw the referee produce a yellow card, the first of six that the Saudis would receive as the half wore on and they became more desperate in defence. Al-Owais continued to impress, coming out quickly to deny Lautaro

Martínez with his feet after the forward had been put through by Ángel Di María. With ten minutes remaining Argentina were awarded a free kick just outside the penalty area – prime location for Messi. As Saudi fans held their breath, he lined up his shot before striking it harmlessly over the bar, frustration etched on his face. Three minutes later a cross found Messi at the far post, but he could only head the ball into the grateful arms of Al-Owais. The clock continued to run down.

As 90 minutes elapsed, Saudi fans were horrified to see the assistant referee indicate ten minutes of added time, which must have felt like a lifetime to all those in green. Nine minutes in, a cross found substitute Julián Álvarez near the far post and his header looped towards the corner before Al-Owais sprang to save the Saudis once again. Then, finally, the referee's whistle blew. Just like 1990, Argentina had suffered an opening-match defeat to a tournament underdog. Football had well and truly come to the Arab world with this result.

Final score
Saudi Arabia 2 (Al-Shehri 48; Al-Dawsari 53)
Argentina 1 (Messi 10 pen)

What was the aftermath?

Unsurprisingly, all the post-match coverage centred on the seismic nature of the shock, given Argentina's long unbeaten run beforehand, along with the possibility that Messi could be seeing his final chance for a World Cup slipping away. Of course, it was also pointed out that, after Argentina had suffered the same fate against Cameroon in 1990, they had then gone on to recover and reach the final. But they had put themselves in an early hole.

Hervé Renard commented, 'Today all the stars in the sky were in a line for us but we can't forget that Argentina are a fantastic team. They came here without losing in 36 games, they are South American champions and they have an amazing player, but this is football. Sometimes something completely crazy can happen.' The Saudis had been extremely well organised after taking the lead and had bravely defended, throwing themselves into challenges with no concern for their own bodily welfare. And Al-Owais had been giant in goal.

Sadly for Saudi Arabia, this was as good as it got for them. Presented with a golden opportunity to progress with this victory, their next two group games saw them go down 2-0 against Poland and 2-1 against Mexico to end the group in last place. 1994 would remain the last time that the Saudis had progressed from the group stage, but they had the consolation of a famous victory that all the players and staff involved will never forget.

As for Argentina, they desperately needed to beat Mexico in their next match to get their campaign on track. If any complacency may have existed in the squad, their opening loss had shaken that away. Manager Lionel Scaloni identified weaknesses and set about fixing them, including looking at players who had not started against Saudi Arabia. Early on against Mexico, the players still looked tense and nervous, unable to breach their opponents across the first 45 minutes, before Messi came to their rescue with a 64th-minute goal before Enzo Fernández added a second three minutes from the end to calm nerves further. They then defeated Poland 2-0 to end up topping the group after all. A win over Australia in the round of 16 set up a quarter-final against the Netherlands, which became a bona fide World Cup classic to be discussed shortly.

Teams

Saudi Arabia: Al-Owais, Abdulhamid, Al-Tambakti, Al-Bulaihi, Al-Shahrani (Al-Breik 90+9), Al-Malki, Al-Buraikan (Al-Amri 89), Al-Faraj (c) (Al-Abed 45+4 [Asiri 89]), Kanno, Al-Dawsari, Al-Shehri (Al-Ghannam 78)
Manager: Renard

Argentina: Martínez, Molina, Romero (Lisandro Martínez 59), Otamendi, Tagliafico (Acuña 71), De Paul, Paredes

(Fernández 59), Di María, Gómez (Álvarez 59), Messi (c), Lautaro Martínez
Manager: Scaloni

Iconic moment

As the Saudis rightfully celebrated their historic achievement, most cameras focused on Messi to gauge his reaction. He could be found in the centre of the field, holding his head in his hands in disbelief. Other Argentine players were slumped on the ground, but Messi just stood in bewilderment, staring into the distance, wondering if his World Cup dream had just gone up in smoke. It was a powerful image that was seen all over the world.

Trivia fact

The victory over Argentina was a great moment for the country as well as manager Hervé Renard. In a globe-trotting career, Renard has, to date, managed Zambia, Angola, Ivory Coast, Morocco, and Saudi Arabia, as well as the French women's national team. He has also overseen club teams in Vietnam and Algeria. But one of his strangest appointments was managing Cambridge United in 2004, where he took charge of just 25 games before being dismissed during a season that saw Cambridge relegated to the Football Conference after 35 years in the Football League. It just shows that you should never give up – from being sacked by Cambridge to beating Argentina 18 years later.

Game 46

2022 World Cup

Germany v Japan

23 November 2022

Khalifa International Stadium, Al Rayyan

Attendance: 42,608

Stage: Group E, Round 1

Why you should watch it

When we last referenced the Germans, it was their shock defeat at the hands of South Korea in the 2018 World Cup and subsequent elimination, even more surprising given their strong form going into that tournament. Following that, Germany played in the inaugural UEFA Nations League, which saw them lose against both the Netherlands and France, meaning *Die Mannschaft* had now lost four of their last six competitive games – unusual for such a historically strong side. In light of this, it was announced in March 2021 that manager Joachim Löw would step down as German manager after Euro 2020 (which had been delayed to the summer of 2021 due to the Covid-19 pandemic). Problems continued as Germany were beaten 2-1 at home by North Macedonia in a World Cup qualifier. Euro 2020 rolled around, and while Germany did get out of the group stage, they were unconvincing. England were their opponents in the round of 16, to be played at Wembley Stadium, where England enjoyed a rare competitive win over their historic rivals with two late goals – German struggles continued.

Post Euro 2020, Bayern Munich manager Hansi Flick came in to take over and normal service was swiftly resumed, with Germany winning all their remaining seven World Cup qualifying games, ending the group with nine wins and just the North Macedonia loss, while scoring 36 goals. Just like that, it seemed that a change of leadership had solved

Germany's problems, allowing them to approach the 2022 World Cup finals with renewed confidence.

Japan had qualified comfortably through the Asian section, finishing second in their final group just behind Saudi Arabia to book their passage. This meant that the Japanese had now qualified for each of the last seven tournaments, in which they had reached the round of 16 three times, that being a hurdle they had not yet crossed. Their squad for 2022 included players who had top-level experience, playing in all the major European leagues.

The Germans and Japanese were placed into group E, along with Spain and Costa Rica. It was a tough Group for Japan, with most pundits predicting that Germany and Spain would easily progress. At the time, both teams were ranked in the top 12 by FIFA, while Japan stood at 24. The opening game would see Germany face Japan – Germany's first World Cup finals match since the 2-0 defeat by fellow Asian power South Korea. Could lightning possibly strike twice?

What happened?

Ahead of kick-off, both teams posed for customary team photos on the field. German players collectively placed their hands over their mouths in a 'gagged' gesture, their way of protesting some of the off-field controversies of hosting the tournament in Qatar and FIFA's involvement therein. There had been anger at FIFA's decision not to allow team captains to wear a OneLove armband, showing their support for tolerance, diversity, and LGBTQ+ rights. And so it was that Germany's interior minister, Nancy Faeser, wore hers proudly as she sat with FIFA president Gianni Infantino in the stands for the duration of the game. The Germans were not going to have their views silenced.

The team lined up in their traditional colours of white shirts for the Germans and blue for the Japanese – *Die Mannschaft* against the Samurai Blue – in front of over 42,000 fans packed into the Khalifa International Stadium, just outside Doha. Right from the start, Japan showed that they were not intimidated by their more illustrious opponents. Just seven minutes in, a Japanese break saw the ball passed out wide to Junya Itō, who whipped in a cross that was tapped in by Daizen Maeda only to be correctly ruled out for offside. But it was a warning to the Germans not to take their opponents lightly.

Germany regained control, with Antonio Rüdiger heading narrowly wide from a corner after 15 minutes. Five minutes later, some neat passing resulted in a vicious shot from Joshua Kimmich which Japan keeper Shūichi Gonda could only deflect away given the power. The Germans kept up the pressure, İlkay Gündoğan seeing his goal-bound effort blocked. It seemed only a matter of time before the Japanese defence would crack.

The German breakthrough finally came after just over 30 minutes. Kimmich, controlling midfield, sprayed a pass out to left-back David Raum who was wide open in the area. Trapping the ball, he turned back as Gonda rushed out to close the angle. As Gonda scrambled after him, he appeared to bundle Raum over and the referee agreed, awarding Germany a penalty that Gündoğan gratefully converted. The Germans were in full flow, Japan just trying to reach half-time without conceding again, and just as the whistle was about to blow Jamal Musiala had a great opportunity to play Thomas Müller in, but overhit the pass slightly. Müller had to switch from a shot to a cross which ended up with Kimmich whose shot was parried by Gonda to Serge Gnabry who fired across the area for Kai Havertz to tap into an open goal. It looked like curtains for Japan until the assistant referee's flag went up – Havertz had just strayed forward a beat too early. Japan were able to get into the changing room just the one goal down, having been thoroughly outplayed. Germany were cruising.

Nothing appeared very different as the second half got underway with Germany still pressing forward. Musiala went on a wonderful jinking run through the Japanese defence that would have been one of the goals of the tournament had he not blazed over at the end. Twelve minutes in, Japan could hardly get out of their own half – they would have to change something if they were to have any chance of getting back into the game. Manager Hajime Moriyasu made the first roll of the dice, bringing on midfielder Kaoru Mitoma and striker Takuma Asano to freshen things up, but straight away Musiala turned provider as he set up Gündoğan whose shot hit the foot of the post.

With 20 minutes remaining, Musiala again created problems for Japan, setting up Kimmich to chip into the area. It was beautifully weighted to Gnabry, who flicked it past Gonda where substitute Jonas Hofmann was positioned. It looked like a second goal was inevitable until Gonda recovered position to throw himself in front of the shot. The play was recycled until a cross found Gnabry unmarked at the far post. His strong downward header was stopped on the line by another fine Gonda save, falling again to Gnabry whose shot was again stopped by the keeper. It was a brilliant double save to keep Japanese hopes alive despite wave after wave of German attack; Gonda seemed on a one-man mission to deny Germany.

Moriyasu went to his bench again, bringing on midfielder Ritsu Dōan. Japan made a rare excursion into the German half, where a lovely slide-rule pass from Wataru Endo found Itō whose shot was parried away by keeper Manuel Neuer as far as defender Hiroki Sakai who had to score. With the goal gaping he showed why he played in defence rather than attack, blasting the ball over. As he slumped to the ground, Japan were left to wonder if their opportunity to equalise had been squandered.

But instead of dropping their heads, it appeared to galvanise Japan. Suddenly the Germans were playing deep as Japan applied the pressure, Mitoma picking up the ball wide and, cutting inside, rolling a cute ball through to Takumi Minamino who had just come on. From Minamino's first-time shot across the six-yard box, Neuer pushed it out one-handed straight to Dōan, who gratefully fired the rebound home. Three of the five Japanese substitutes had dragged their team level – inspired changes by Moriyasu. Suddenly, having been second best for 75 minutes, it was game on.

Maybe memories of 2018 resurfaced as now, with 15 minutes left, the Germans looked nervous. Japan's fans amped up the volume as their team went looking for more, sensing that Germany were rattled, and with seven minutes remaining, a long ball from defence dropped to Asano whose first touch was sublime. Battling into the area with German defender Nico Schlotterbeck, Asano was able to muscle him off and get enough space to fire a shot over Neuer at his near post. In the space of just eight minutes, two replacements had scored and turned the game completely on its head.

Germany were simply shocked. Even with seven additional minutes added on, giving them a quarter of an hour to respond, they couldn't threaten. They screamed for a second penalty at one stage in desperation, but nothing came of it. The final whistle blew, and it was 2018 all over again – Germany beaten in their opening game, this time by Japan rather than Mexico, Moriyasu reaping the reward for his second-half changes.

Final score
Japan 2 (Dōan 75; Asano 83) Germany 1 (Gündoğan 33 pen)

What was the aftermath?

Japanese media quickly dubbed the game 'The Miracle of Doha'. Coming the day after Saudi Arabia had beaten Argentina, resulting in the declaration of a public holiday there, the Japanese public demanded the same from their prime minister, who had already irked them by tweeting that he was visiting the imperial palace during the match, instead of watching it.

Hajime Moriyasu was loudly praised for his five inspired changes during the second half which had helped to turn the tide Japan's way. There was also much commentary on the fact that the two Japanese goalscorers, Dōan and Asano, both ironically played for German club sides, SC Freiburg and VfL Bochum respectively.

As for Germany, they once again faced an uphill battle, like 2018 when South Korea had inflicted the killer blow after the Mexico defeat. And this time they had to play Spain next – a Spain who had just defeated Costa Rica 7-0 in their opening match. The signs were ominous.

Coach Hansi Flick admitted Germany were 'under pressure, no question about it'. Some media pundits tried to blame the pre-match protests, saying that it had distracted the German players who should have been 100 per cent focused on the game.

There was also criticism of Flick's substitutions, in particular the removal of Gündoğan and Musiala, both of whom had been central to German chances. Starting the relatively inexperienced Schlotterbeck was also questioned, especially considering being outmuscled by Asano for Japan's winner. But as always, it is easy after the event to second-guess decisions made in the heat of the moment.

The German team themselves called an internal angry team meeting after the defeat – a chance to air grievances behind closed doors and clear the air. With Spain upcoming it was clear that they needed to improve quickly. Group E would not disappoint – there was much more drama to come.

Teams

Japan: Gonda, Sakai (Minamino 75), Itakura, Yoshida (c), Nagatomo (Mitoma 57), Endo, Tanaka (Dōan 71), Itō, Kamada, Kubo (Tomiyasu HT), Maeda (Asano 57)
Manager: Moriyasu

Germany: Neuer (c), Süle, Rüdiger, Schlotterbeck, Raum, Kimmich, Gündoğan (Hofmann 67), Gnabry (Moukoko 90), Müller (Goretzka 67), Musiala (Götze 79), Havertz (Füllkrug 79)
Manager: Flick

Iconic moment

The game finished around midnight Japanese time and sent the country into mass celebration. Crowds congregated throughout, but especially in Tokyo where many converged at the street crossing in Shibuya, famous as one of the world's busiest. With typical Japanese respect, fans waited until the signals indicated they could walk before massing in the intersection in a joyful huddle. Video footage quickly went viral and became synonymous with Japan's famous evening.

Trivia fact

As the Japanese supporters partied outside the stadium, there were many older members among them for whom winning in Doha brought particular joy. Almost three decades prior, Japan had travelled there to take on Iraq for a spot at the 1994 finals in the USA. As stoppage time came, Japan were leading and on their way to their first World Cup until a last-gasp equaliser shattered the dream. The game became known in Japan as 'The Agony of Doha'. Now they had returned and beaten Germany in their opening game, helping to exorcise that painful memory, especially for Hajime Moriyasu who ironically had been one of the players for Japan on that fateful occasion.

Games 47/48
2022 World Cup

Japan v Spain

1 December 2022
Khalifa International Stadium, Al Rayyan
Attendance: 44,851
Stage: Group E, Round 1

Costa Rica v Germany

1 December 2022
Al Bayt Stadium, Al Khor
Attendance: 67,054
Stage: Group E, Round 1

Why you should watch them

Following on from Japan's win over Germany in the opening match, subsequent results had set Group E up for a grandstand finish. After Japan celebrated their historic victory, Spain demolished Costa Rica 7-0, representing their record win at a World Cup.

Spain had cruised into the 2022 tournament, winning six of their eight qualification games to win their group ahead of Sweden and Greece, among others. They had reached the semi-final of Euro 2020, losing to eventual champions Italy on penalties, as well as reaching the final of the 2021 UEFA Nations League, losing to a late Kylian Mbappé goal against France. They were playing well ahead of Qatar 2022, managed by ex-playing legend Luis Enrique, entering the tournament ranked by FIFA number seven in the world, ahead of Germany at 11, making them group favourites.

Japan dominated against Costa Rica in their next game but couldn't find a way through when, to their horror, Keysher Fuller grabbed a late goal for the South Americans, undoing all of Japan's great work against Germany. Germany, meanwhile, faced Spain knowing that they needed a win to get back into contention. After a goalless first half, Spain took the lead on 62 minutes through Álvaro Morata, placing *Die Mannschaft* in a perilous position. Luckily, they managed to equalise through substitute Niclas Füllkrug with seven minutes remaining, and then almost snatched a winner at the death when Leroy Sané went close. In the end Germany had to settle for a point, which left the table going into the last set of games with Spain on four points and a goal difference of +7, Japan on three points and a goal difference of 0, Costa Rica also on three points but -6 for goal difference, and Germany on one point and -1.

The final group matches would see Japan take on Spain while Germany faced Costa Rica. If the favourites both won their matches then they would both move on to the knockout stages as expected ahead of the tournament. But if we had learned anything from the first two rounds of this group, it was that nothing ever went to plan. And what happened over the next 90 minutes did not disappoint, with enough twists and turns to provide great drama.

What happened?

As the teams lined up in the Khalifa International Stadium, Japan could at least take solace that they were walking back on to the same pitch on which they had shocked Germany just a week before. Their usual colourful fans were out in force, a group that always brought such joy to the tournament with their amazing costumes and painted faces. At the same time, Germany kicked off against Costa Rica, knowing that they needed at least a win to have a chance of moving on. Fans in both stadiums would be busy watching their phones from the corner of their eyes to check in on the other match.

Spain almost gifted Japan a dream start after just seven minutes when a sloppy touch by captain Sergio Busquets turned over possession in the penalty area. Japan managed to work the ball out to Junya Itō whose close-range shot narrowly missed the near post. Then, three minutes later, came news of a first goal over in Al Khor where Serge Gnabry gave Germany an early lead, meaning the live table became:

Spain 5 pts, +7
Japan 4 pts, 0
Germany 4 pts, 0
Costa Rica 3 pts, -7

It was looking as if Germany were going to easily pick off Costa Rica as Spain had, which would mean Japan would need to beat *La Roja* to progress. Japan fans would have felt a feeling of doom.

As the Japanese fans processed the German goal and its implications, that feeling would suddenly become a sickening sensation. Almost immediately, a period of Spanish possession on the edge of the Japanese penalty area saw defender César Azpilicueta send a cross towards the back post, where an unmarked Morata headed home with ease. In the space of two minutes, Japan's world was crumbling as they refreshed their phones to see the latest live table:

Spain 7 pts, +8
Germany 4 pts, 0
Japan 3 pts, -1
Costa Rica 3 pts, -7

It was all Spain as they pushed forward for a second. Gavi set up another chance for Morata but this time his shot was comfortably saved by opening-game hero Shūichi Gonda. Morata then turned provider as he set up Dani Olmo, whose shot was deflected over. Japan managed to weather the storm and get into the half-time break just the one goal down, while things also remained unchanged in Al Khor, meaning Hajime Moriyasu would have to inspire another second-half comeback like against Germany.

Moriyasu made two changes, bringing on Ritsu Dōan, who had scored the vital equaliser against Germany after coming on in the second half of that match, as well as Kaoru Mitoma. And once again Dōan delivered, controlling the ball beautifully just outside the area before firing in a vicious shot that Spanish keeper Unai Simón could only parry into the roof of the net. Just three minutes had elapsed in the second half and yet again a Moriyasu substitution had changed the game, bringing Japan ahead of Germany once more in the live table:

Spain 5 pts, +7
Japan 4 pts, 0
Germany 4 pts, 0
Costa Rica 3 pts, -7

Once again Japan had come back from a first-half deficit, just like a week prior. The news filtered quickly to German management and fans alike – they needed at least another goal in their game.

Then, just three minutes later, arose one of the most controversial moments of the whole 2022 tournament. Japan were flying forwards at the shocked Spaniards and a pass out to Dōan saw him hit the ball across the face of the area where Mitoma sprinted to keep it in play. Throwing himself forward, left leg fully stretched out, he managed to hook the ball back into the six-yard box for Ao Tanaka to bundle home. The Japanese fans went ballistic, only for their celebrations to be swiftly halted as the referee signalled for a VAR review, suspecting that the ball may have gone out of play just before Mitoma reached it. All eyes turned to the replay.

It looked incredibly close. On first view, from the side, the ball looked fractionally out. Japan fans stood, several with hands in prayer, as every angle was studied. And then finally the referee blew his whistle and pointed to the centre circle. They could finally release their breath in an outpouring of pure joy – yet again Japan had risen from the dead in the second half. And now the live table made much better reading for them:

Japan 6 pts, +1
Spain 4 pts, +6
Germany 4 pts, 0
Costa Rica 3 pts, -7

For Spanish fans, a little unease started to creep in, but still, Germany would need another six goals against Costa Rica to trouble them. So surely they could relax despite going behind.

But then came through news that Spain could not have been expecting. Rather than Germany beginning to pile up goals, Costa Rica scored. Manuel Neuer could only parry a fierce close-range header from Costa Rican defender Kendall Waston and Yeltsin Tejeda was first to react, sweeping the ball home to send his team's supporters into ecstasy. The Spanish supporters quickly realised that, instead of worrying about German goals, another goal by Costa Rica was now the biggest concern, given that the live table now stood at:

Japan 6 pts, +1
Spain 4 pts, +6
Costa Rica 4 pts, -6
Germany 2 pts, -1

German fans, meanwhile, could only watch in horror as they slipped to the bottom of the standings. Calculators on many phones were going into overtime.

The German players threw themselves back at Costa Rica, Jamal Musiala seeing his shot come back off the post. They knew they had to regain the lead but, with 20 minutes remaining, more craziness followed as a floated free kick into the German area was headed back into the danger area by Waston. A seemingly harmless upward header occurred in the six-yard box where keeper, defenders and attackers converged under. It dropped, bobbled around players' feet, and somehow ended up in the net, coming off Juan Pablo Vargas's boot last. Against all the odds, pandemonium broke out as Costa Rica were now heading to the knockout stage. Meanwhile, back in Al Rayyan, Spanish management tried to let their players know they were facing elimination and to push forward harder as watching fans all over the world were setting up TVs and laptops to watch the duelling action unfold. As they refreshed their live standings, they would have seen:

Japan 6 pts, +1
Costa Rica 6 pts, -5
Spain 4 pts, +6
Germany 1 pt, -2

Two of the biggest teams in world football were 20 minutes from elimination.

This shocking statistic only lasted for all of three minutes. Germany were now pushing everyone forward and a lovely flick found Kai Havertz alone by the penalty spot, where one touch to control followed by a little chip saw Germany level again, putting the standings back to:

Japan 6 pts, +1
Spain 4 pts, +6
Costa Rica 4 pts, -6
Germany 2 pt, -1

Spanish fans could breathe again but Germany still needed a win – and to then hope that Spain could pull one back against Japan. With five minutes remaining, a low cross from Serge Gnabry found Havertz open again, this time at the far post, with an easy tap-in to give Germany a 3-2 lead. Calculators overheating, the live standings now changed to:

Japan 6 pts, +1
Spain 4 pts, +6
Germany 4 pts, 0
Costa Rica 3 pts, -7

With Germany back in the lead, their supporters now had to hope that Spain could draw level with Japan and that Germany could score one more goal.

And with one minute remaining, the second of these requirements occurred. A ball in to Havertz saw him chest it down to an open Niclas Füllkrug to put German goal difference up to +1. That meant that if Spain could score, Japan would be level on points with Germany but with a zero goal difference. Every German fan now moved away from their game and willed Spain to get a stoppage-time equaliser. The problem was, as things stood, Spain had little incentive to do so – they were on track to move on with Japan. But there were moments to give Germany hope such as when Olmo got through on 89 minutes only to see his shot smothered by Gonda. Japanese fans sweated through seven minutes of stoppage time before the final whistle set off wild celebrations for both sets of supporters. Japan had beaten both Germany and Spain to top the group while, despite their loss, Spain would also go through. The mighty Germans were out. It was the end of one of the wildest evenings a World Cup had ever seen.

Final scores
Japan 2 (Dōan 48; Tanaka 51) Spain 1 (Morata 11)
Germany 4 (Gnabry 10; Havertz 73, 85; Füllkrug 89)
Costa Rica 2 (Tejeda 58; Vargas 70)

What was the aftermath?

Following on from 'The Miracle of Doha' where Japan had beaten Germany, they had now returned to the same venue and beaten Spain – and so naturally it was quickly dubbed 'The Miracle of Doha 2.0'. The Japanese media were smart enough to acknowledge that luck had been on their side, especially with the Mitoma cross, but also pointed out how their team had now become the darlings of world media when before no one expected much from them going into the tournament. Seth Levine of *The Guardian* summed Japan's performance up beautifully, saying, 'Not sure I've ever been more pleased for any side in any sport. Love the way they play.

No histrionics. Brilliant fans. Excellent tactically. Manager wears a charcoal three-piece suit. What's not to love?' As with the Germany game, this one was played early in the morning local time, meaning that morning commuters in Tokyo were met by high fives from bleary-eyed fans still hanging around Shibuya.

Japan's reward for topping the group were tough round of 16 opponents in Croatia. Unlike their group matches, Japan took the lead this time before Ivan Perišić levelled after 55 minutes. That would be all the scoring, leading to a penalty shoot-out. Sadly for Japan, their first four kicks included three of the worst penalties you could imagine, all saved by Croatian keeper Dominik Livaković. Yet again their World Cup dream died in the round of 16, but Japanese fans were full of pride for their team whose two victories will live on in legend for many decades.

On the Spanish side, Luis Enrique created some raised eyebrows from journalists when he said after the match not to have known that Spain were at one point in peril of elimination. When asked how he was feeling during those three minutes, he claimed to have been unaware, saying that he was fully concentrated on Spain's match and not getting updates on what was going on elsewhere. He even added that if he had known he 'would have had a heart attack'. What made the statement more surprising is that the Costa Rica score had been put up on the video display during the Spain game – supporters and some players said that they were aware of the situation. But whatever the truth, Spain had made it through to the knockout stages where they would face Morocco rather than Croatia. Many pundits felt that Spain had lucked out by coming second with Morocco seen as an easier opponent.

But it wasn't to be. After a scoreless 120 minutes, Spain and Morocco went into a penalty shoot-out. The Spanish then proceeded to miss their first three, meaning that the shoot-out was ended when Achraf Hakimi scored Morocco's third with a cute Panenka followed by his penguin dance celebration. Second place in the group had cost Spain after all.

The reactions in Germany to their elimination were savage. This was now the second World Cup in succession where *Die Mannschaft* had fallen at the group stage – an unthinkable situation for such a historically successful team. Newspaper headlines included 'winter nightmare', 'new low point' and 'football dwarf'. Legendary former player Bastian Schweinsteiger suggested that German players didn't have the burning desire to win anymore, and that more leadership was needed on the field. The newspaper *Die Welt* summed it up: 'What remains is an embarrassing World Cup exit from a group containing Japan and Costa Rica. The German national team has once again fallen far short of its own aspirations, it has arrived in grey mediocrity.' Hansi Flick also came in for criticism, especially his decision to substitute Gündoğan in all three matches, although the German Football Association stuck by their appointment at least, leaving Flick in charge after the tournament despite their elimination.

Teams

Japan: Gonda, Itakura, Yoshida (c), Taniguchi, Itō, Morita, Tanaka (Endo 87), Nagatomo (Dōan HT), Kamada (Tomiyasu 68), Maeda (Asano 62), Kubo (Mitoma HT)
Manager: Moriyasu

Spain: Simón, Azpilicueta (Carvajal HT), Rodri, P. Torres, Balde (Alba 68), Busquets (c), Gavi (Fati 68), Pedri, Williams (F. Torres 57), Morata (Asensio 57), Olmo
Manager: Luis Enrique

Germany: Neuer (c), Kimmich, Süle (Ginter 90+3), Rüdiger, Raum (Havertz 66), Goretzka (Klostermann HT), Gündoğan (Füllkrug 55), Sané, Musiala, Gnabry, Müller (Götze 66)
Manager: Flick

Costa Rica: Navas (c), Waston, Duarte, Vargas, Fuller (Matarrita 74), Oviedo (Contreras 90+3), Campbell, Borges,

Tejeda (Wilson 90+3), Aguilera (Salas HT), Venegas (Bennette 74)
Manager: Suárez

Iconic moment

Not surprisingly, every report of Japan v Spain contained a photo of the Mitoma cross. There was endless debate about whether the ball had gone out of play or not. The problem was, when you looked at the side-on photo, the base of the ball was clearly over the line, and so it surely had to be the wrong decision. But what thousands of people had seemingly forgotten was that a ball is not square but spherical. Therefore, the middle is wider than the base. If you looked at a camera angle that was above the ball, you could just see that the bulge of the ball in the middle did break the plane of the goal line – albeit by a minute degree. VAR had multiple angles to use and had seen this view which guided their decision. Post-match, FIFA tweeted out the image to answer the question once and for all. Yes, the ball had stayed in play and yes, the Japanese goal was valid by a hair's breadth. Football is often a game of fine margins.

Trivia fact

Post-match statistics showed that, for Japan v Spain, Japan had averaged possession for just 18 per cent of the 90 minutes, the lowest possession percentage ever tracked for a World Cup victory, while completing 175 passes to Spain's 991. Just another example of 'it's not how much you have the ball, it's what you do with it that matters'. For all of Spain's technical ability, they had found it hard to break down the Japanese defence, while Japan took their chances when presented. There is still only one stat that matters at the end of the day – the final score.

Game 49

2022 World Cup

Argentina v The Netherlands

9 December 2022

Lusail Stadium, Lusail

Attendance: 88,235

Stage: Quarter-Finals

WORLD CUP CLASSIC

Why you should watch it

Following on from Argentina's shock opening loss to Saudi Arabia, I described earlier how they then recovered to reach the quarter-final stage, where their opponents would be their old foes, the Netherlands. Argentina and the Netherlands have a historic rivalry based upon many high-profile World Cup encounters – two of which have been covered in this book already. The Netherlands put on a masterclass to thrash Argentina 4-0 in 1974, with Johan Cruyff in his pomp, before Argentina took revenge in the 1978 final. Their 1998 quarter-final was settled by the last-minute piece of magical finishing from Dennis Bergkamp before a couple of goalless draws in the 2006 group stage and 2014 semi-final, won by Argentina on penalties. So after five games it was two wins for the Netherlands, one draw and two wins for Argentina; all square overall.

While Argentina had suffered an initial group scare, the Netherlands had topped their group relatively comfortably. Opening with a 2-0 win over Senegal, albeit with two late goals, they then drew with Ecuador before beating hosts Qatar 2-0. This had set them up to play the USA in the round of 16, which again was comfortable, 3-1 being their margin of victory, resulting in the next instalment of their rivalry with Argentina.

The Netherlands were managed by the legendary Louis van Gaal, a larger-than-life character with considerable experience. He became famous when leading a young Ajax team to an incredible 1995 season in which they won both the Eredivisie and the Champions League without losing a single game in either competition. That resulted in a move to Barcelona in 1997, where he took them to two La Liga titles, before spending a couple of stints in charge of the Netherlands in between managerial posts at such clubs as AZ Alkmaar, Bayern Munich and Manchester United. His first spell was unsuccessful, as the Dutch failed to qualify for the 2002 World Cup under his watch, but his second was a success as he led the team to qualification for the 2014 World Cup before then managing them to the semi-finals and that painful loss on penalties to Argentina. In early 2019, he decided to finally retire from management aged 67, but following on from the dismissal of Frank de Boer after a poor 2020 Euros, Van Gaal returned to lead the Netherlands for a third time. Coming into the Argentina game, he had been in charge for 19 internationals, with no losses, showing his legendary touch had not deserted him.

In early 2022, ahead of the tournament, Van Gaal shocked the world by announcing that he was suffering from prostate cancer. Typical of the great man, he continued to work, saying in August that the radiation treatment had proved successful, allowing the world to breathe a sigh of relief that once again Van Gaal would be able to grace the global stage – one of football's greatest characters.

In typical Van Gaal 'I'll say what I like' mode, his comments to press ahead of the quarter-final helped build the already tense atmosphere regarding this rivalry. While Argentine manager Lionel Scaloni praised Van Gaal as a legend, Van Gaal commented, 'We've got a score to settle with Argentina for what happened two World Cups ago.' The shoot-out defeat in Brazil was still eating away at him. He also told Dutch publication *NOS*, 'Messi is indeed the most dangerous player who creates the most chances and also makes them himself. But on the other hand he does not play much with the opponent when he has possession of the ball. That is also where our chances lie.' The tension was slowly being ratcheted.

So as the two teams stepped out into the Lusail Stadium, a global audience prepared to watch game six of this World Cup rivalry. Would it be a goalless draw like eight years previous or would there be fireworks? Oh, there were fireworks aplenty.

What happened?

In a stadium awash in blue, white and orange, the game got underway with memories of Cruyff, Kempes and Bergkamp swimming around minds. The referee chosen to oversee this fixture was Spanish official Antonio Mateu Lahoz, who had a wealth of experience but also a reputation for being talkative with players and sometimes allowing games to get out of control. Given the two teams he was presiding over, it would be important that he keep a tight leash over any possible boiling points. Señor Lahoz would be in for a very busy evening indeed.

Given the respect the two sides had for each other, the game was cagey early on, without the creation of many chances. The opening half an hour saw neither goalkeeper troubled as occasional shots either flew wide or were comfortably saved. It did, however, see the first yellow card, given to Wálter Samuel, Argentina's assistant manager. Then came a moment of Messi magic.

Picking up the ball in midfield, the little wizard turned his marker before edging towards the area. Sizing up the Dutch defence before him, he suddenly slipped a perfect reverse pass through to right-back Nahuel Molina who had made a run through the offside trap. It just took one touch from Molina and then a poke past Dutch keeper Andries Noppert and, just like that, Argentina were 1-0 up. Messi's pass had been perfection – it almost appeared to be no-look as he caught out the Dutch – and the stadium exploded in an orgy of blue and white celebration.

Shortly afterwards, Messi got himself into another good position, this time getting in a shot that was easily covered by Noppert. Then the first minor flashpoint arose. A tackle on Denzel Dumfries by Marcos Acuña saw the Argentine become the first outfield player to receive a yellow card. Dutch defender Jurriën Timber took offence, pushing Acuña to the ground and receiving a yellow himself, a signal of the needle between the two teams beginning to build. Memphis Depay was then involved in jumping for a ball which Argentine defender Cristian Romero decided to swat away with his hand, earning him a booking. There was still time for Dutch substitute Wout Weghorst to be cautioned for protesting a foul while on the bench before the half-time whistle blew. A relatively quiet first half had seen one moment of magic from Messi provide Argentina with a lead, and five yellow cards, two of which were for personnel not even on the field. The game was gently simmering.

The second half started like the first with little action of note. It took 15 minutes until a free kick from Messi flew narrowly over. Then, on 73 minutes, Acuña turned back on Dumfries in the area, causing the midfielder to catch his trailing leg and referee Lahoz pointed to the penalty spot as Messi picked up the ball and strode over. The captain delivered again and, with just 17 minutes remaining, it looked like Argentina were going to progress courtesy of a not very memorable game.

Dutch tempers began to rise in frustration at the penalty award and impending defeat. A cross into the area saw substitute Luuk de Jong tussle with goalkeeper Emiliano Martínez, followed by some shoving among nearby players. The result was yellow cards for Depay and Lisandro Martínez. As both sides made changes, Van Gaal's included throwing on striker Weghorst and, with just seven minutes remaining, the big man made his mark, jumping at the near post to head the Netherlands back into the game. What had looked like an easy evening for Argentina suddenly became nervy.

The Dutch realised that the high balls to the tall forwards were creating problems for Argentina. Straight after Weghorst's goal, another cross saw a knock-down fall to substitute Stephen Berghuis whose vicious shot rippled the side-netting. A Messi run was halted by an unsubtle shove from Berghuis, who earned a yellow card. As Argentine nerves grew, Dutch defender Nathan Aké was chopped down by substitute Leandro Paredes right in front of the team benches. It was a crude challenge and suddenly all the pent-up frustrations exploded. Paredes clouted the ball towards the Dutch dugout before trying to exit the scene, a picture of innocence, after which captain Virgil van Dijk flew into him, sending him sprawling over as the bench rushed on to the pitch seeking revenge. As the referee frantically blew, a mass shoving match took place and, when things finally settled, a yellow card was awarded to Paredes, Van Dijk somehow escaping punishment.

The assistant referee's board went up to indicate a minimum of ten minutes of additional stoppage time, sending the tension level sky high and leading to a yellow card for Lionel Scaloni as he protested vehemently. As eight minutes of injury time had elapsed, celebrations began among the Argentina fans who could sense a semi-final place. Their team just had to do nothing stupid in the remaining two minutes.

And then Paredes and substitute Germán Pezzella combined to bundle Weghorst over just outside their own area. It was unnecessary and gifted the Netherlands a last free-kick opportunity to try and tie the game. Nerves were shredded as Argentina formed their wall, Messi getting a yellow card for his protestations. It was all or nothing as the world watched substitute Tuen Koopmeiners step up to take the kick. Would he go for the top corner or a low drive? The crowd held its breath.

Koopmeiners slowed his run-up and passed the ball to the side of the wall where Weghorst was lurking. As brains still tried to comprehend what was happening, Weghorst took a touch to control and then slid the ball past Martínez. The Dutch rushed towards the corner in celebration, stunned Argentine fans trying to understand what they had just witnessed. With the last kick of the game, the Dutch had implemented a training-ground routine that had completely fooled them. It was brave, it was ballsy, it was inspirational. We were heading for extra time and even as the teams congregated on the field to prepare, players had to be separated as tempers flared.

After 101 minutes, four goals, a deep stoppage-time trick-play equaliser and 13 yellow cards, what would the next 30 hold in store?

Given the intensity of the last half an hour, it was only natural that the game would slow down during the first half of extra time. That still didn't stop the bookings, however, with substitute Gonzalo Montiel receiving a yellow card just three minutes after coming on for something he said. Three minutes later Pezzella joined him after what looked a fair challenge on Cody Gakpo. The only real chance of extra time fell to Lautaro Martínez, who saw his goal-bound shot fly narrowly wide following a deflection. But as the game drew towards penalties, Argentina were in command, and as we went into stoppage time again, Enzo Fernández saw his shot rebound off the post. The epic struggle would be decided from 12 yards, just like their last meeting back in 2014.

First up was Van Dijk who struck his penalty well, only to see Martínez guess correctly. Messi then stroked in the calmest, gentlest penalty you have ever seen to put Argentina ahead. Martínez then repeated his heroics to stop the kick from Berghuis and, with Paredes then scoring, the momentum was with *La Albiceleste*. Koopmeiners and Montiel both scored to take it to 3-1 after three kicks each. Weghorst continued his scoring streak to keep the Netherlands alive before Fernández stepped up with the potential winning kick. The tension was white-hot as some words were exchanged between players before he pulled his effort wide, giving the Netherlands a glimmer of hope again. Luuk de Jong did what he had to do and it all came down to Lautaro Martínez. Score and Argentina were through, miss and it was heading to sudden death.

Martínez swept his kick towards Noppert's left but the keeper dived to the right. The ball nestled in the corner and Argentina were into the semi-finals, but even then, as the celebrations began, the animosity spilled over yet again. With Argentina running past the Dutch and mocking them while celebrating, some *Oranje* players took offence and squared up to their opponents, while others, such as Weghorst, were in a heap, uncontrollably sobbing. It had been another classic duel between these two great football nations that had everything – goals, drama, spiciness, penalties, and yellow cards galore.

Final score
Argentina 2 (Molina 35; Messi 73 pen) Netherlands 2 (Weghorst 83, 90+11)
After extra time; Argentina win 4-3 on penalties

What was the aftermath?

Given the animosity during and after the game, it was quickly dubbed by the media as 'The Battle of Lusail'. When everything had settled, the final count showed that referee Antonio Mateu Lahoz had issued a World Cup-record 18 yellow cards and one red. The dismissal had occurred right at the end of the game, when Denzel Dumfries, who had been shown a yellow for unsporting behaviour towards Lautaro Martínez as he went to take the decisive penalty, again squared up to the celebrating Argentinian players, earning a second yellow. There was criticism of Lahoz, mainly for issuing so many yellow cards but never a red until after the match despite all the flare-ups. Some players also made it known that they were not impressed by his performance. It would be his last refereeing gig at the 2022 tournament.

At the end of the game, Messi had exchanged words with Louis van Gaal while Emiliano Martínez had also hurled obscenities at both him and the Dutch bench. Tempers remained hot as players spoke to the media. Most notably, while Messi was being interviewed, Weghorst tried to congratulate him. Messi misunderstood and told him the rough equivalent of, 'What are you looking at, fool?' Messi would then go on to tell reporters that the Dutch spoke too much during the game and that Van Gaal had gone for a long-ball approach. He later expressed regret for some comments, blaming the heat of the moment.

The quest to provide Messi with a historic World Cup triumph continued for *La Albiceleste*. The semi-final against Croatia saw Messi score again as Argentina cruised to a 3-0 win, setting them up for a final against the French. And that is the final game of this book.

Teams

Argentina: E. Martínez, Romero (Pezzella 78), Otamendi, Lisandro Martínez (Di María 112), Molina (Montiel 106), Acuña (Tagliafico 78), De Paul (Paredes 67), Fernández, Mac Allister, Álvarez (Lautaro Martínez 82), Messi (c)
Manager: Scaloni

Netherlands: Noppert, Timber, Van Dijk (c), Aké, Dumfries, de Roon (Berghuis HT), F. de Jong, Blind (L. de Jong 64), Gakpo (Lang 113), Depay (Weghorst 78), Bergwijn (Koopmeiners HT)
Manager: Van Gaal

Iconic moment

The Dutch equaliser with nearly the last kick of the match was a moment of pure audacity. Just think about it – it is your final chance to score, with the world watching you, and you try what is almost a trick play. You can imagine the howls that would have arisen had they tried it and Argentina had intercepted and cleared the ball. The safe approach was to take a shot, either full power or curling around the wall. But the Dutch didn't want to take the safe approach and were rewarded for their bravery. It was breathtaking and just added to the narrative of an incredible game.

Trivia fact

While viewers may have been stunned by the audacity of Weghorst's equaliser and that free-kick routine, it was not the first time that he had pulled off this trick. In 2020 he scored a similar goal for Wolfsburg against Arminia Bielefeld in the German Bundesliga. It seems that practice does in fact make perfect.

Game 50

2022 World Cup

Argentina v France

18 December 2022

Lusail Stadium, Lusail

Attendance: 88,966

Stage: Final

WORLD CUP CLASSIC

Why you should watch it

And so we get to the 50th and last game of the book, which fittingly enough is the last World Cup game played at the time of writing, 2022's showpiece between Argentina and France.

We saw earlier how Argentina survived an epic encounter with the Dutch to reach the semi-finals, after which they saw off Croatia to reach their sixth final. Their record up to 2022 – two wins in 1978 and 1986, and three defeats in 1930, 1990 and 2014. Having got this far, it was all now about whether one of the greatest players of all time, Lionel Messi, could cap an incredible career with the one major trophy he was lacking and become a legend by leading *La Albiceleste* to a World Cup victory. Ever since 1986, Diego Maradona had been revered in Argentina for leading them to the title. Messi had achieved more at a club level than Maradona, but that was all in Europe, principally for Barcelona; therefore there was still a feeling back in Argentina that he hadn't quite achieved greatness when playing for them. This had been partially softened by Messi leading them to 2021 Copa América success, but the World Cup was the big one. The narrative now was would this be Messi's crowning moment of a glorious career – it would probably be his last chance given he was 35 years old. Many neutrals were hoping Messi would be lifting the trophy at the end of the game, something no South American side had done since Brazil in 2002.

But Argentina faced tough opponents in France. They had topped their group, albeit while suffering a surprising loss to Tunisia, but at that stage they had already qualified for the knockout rounds and were not fielding a full-strength side. Kylian Mbappé had scored three of their six group goals, continuing where he left off in 2018. The round of 16 saw France overcome Poland 3-1, Mbappé again making his mark with two goals, before England proved tougher opposition in the quarter-finals, with an Olivier Giroud winner near the end seeing France over the line. The semi-final had seen France face the surprise story of the tournament, Morocco, who had become the first African team to reach that stage, and they proved too strong and experienced, posting a 2-0 victory to put them into their second successive final.

Heading into the final, Messi and Mbappé were the tournament's leading goalscorers with five goals each. While both teams had strong sides with many fine players, all the talk was of Messi vs Mbappé, maybe the best two players at that time and also team-mates at Paris Saint-Germain, facing off on a global stage. There was the memory of their last World Cup encounter in 2018 when France won 4-3 in one of the greatest games ever, discussed earlier in this book – in which Mbappé had scored as a precocious teenager. If the final could be half as good as that encounter, then the world was in for a treat. But most finals are notoriously edgy, tight affairs. Would this one buck the trend and would Messi and Mbappé play at their best? We should never have doubted it.

What happened?

The usual pre-match tournament closing ceremony took place before 88,000 fans, several leading dignitaries and a huge global audience within the impressive Lusail Stadium, under a setting Arab sun. A pyrotechnic display lit up a huge World Cup trophy in the middle of the pitch as fans of both teams cranked up the atmosphere. The national anthems were sung, with 'La Marseillaise' sounding as stirring as ever, and then the 2022 World Cup Final was underway.

Right from the start, Argentina took control. Buzzing within the France half, they created a few half-chances but never troubled Hugo Lloris, while *Les Bleus* were finding it hard to even get out of their own territory. The pressure finally paid off as, after 23 minutes, a piece of magic from Ángel Di María saw him cut into the box before going down under a challenge from Ousmane Dembélé. It was clumsy and the referee had no hesitation in pointing to the spot. Of course, there was only ever going to be one man entrusted with a World Cup Final penalty for Argentina. It was Messi's first chance to make his mark in the game and, sending Lloris the wrong way, he coolly converted to give Argentina a well-deserved lead given their early domination of the match. It was his 97th international goal and maybe the most important.

As the match rolled on to the 36th minute, France were still struggling with Mbappé having little influence on play thus far. He received a pass which he swung infield, but straight to a defender and suddenly Argentina were in full flow. A first-time pass found Messi in midfield, who flicked a cute ball out to Julián Álvarez which he immediately struck into the empty space in front of a breaking Alexis Mac Allister, who also moved the ball on first time to Di María at the far post. As Lloris rushed out, Di María chipped the ball over him to double Argentina's lead. The whole move up the field had been lightning fast – quick first-time balls pulling the French defence apart. It was beginning to look like a romp for *La Albiceleste*, whose fans were in dreamland.

France manager Didier Deschamps was troubled, deciding to make a double substitution after just 41 minutes to try and wake his team up. But as the half-time whistle blew, his team looked shell-shocked, having been thoroughly outclassed for 45 minutes and now facing a two-goal deficit. Mbappé had been practically non-existent.

Argentina continued where they had left off as the second half got underway, with midfielder Rodrigo De Paul hitting a sweet volley straight at Lloris. Álvarez tried his luck next, forcing Lloris into a low save at his near post. A couple of last-ditch tackles denied first Messi and then Mac Allister as Argentina continued to sweep forward in waves. If any team was going to score, it looked likely to be those in striped shirts at this stage – it was one-way traffic.

Going into the final half an hour, Di María was withdrawn to great applause, having played a huge part in both goals. With 20 minutes left Mbappé reminded everyone of his presence, cutting across the Argentinian defence only to see his snap-shot sail over. But it was a reminder – he was still out there, and he could produce something in a heartbeat.

With the clock down to just ten minutes remaining, Mbappé hit a ball behind the Argentina defence which Nicolás Otamendi seemed to have covered. But an acceleration from substitute Randal Kolo Muani took him past Otamendi as they entered the penalty area, leading to an entanglement. The referee pointed to the spot and suddenly France had a glimmer of hope. And like Messi earlier, there was only going to be one man France would trust with this kick. Up stepped Mbappé.

He struck it low and hard towards the corner, but keeper Martínez threw himself to that side, getting a hand to it but unable to keep it out. As French president Emmanuel Macron punched the air in delight, Mbappé grabbed the ball and hurried back to the centre circle. Ten minutes left and game on.

Suddenly the French were faster, more determined and first to every ball – they looked a different team. Messi was caught in possession out wide and robbed by substitute Kingsley Coman who set off down the wing before passing inside. The ball made its way to Mbappé outside the Argentine area, where he flicked a header to Marcus Thuram before sprinting into the penalty box as a first-time return pass fell to him on the volley. He struck a beauty into the bottom corner and in under 90 seconds France were level. Fans of *Les Bleus* went crazy in the stands, unable to completely believe their eyes.

France were now flying as a shell-shocked Argentina tried to regain their heads. Thuram went down under a challenge from Enzo Fernández that looked like a penalty, only for the referee to deem it a dive and book the substitute forward. But Argentina were seriously rocking, desperately hanging on. The board went up to indicate a minimum eight minutes of stoppage time to Argentine groans as they resembled a boxer, sticking by the ropes and absorbing punches in hope of the bell. Mbappé had another attempt deflected over before Adrien Rabiot found a patch of space in the area. His shot was pushed out by Martínez, who then gratefully saw Romero drop to his knees to deflect the ball back into his arms. It was frantic stuff. And then, just as stoppage time was ending, Messi carved one more chance, his fierce shot pushed over by an alert Lloris. The whistle blew, allowing everyone to finally take a moment and catch their breath, mesmerised by the last 20 minutes. The good news for the neutrals was that we were going to get 30 minutes more.

Maybe unsurprisingly given the pace of those last 20 minutes, the first half of extra time saw both teams also catching their breath, until just before the break when a Messi one-two resulted in a chance for substitute Lautaro Martínez, whose shot was superbly blocked by Dayot Upamecano before the follow-up effort was headed over by Rabiot. Martínez still had time for one more effort before the break which went narrowly wide.

The game went into the second period of extra time, and three minutes in some neat passing put Martínez on goal again. Lloris could only parry his vicious shot and Messi pounced on the rebound, only to see his shot cleared off the line. Argentina appealed and all eyes turned to the referee who, looking at his watch, indicated that the ball had crossed the line. Messi had done it again, putting Argentina back into the lead and grabbing his second. It seemed like Mbappé and Messi were locked in a personal duel out there.

The clock ticked down to five minutes remaining as Mbappé took a shot from outside the area, which was blocked by Gonzalo Montiel. The replay showed that it had clearly struck Montiel's arm, but was it in an unnatural position? The referee thought so and a stunned crowd looked on as yet again he pointed to the spot. It would all be down to Mbappé and whether he could keep his cool under the most pressurised of situations. Yes, he could – he sealed his hat-trick and France were once again level, the duel continuing in this see-saw match.

With ten seconds of regular time left, Mbappé swung a cross in that found Kolo Muani unmarked. It looked like France were going to grab a dramatic winner, but his header down into the ground just bounced wide of the Argentine goal. Three minutes of stoppage time were added on and then, right as those three minutes elapsed, Kolo Muani found himself through on goal. Time seemed to slow as the World Cup came down to Kolo Muani vs Emiliano Martínez.

Kolo Muani hit it hard and low towards the corner. Martínez spread himself and threw out a leg. The whole world held its breath.

Martínez's leg was strong enough and the ball was picked up by Argentina who then launched a counterattack which resulted in a cross to Martínez who looked like he could score, only to get his header wrong and see it fly well wide. It was an insane ending where both sides could have won it at the death. But neither did and it was off to the dreaded penalty shoot-out.

France would go first and who else but Mbappé stepped up to take it, his third spot-kick of the match. And his third conversion as he put it in the corner. In reply, Argentina sent Messi over to take their first, and his second. His second conversion followed as he rolled it so coolly, almost slowly, into the net. The two leading men had gone, and both had scored. It was now down to the supporting cast.

First up was Coman but he saw his effort saved by Martínez, who ran off punching the air in delight. Paulo Dybala hit his penalty straight and true down the middle to give the advantage to Argentina. Aurélien Tchouaméni then dragged his kick wide before Leandro Paredes gave the South Americans a two-goal advantage. Kolo Muani had to score to keep French hopes alive – and he did just that, blasting the ball down the middle. But now Montiel had the chance to win the World Cup.

He shot to Lloris's right – and Lloris dived to his left – Argentina were world champions for the third time. Messi had scored twice and could now rightly stand with Diego Maradona as an *Albiceleste* legend. The party could commence.

Final score
Argentina 3 (Messi 23 pen, 108; Di María 36)
France 3 (Mbappé 80 pen, 81, 118 pen)
After extra time; Argentina win 4-2 on penalties

What was the aftermath?

Messi had finally done it – he could now bask in having achieved greatness by leading his nation to World Cup success. After so many tense, edgy finals, the world had been given one of the greatest of all time. It had served up everything anyone could want, including that fantastic duel between two of the greatest players of their generation, Messi and Mbappé.

The World Cup trophy was brought out on to a swiftly erected stage in the centre of the pitch, placed on a pedestal backlit by a light show. FIFA president Gianni Infantino strode over, resplendent in his suit and white sneakers, accompanied by Qatari Emir Tamim bin Hamad Al Thani, French president Emmanuel Macron and Argentine Football Association president Claudio Tapia, among others. Individual awards were given out first, including the Golden

Glove to Emiliano Martínez, whose subsequent pose with the trophy was not exactly classy. A disappointed Mbappé came up to receive the Golden Boot for his eight tournament goals, one ahead of Messi – he had also become the first person to have scored four goals in World Cup Finals following his one in 2018 and hat-trick four years later.

The Golden Ball for player of the tournament, unsurprisingly, went to Messi, making him the first player to win that award twice. The final had represented Messi's 26th World Cup game, setting a record ahead of Germany's Lothar Matthäus.

There was then a wait as the whole French squad came up to pick up their medals, disappointment etched on their faces. But finally the Argentinian squad collected their medals, captain Messi bringing up the rear. He was led over to the trophy before the slightly bizarre image of a bemused-looking Messi being wrapped in a bisht (a traditional Arab cloak) by the Qatari Emir. Picking up the trophy, Messi gave it a kiss and a rub before carrying it over to the waiting squad, bouncing in anticipation. The prize was held aloft, fireworks shot into the night sky and Argentinian fans the world over could celebrate.

Teams

Argentina: E. Martínez, Molina (Montiel 91), Romero, Otamendi, Tagliafico (Dybala 120+1), Fernández, De Paul (Paredes 102), Mac Allister (Pezzella 116), Messi (c), Álvarez (Lautaro Martínez 102), Di María (Acuña 64)
Manager: Scaloni

France: Lloris (c), Koundé (Disasi 120+1), Varane (Konaté 113), Upamecano, Hernandez (Coman 71), Tchouaméni, Rabiot (Fofana 96), Dembélé (Kolo Muani 41), Griezmann (Camavinga 71), Mbappé, Giroud (Thuram 41)
Manager: Deschamps

Iconic moment

If anything summed up this epic match, it was that final minute of extra time when Randal Kolo Muani almost won it for France, only for Argentina to immediately break and almost win it themselves through Lautaro Martínez. It encapsulated the back and forth between these two great sides where you just couldn't tell where the game would flow next.

Trivia fact

Qatar 2022 saw Messi become the first player to score in the group stage, round of 16, quarter-final, semi-final and final in a single tournament – a remarkable feat that shows how dominant he was, although helped by being Argentina's penalty taker. Not bad for a 35-year-old.

Afterword

There you have it, my humble attempt to select 50 great World Cup games for you to watch. Going through this exercise, it has been interesting to see conclusions develop within myself. When I started, I had certain ideas about each World Cup in terms of quality and drama but had not revisited many for some time and so writing this book has helped to crystallise those opinions.

For starters I, like many English people of my age, remember Italia '90 with fondness. There were the incredible stadia, such as the glorious San Siro – so ahead of anything we had ever seen at that time. There was Des Lynam, the BBC and 'Nessun Dorma'. There was Gazza and that game against the Germans. But looking back at the tournament with more neutral, and older, eyes I now realise that it was one of the poorest in terms of quality. Many games were dull and often went to penalty shoot-outs. England themselves were unexciting in the group stage before enjoying some luck in their games against Belgium and Cameroon, saving their best performance for the semi-final. But that just shows how emotion is important in watching this game that we love – because of my age at the time and that semi-final run, Italia '90 will always have a special place in my heart.

Looking over how many games I included for each tournament and how many of those I have labelled as classics, I can see which stand out. Of course, one needs to remember that the earlier World Cups in this book had significantly fewer games than the later ones and so automatically would be expected to have fewer standout matches. 1974 will always be remembered for the Netherlands and Johan Cruyff – those long-haired footballing rebels who seemed to redefine the game – and best summed up by that thrashing of Argentina. In the end, the final against West Germany in Munich was one step too far, and the Germans deserve full credit for their win, but in a way the Dutch team has become almost more loved because of that failure. 1978 was the ticker tape pouring off the terraces while Kempes galloped through defences – a tournament surrounded by controversy given the regime at the time and the Argentina vs Peru game but, as a child, I was unaware of that and was busier following the Scottish farce.

I would argue that 1982 and 1986 were two of the greatest tournaments. 1982 will forever be remembered for two great games that both ended in heartbreak for so many neutrals. The Brazil team containing Zico, Falcão, Sócrates and Éder was one of absolute beauty, playing with a swagger and style that lifted the heart, but Italy were ruthless on the day and Paolo Rossi had the game of his life. And then France, with Platini, Tigana, Giresse and Rocheteau, were cruelly beaten by West Germany, assisted by the callousness of Harald Schumacher. 1986, meanwhile, saw the zenith of one of the greatest players of all time, Diego Armando Maradona, including his magical goals against England and Belgium as well as his infamous 'Hand of God'. Brazil and France still both had great sides, and no one should forget the Danish Dynamite, who shone so brightly, but sadly so briefly, while sporting shirts that were works of art.

1994 was a good tournament until the final stages which mar the memory – a World Cup that many were sceptical about given the perceived lack of interest for football in the USA, but where crowds were high – if Americans like anything, it is a spectacle. And we did get to see the eastern European geniuses of Gheorghe Hagi and Hristo Stoichkov, as well as the sublime skills of Roberto Baggio. 1998 saw that wonder goal from teenage sensation Michael Owen, the ups and downs of the Ronaldo saga and a multicultural French team unite a nation.

The 2002 tournament saw Asia host for the first time and the South Korean run, surrounded by both controversy and a passionate fanbase, along with a perfect ending as Ronaldo enjoyed the ultimate redemption story. 2006 in my mind was one of the poorer instalments, although the party atmosphere that was generated in Germany was great to see. 2010 took us to Africa for the first time, with colour, dancing and vuvuzelas, along with Ghanaian heartbreak as they came so close to becoming the first African nation to reach the semi-final stage.

The 2014 tournament will always be remembered for that astonishing night when Brazil crashed so spectacularly in front of their shocked fans, before 2018 saw the World Cup move to Russia – one of FIFA's more controversial choices of venue – and the emergence of Kylian Mbappé as the latest global superstar.

Which takes us to 2022. All the talk ahead of the tournament was about the choice of Qatar as hosts. Why play a World Cup in a country with such little footballing history? Why play in a country marred by migrant worker issues, LGBTQ+ issues etc? And all of those were, and remain, fair criticisms. But, and maybe this is recency bias, what a tournament they delivered. A great advert for the beauty of the four-team groups along with arguably the greatest final of all time, although the Brazilian boys of 1970 may wish to challenge that. A reminder of everything we love about this game – thrilling matches, jeopardy, heroes, and villains – as well as everything we dislike about modern football – politics, over-expansion, egos, and the smell of corruption.

I hope you enjoy reading these 50 summaries as much as I enjoyed researching and writing them. If you discover a past game that brings you joy and maybe further research, then this book will have achieved its aim. Naturally everyone will have their own opinion on the 50 chosen and the classic nominations – football is subjective and in the eyes of the beholder. I expect every reader to come up with at least one game that they feel was wrongly omitted – it is tricky to select a set number and there were certain matches that I agonised over not including (for example, Argentina v Croatia in 2018). But once you decide on 50, you must draw the line somewhere.

Thank you for joining me in this journey and may you enjoy many hours of pleasure on YouTube. I hope that this book gives you some context about the games you are watching and how they fit into football at the time, their legacy, and their importance.

And, from someone who was 16 in 1982, prime age for falling in love for the first time and with the time to watch every game, Brazil and France will always have a special place in my heart. Zico and Platini – thanks for the memories.

Bibliography

Books

Holt, N., *The World Cup, The Definitive Guide 1930–2018* (London: Robinson, 2018)

Smyth, R., Eriksen, L., and Gibbons, M., *Danish Dynamite, The Story of Football's Greatest Cult Team* (London: Bloomsbury, 2015)

Websites

bbc.co.uk
theguardian.com
wikipedia.org
youtube.com
thesefootballtimes.co
fourfourtwo.com
mirror.co.uk
dailymail.co.uk

Podcasts and YouTube channels

FIFA
RptimaoTV2
DEL PIERO 10
Football Flashback 6
The Golden Age
VintageHDtv
L.N.D Fo0tY
sp1873